INDUSTRIAL PHARMACY-I

FROM THEORY TO PRACTICE

DR. SANTHI SREE VEMULAPALLI, DR. ANVESH RAJ MOTURI, DR. J. DINESH BABU

Contents

Preface

Industrial Pharmacy-I: From Theory to Practice

The world of pharmaceutical science is always changing, with new advancements improving healthcare every day. This field needs professionals who understand both the theory and practical applications of pharmacy. "Industrial Pharmacy-I: From Theory to Practice" is created to be a complete guide for students and professionals, helping them gain the necessary knowledge and skills.

Purpose and Vision

This book was created to fill a gap in pharmaceutical education. As teachers, we have seen the difficulty students face in finding detailed and easy-to-understand reference materials. Our aim is to provide a single, comprehensive resource that covers everything in the Industrial Pharmacy-I curriculum. This book is designed to help students learn and apply their knowledge effectively without needing to look for additional resources.

Content Overview

The book is divided into ten detailed chapters, covering all important aspects of industrial pharmacy. It starts with preformulation studies and goes through the manufacturing processes for different dosage forms like tablets, capsules, and parenterals. Each chapter includes information on quality control and regulatory requirements, ensuring a complete understanding of the field. We have included practical examples, case studies, and real-world applications to make the learning process easier and more engaging.

Educational Approach

Our approach is to make education clear, simple, and comprehensive. We have presented the information in an engaging and informative way, avoiding unnecessary complexity. This book is a reliable guide for pharmacy students at all levels and a valuable reference for professionals looking to refresh their knowledge.

Gratitude and Acknowledgments

We are very grateful to our colleagues, students, and the academic community for their continuous support and encouragement. Special thanks to Vijaya College of Pharmacy for providing an environment that supports academic growth and innovation. We are highly grateful to Dr. Muralidhar Rao Akkaladevi, Principal of St. Mary's College of Pharmacy, for his guidance and support in the completion of this book. His insights and encouragement have been instrumental in shaping the final manuscript. We also want to thank our families for their unwavering support throughout the creation of this book.

We hope that "Industrial Pharmacy-I: From Theory to Practice" will be a valuable resource for your studies and professional growth. This book aims to guide you towards excellence in the field of industrial pharmacy.

Dr. Santhi Sree Vemulapalli

Dr. M. Anvesh Raj

Dr. J. Dinesh Babu

Industrial Pharmacy-1 From Theory To Practice

Dr. Santhi Sree Vemulapalli
Professor
Vijaya College of Pharmacy
Hayatnagar, Munagnoor
India
Dr. M. Anvesh Raj
Associate Professor
Vijaya College of Pharmacy
Hayatnagar, Munagnoor
India
Dr. J. Dinesh Babu
Associate Professor
Vijaya College of Pharmacy
Hayatnagar, Munagnoor
India
Edited by
Dr. Muralidhar Rao Akkaladevi
Principal, St. Mary's College of Pharmacy
Secunderabad

Published by Notion Press
Notion Press, Inc.
800, West EI Camino Real #180,
California USA 94040
Notion Press Media Pvt Ltd
#7, Red Cross Road,
Egmore, Chennai, Tamil Nadu 600008
Email ID: publish@notionpress.com
Phone Number: +91 44 46315631
July 2024

CHAPTER ONE

Preformulation studies

1.1 Introduction to Preformulation

Goals and Objectives

The **primary goals and objectives** of **preformulation studies** in pharmaceutical development are multifaceted and crucial for the successful advancement of a drug candidate. Preformulation studies aim to characterize the physical, chemical, and biological properties of a **drug substance**. This characterization helps in understanding how the drug behaves under various conditions and predicts its interactions with potential formulation components. By identifying these properties early in the development process, preformulation studies help in designing an optimal **dosage form** that ensures the drug's **efficacy, safety,** and **stability**.

One of the specific aims of conducting preformulation studies is to determine the **solubility profile** of the drug. Solubility is a critical factor that influences the drug's bioavailability and therapeutic effectiveness. By studying the solubility in different solvents and at various pH levels, researchers can anticipate how the drug will dissolve in the human body. Additionally, preformulation studies evaluate the **drug's stability** under different environmental conditions such as temperature, humidity, and light. This helps in identifying potential degradation pathways and formulating strategies to enhance the drug's shelf life.

Preformulation studies also play a vital role in assessing the **compatibility** of the drug with **excipients**—the inactive ingredients used in drug formulations. By identifying compatible and incompatible excipients, these studies guide the formulation process, ensuring that the final product is both effective and stable. Furthermore, preformulation studies help in understanding the **pharmacokinetics** of the drug, including absorption, distribution, metabolism, and excretion (ADME) properties. This comprehensive understanding aids in optimizing the drug's dosage regimen and delivery system.

Importance in Drug Development

Preformulation studies are critical in the early stages of **drug development** because they provide a foundation for subsequent formulation and development activities. By characterizing the **physicochemical properties** of the drug, preformulation studies help in predicting potential challenges and addressing them proactively. This early identification and mitigation of issues can significantly reduce the time and cost associated with drug development, leading to more efficient and successful outcomes.

One of the key impacts of preformulation studies on the design and formulation of drug products is the ability to select the most suitable dosage form. For instance, if a drug exhibits poor solubility in water, researchers might consider formulating it as a **solid dispersion** or using **nanotechnology** to enhance its solubility and bioavailability. Similarly, if a drug is unstable under certain conditions, preformulation studies can guide the development of **protective packaging** or the inclusion of stabilizing agents.

Preformulation data has a profound influence on the development of successful pharmaceutical products. For example, the formulation of **Amorphous Solid Dispersions (ASDs)** for drugs with poor water solubility has led to significant improvements in their bioavailability and therapeutic efficacy. Another notable example is the use of **lipid-based formulations** to enhance the absorption of poorly water-soluble drugs, thereby improving their clinical outcomes. By providing detailed insights into the drug's properties, preformulation studies enable the development of innovative and effective drug formulations that meet the desired therapeutic objectives.

1.2 *Study of Physicochemical Characteristics of Drug Substances*

1.2.1 Physical Properties

Physical Form (Crystal & Amorphous)

Differences between Crystalline and Amorphous Forms

Crystalline and **amorphous** forms of drug substances exhibit distinct structural characteristics that significantly impact their performance. Crystalline drugs possess a well-ordered arrangement of molecules in a fixed geometric pattern, leading to a highly structured and stable form. This orderly arrangement contributes to the **high melting points** and **distinctive solubility profiles** typically observed in crystalline drugs. In contrast, amorphous drugs lack this ordered molecular arrangement, resulting in a disordered and irregular structure. This lack of organization in amorphous forms often leads to lower melting points and higher solubility compared to their crystalline counterparts.

The crystalline form is generally more stable due to its well-defined lattice structure, which resists changes in environmental conditions such as temperature and humidity. However, this stability often comes at the cost of lower solubility and slower dissolution rates. On the other hand, the amorphous form, while less stable and more prone to recrystallization, offers higher solubility and faster dissolution rates, which can enhance the drug's bioavailability.

Effect on Solubility and Stability

The physical form of a drug profoundly affects its **solubility** and **stability**, two critical factors in pharmaceutical development. Crystalline drugs, due to their ordered molecular structure, tend to have lower solubility and slower dissolution rates. This can limit their absorption in the gastrointestinal tract and reduce their overall bioavailability. However, their high stability makes them less susceptible to degradation during storage, ensuring a longer shelf life.

In contrast, amorphous drugs, with their disordered structure, exhibit higher solubility and faster dissolution rates, enhancing their absorption and bioavailability. This increased solubility is particularly beneficial for drugs with poor water solubility, as it can improve their therapeutic efficacy. However, the amorphous form's lack of stability can pose challenges during storage, as it is more prone to recrystallization and degradation over time. Formulation strategies such as the use of **stabilizing excipients** and **protective packaging** are often employed to mitigate these stability issues.

Examples and Implications on Drug Performance

Several drugs exist in both crystalline and amorphous forms, each exhibiting unique performance characteristics. **Indomethacin,** a nonsteroidal anti-inflammatory drug (NSAID), is available in both forms. The crystalline form of indomethacin is highly stable but has poor solubility, leading to limited bioavailability. Conversely, the amorphous form of indomethacin offers improved solubility and faster dissolution rates, resulting in better absorption and enhanced therapeutic effects. However, the amorphous form requires careful handling and storage to maintain its stability.

Another example is **ritonavir**, an antiretroviral drug used in the treatment of HIV/AIDS. Initially, ritonavir was developed in its crystalline form, but issues with polymorphism and solubility limited its effectiveness. The development of an amorphous solid dispersion of ritonavir significantly improved its solubility and bioavailability, making the drug more effective in clinical use.

Similarly, **nifedipine**, a calcium channel blocker used to treat hypertension and angina, exhibits different performance characteristics in its crystalline and amorphous forms. The crystalline form of nifedipine is stable but poorly soluble, whereas the amorphous form offers higher solubility and faster onset of action. The choice between these forms depends on the specific therapeutic requirements and formulation strategies employed.

Particle Size and Shape

Importance in Preformulation Studies

Particle size and **shape** are fundamental parameters in preformulation studies because they profoundly impact the **drug's performance** and the efficiency of the **manufacturing process**. The size of the particles affects not only the drug's dissolution rate and bioavailability but also the uniformity of the final product. Smaller particles tend to have a larger surface area relative to their volume, which can enhance the dissolution rate. This is particularly critical for drugs with poor water solubility, as increasing the dissolution rate can improve bioavailability and, consequently, therapeutic effectiveness. The shape of the particles influences the flow properties, compressibility, and packing behavior of the powder, which are essential for consistent manufacturing.

For instance, spherical particles typically exhibit better flow properties than irregularly shaped particles. Good flow properties are crucial for ensuring uniformity in dosage forms like tablets and capsules. Irregularly shaped particles may lead to poor flow, resulting in variations in the weight and content uniformity of the final product. This can affect the drug's quality and efficacy. Therefore, understanding and controlling particle size and shape is vital for developing a robust and reproducible drug formulation.

Influence on Dissolution Rate and Bioavailability

The **particle size** of a drug directly influences its **dissolution rate** and **bioavailability**. According to the Noyes-Whitney equation, the dissolution rate of a solid is proportional to its surface area exposed to the dissolution medium. Smaller particles have a larger surface area-to-volume ratio, which increases the contact area with the dissolution medium, leading to a faster dissolution rate. This is particularly beneficial for drugs with poor solubility, as rapid dissolution can enhance the drug's absorption in the gastrointestinal tract and improve its bioavailability.

For example, **griseofulvin**, an antifungal drug, exhibits significantly improved bioavailability when formulated with smaller particle sizes. Reducing the particle size increases the drug's surface area, enhancing its dissolution rate and allowing for more rapid absorption. Similarly, **fenofibrate**, a lipid-lowering agent, demonstrates higher bioavailability when micronized, leading to improved therapeutic outcomes.

On the other hand, larger particles dissolve more slowly, which can limit the drug's absorption and reduce its bioavailability. This can be particularly problematic for drugs with narrow therapeutic windows, where precise dosing is critical. In such cases, ensuring an optimal particle size distribution is essential to achieve consistent and predictable drug release profiles.

Techniques to Measure Particle Size and Shape

In pharmaceutical development, accurately measuring the **particle size** and **shape** of drug substances is crucial for ensuring the consistency, quality, and performance of the final product. Several advanced techniques are employed to characterize these properties, each offering unique advantages and insights.

Laser Diffraction

Laser diffraction is one of the most widely used techniques for measuring particle size distribution. It works on the principle of **light scattering**, where a laser beam passes through a dispersed sample of particles. The angle and intensity of the scattered light are analyzed to determine the particle size distribution. Laser diffraction can measure a broad range of particle sizes, typically from submicron to several millimeters. Its advantages include rapid analysis, high reproducibility, and the ability to handle a wide range of sample types, from dry powders to liquid suspensions.

Dynamic Light Scattering (DLS)

Dynamic light scattering, also known as photon correlation spectroscopy, is particularly useful for measuring the size of small particles in suspension or solution, typically in the nanometer to micrometer range. DLS measures the fluctuations in light scattering due to the Brownian motion of particles. By analyzing these fluctuations, the technique determines the hydrodynamic diameter of the particles. DLS is highly sensitive and provides precise measurements of small particles, making it suitable for characterizing nanoparticles and colloidal systems.

Microscopy (Optical and Electron Microscopy)

Optical microscopy and **electron microscopy** (scanning electron microscopy [SEM] and transmission electron microscopy [TEM]) are essential techniques for directly observing and measuring the size and shape of particles. Optical microscopy is useful for larger particles and provides visual images that can be analyzed for size and shape. SEM and TEM offer much higher resolution, allowing detailed examination of the surface morphology and internal structure of particles. These techniques are invaluable for understanding the shape, texture, and aggregation state of particles.

Sieving

Sieving is a traditional and straightforward method used to separate particles based on size. A series of sieves with different mesh sizes are stacked, and the sample is passed through them. Particles are sorted into size fractions according to the mesh sizes. While sieving is limited in its precision compared to modern techniques, it remains useful for larger particles and bulk materials. It is simple, cost-effective, and provides a direct measure of particle size distribution.

Image Analysis

Image analysis involves capturing images of particles using microscopy techniques and analyzing these images with specialized software. This method allows for detailed measurement of particle size and shape parameters, such as aspect ratio, circularity, and surface roughness. Image analysis is particularly valuable for characterizing irregularly shaped particles and providing comprehensive shape descriptors that other techniques might not capture.

Coulter Counter

The Coulter counter, also known as electrical sensing zone method, measures particle size by detecting changes in electrical resistance as particles pass through a small aperture. Each particle displaces a volume of electrolyte solution, causing a change in resistance proportional to the particle's size. The Coulter counter is effective for measuring the size distribution of particles in suspension and can handle a wide range of particle sizes, from submicron to hundreds of micrometers.

X-ray Powder Diffraction (XRPD)

While primarily used for identifying crystalline structures and polymorphs, XRPD can also provide information on particle size through the analysis of peak broadening in diffraction patterns. Scherrer's equation is commonly used to estimate particle size from XRPD data. This technique is particularly useful for characterizing nanoparticles and understanding the crystalline properties of drug substances.

Flow Properties

Definition and Significance in Drug Formulation

Flow properties refer to the behavior of powdered or granulated materials when subjected to various forces. These properties are essential in understanding how a material moves, settles, and interacts with equipment during the manufacturing process. In drug formulation, flow properties are crucial because they directly influence the efficiency, consistency, and quality of the production process, particularly for solid dosage forms such as tablets and capsules.

Why Flow Properties Are Significant in Drug Formulation

1. Ensuring Uniformity and Consistency

Good flow properties are vital for ensuring uniformity in the distribution of active pharmaceutical ingredients (APIs) and excipients. Uniform flow ensures that each dose contains the correct amount of API, which is critical for the drug's efficacy and safety. Inconsistent flow can lead to weight variations in tablets and capsules, resulting in dose inaccuracies that can compromise therapeutic outcomes.

2. Enhancing Manufacturing Efficiency

Efficient flow properties facilitate smooth operation during the manufacturing process, reducing downtime and minimizing the risk of mechanical issues. Materials with good flow characteristics can easily move through hoppers, feeders, and die cavities without clogging or bridging. This leads to a more efficient production process with fewer interruptions, ultimately reducing production costs and time.

3. Improving Compressibility and Compaction

Flow properties affect the compressibility and compaction behavior of powders. Materials that flow well can be more uniformly compressed, resulting in tablets with consistent hardness and disintegration profiles. Poor flow can cause uneven compression, leading to tablets with variable hardness, which can affect dissolution rates and bioavailability.

4. Preventing Segregation

Segregation occurs when different components of a powder blend separate due to differences in particle size, shape, or density. Good flow properties help maintain a homogeneous blend, preventing segregation and ensuring that each dosage unit contains the intended formulation. Segregation can lead to dosage units with varying concentrations of the API, affecting the drug's efficacy and safety.

5. Facilitating Packaging and Storage

Flow properties also play a role in the packaging and storage of pharmaceutical products. Powders with good flow characteristics can be efficiently filled into containers, sachets, or blister packs without significant spillage or wastage. Additionally, good flow properties help in maintaining the integrity of the product during storage and transportation, ensuring that the drug remains effective until it reaches the patient.

6. Enhancing Patient Compliance

Uniformity in the size and shape of dosage forms, achieved through good flow properties, can enhance patient compliance. Tablets and capsules with consistent appearance are more likely to be accepted by patients, leading to better adherence to prescribed treatment regimens.

Impact on the Manufacturing Process of Solid Dosage Forms

Flow properties play a crucial role in the manufacturing process of solid dosage forms such as tablets and capsules. The efficiency, consistency, and quality of the final product are significantly influenced by how well the powdered materials flow through various stages of production. Here's a detailed explanation of how flow properties affect different aspects of the manufacturing process:

1. Mixing and Blending

During the initial stages of manufacturing, the active pharmaceutical ingredient (API) and excipients need to be thoroughly mixed to ensure a uniform distribution of the API throughout the batch. Good flow properties ensure that the powders mix homogeneously, which is essential for dose uniformity. Poor flow can lead to segregation, where different components separate based on size or density differences, resulting in inconsistent API distribution and dosage variations in the final product.

2. Hopper Flow

In many manufacturing processes, powders are fed from a hopper into processing equipment. Powders with good flow properties move smoothly through the hopper, preventing issues like bridging (where particles form a bridge across the hopper outlet) or rat-holing (where a hole forms in the center of the powder, causing material to stop flowing). Such issues can cause interruptions in the manufacturing process, leading to downtime and reduced efficiency.

3. Die Filling

In tablet manufacturing, the powder blend needs to flow consistently into the tablet press dies. Uniform die filling is crucial for producing tablets with consistent weight and content. Powders with poor flow properties may not fill the dies evenly, leading to tablets with variable weights and potentially incorrect dosages. This inconsistency can result in out-of-specification products that must be rejected, increasing waste and production costs.

4. Compression

The flow properties of powders also affect their behavior during compression. Powders with good flow characteristics tend to compress more uniformly, resulting in tablets with consistent hardness and density. Uniform compression ensures that each tablet has the same dissolution and disintegration profile, which is important for predictable drug release and bioavailability. Poor flow can lead to uneven compression, causing tablets to vary in hardness and potentially affecting their performance.

5. Encapsulation

For capsule filling, powders must flow smoothly into the capsule dosator or filling machine. Good flow properties ensure that each capsule receives the correct amount of powder, maintaining dose accuracy and uniformity. Powders that do not flow well can cause inconsistent filling, leading to capsules with varying API content and potential dose inaccuracies.

6. Packaging

Flow properties also impact the efficiency of the packaging process. Powders with good flow can be easily transferred into packaging containers, such as sachets or blister packs, without spillage or wastage. Consistent flow ensures that each package contains the correct amount of product, which is essential for maintaining dose accuracy and product integrity.

7. Storage and Handling

Good flow properties facilitate the handling and storage of powders. Powders that flow well are less likely to agglomerate or form lumps, which can complicate subsequent processing steps. Consistent flow also ensures that powders can be easily transferred between containers or processing equipment, reducing the risk of contamination or material loss.

Methods to Evaluate Flow Properties

Several methods are used to evaluate the flow properties of powdered drug substances:

- **Angle of Repose:** Measures the maximum angle at which a pile of powder remains stable. A smaller angle indicates better flow properties.
- **Carr's Index and Hausner Ratio:** Calculated from the bulk and tapped densities of the powder. Lower values indicate better flowability.
- **Flow Rate through an Orifice:** Measures the time it takes for a specific amount of powder to flow through an orifice of known diameter.
- **Powder Rheometers and Shear Cell Testers:** Provide detailed insights into the flow behavior of powders under different conditions, such as consolidation, aeration, and shear.

Methods to Evaluate the Flow Properties of Powdered Drug Substances

Evaluating the **flow properties** of powdered drug substances is essential to ensure efficient and consistent manufacturing of solid dosage forms. Several methods are employed to assess these properties, each providing valuable insights into the behavior of powders under different conditions. Here are the commonly used techniques:

1. Angle of Repose

The **angle of repose** measures the maximum angle at which a pile of powder remains stable without collapsing. This method involves pouring the powder through a funnel onto a flat surface and measuring the angle formed between the surface and the slope of the powder heap. A smaller angle of repose indicates better flow properties, as the powder forms a flatter heap. This simple and quick method provides an initial indication of a powder's flowability.

2. Carr's Index (Compressibility Index) and Hausner Ratio

These indices are calculated based on the bulk density and tapped density of the powder:

- **Bulk Density:** The mass of the powder divided by its volume in a loose state.
- **Tapped Density:** The mass of the powder divided by its volume after being tapped or packed down.

Carr's Index is calculated as: Carr's Index=(Tapped Density–Bulk Density/Tapped Density)×100

Hausner Ratio is calculated as: Hausner Ratio=Tapped Density/Bulk Density

A lower Carr's Index (below 20%) and Hausner Ratio (close to 1) indicate better flow properties. These indices are widely used due to their simplicity and effectiveness in assessing powder flowability.

3. Flow Rate through an Orifice

This method measures the time it takes for a specific amount of powder to flow through an orifice of known diameter. The powder is placed in a funnel or hopper with an orifice at the bottom, and the flow rate is determined by measuring the mass or volume of powder that passes through the orifice over a given time period. This test provides direct information about the powder's flow behavior under gravity.

4. Powder Rheometers

Powder rheometers are sophisticated instruments that measure the flow properties of powders under various conditions, such as aeration, consolidation, and shear. They provide detailed data on parameters like cohesion, flow energy, and permeability. Rheometers can simulate different processing environments, offering insights into how powders will behave during manufacturing. This method is particularly useful for understanding complex flow behaviors and optimizing powder formulations.

5. Shear Cell Testers

Shear cell testers measure the flowability of powders by determining their yield strength under different applied stresses. The powder is placed in a shear cell, and a controlled stress is applied to induce flow. The yield strength is then measured as the point at which the powder starts to flow.

This method is valuable for assessing the powder's behavior under compression and during storage, where consolidation can affect flow properties.

6. Compressibility Testing

Compressibility testing involves compressing a known volume of powder in a die and measuring the pressure required to achieve a certain volume reduction. This test provides information on the powder's compressibility and compactibility, which are important for tablet formulation. Powders with good compressibility and compactibility tend to have better flow properties, as they can form cohesive and uniform compacts.

7. Granulometry

Granulometry involves analyzing the size distribution and shape of powder particles using techniques like laser diffraction and image analysis. While primarily used to determine particle size, granulometry can also provide insights into flow properties. Powders with a narrow size distribution and uniform shape typically exhibit better flow characteristics.

8. Angle of Fall, Angle of Spatula, and Angle of Difference

These are less commonly used methods but still provide valuable information about powder flow:

- **Angle of Fall:** The angle at which a powder stops flowing and starts to settle.
- **Angle of Spatula:** The angle formed when a powder is scooped and then released from a spatula.
- **Angle of Difference:** The difference between the angle of repose and the angle of fall.

These angles provide additional data on the dynamic flow behavior of powders.

Solubility Profile (pKa, pH, Partition Coefficient)

Significance of Solubility Profiles in Preformulation Studies

The **solubility profile** of a drug substance is a crucial aspect of preformulation studies, significantly impacting the drug's development and ultimate success. Solubility determines the rate and extent of the drug's dissolution, which in turn affects its **absorption, bioavailability,** and **therapeutic efficacy.** Understanding the solubility profile helps in designing appropriate formulation strategies, ensuring optimal drug delivery and performance.

1. Predicting Bioavailability

Solubility is a key determinant of a drug's **bioavailability**, which is the proportion of the drug that enters the systemic circulation and reaches the target site. Poorly soluble drugs often exhibit low bioavailability because they dissolve slowly in the gastrointestinal tract, limiting the amount of drug absorbed. By understanding the solubility profile, formulation scientists can employ techniques like particle size reduction, salt formation, or the use of solubilizing excipients to enhance the drug's solubility and improve bioavailability.

2. Guiding Formulation Development

The solubility profile informs the selection of the most suitable **dosage form** and **formulation strategy**. For instance, a drug with poor water solubility might be formulated as a **solid dispersion** or incorporated into a **lipid-based delivery system** to enhance its solubility. Conversely, a highly soluble drug may be formulated as a simple solution or suspension. By tailoring the formulation to the drug's solubility characteristics, scientists can optimize the drug's performance and ensure consistent therapeutic outcomes.

3. Ensuring Stability

The solubility profile also provides insights into the drug's **stability** under various conditions. Some drugs may degrade or precipitate out of solution at certain pH levels or in the presence of specific ions. Understanding these solubility-related stability issues allows for the development of formulations that protect the drug from degradation, ensuring its efficacy throughout its shelf life. Stabilizing agents or protective packaging can be employed to maintain the drug's stability.

4. Facilitating Regulatory Compliance

Regulatory agencies require comprehensive data on the solubility and stability of drug substances to ensure their **safety** and **efficacy**. A well-characterized solubility profile supports the regulatory submission process by providing evidence of the drug's performance under various conditions. This data is essential for gaining approval from regulatory bodies and bringing the drug to market.

5. Optimizing Drug Delivery

The solubility profile influences the choice of **drug delivery systems** and **administration routes**. For example, a drug with poor solubility in water but good solubility in lipids may be better suited for a lipid-based formulation like a softgel capsule. Understanding the solubility characteristics enables the development of delivery systems that maximize the drug's therapeutic potential.

6. Enhancing Patient Compliance

By optimizing the solubility profile and ensuring consistent drug release, formulations can be designed to enhance **patient compliance**. Improved solubility can lead to faster onset of action and more predictable therapeutic effects, making it easier for patients to adhere to their prescribed treatment regimens. Patient-friendly dosage forms, such as orally disintegrating tablets or liquid formulations, can also be developed based on solubility data.

7. Reducing Development Costs and Time

Identifying and addressing solubility issues early in the drug development process can reduce **development costs** and **time**. By understanding the solubility profile, potential challenges can be anticipated and mitigated before they become significant obstacles. This proactive approach streamlines the development process and increases the likelihood of success in later stages of development.

Influence of pKa, pH, and Partition Coefficient on Solubility

1. pKa

Definition and Role

The **pKa** of a drug substance is the pH at which the drug exists in equal proportions of ionized and non-ionized forms. It is a critical parameter because the ionization state of a drug influences its solubility, absorption, and overall bioavailability.

Influence on Solubility

- **Ionization and Solubility:** Drugs that ionize more readily in a given pH range are usually more soluble in aqueous solutions. Ionized drugs are more hydrophilic, which enhances their solubility in water. For instance, a weak acid will be more ionized and hence more soluble in a basic environment (higher pH), whereas a weak base will be more ionized and more soluble in an acidic environment (lower pH).
- **Formulation Strategy:** Knowing the pKa helps in selecting the optimal pH for formulation to maximize solubility. For example, if a drug has a pKa of 5, adjusting the formulation pH to around 7-8 (basic) will increase the solubility of an acidic drug by ensuring it is predominantly in its ionized form.

2. pH

Definition and Role

The **pH** of the environment, such as the gastrointestinal (GI) tract, affects the ionization state of a drug, and consequently, its solubility and absorption. Different parts of the GI tract have varying pH levels, influencing the solubility of drugs at different locations.

Influence on Solubility

- **pH-Dependent Solubility:** The solubility of a drug can change significantly with pH. For weak acids and bases, solubility is highly pH-dependent. Weak acids are more soluble at higher pH (alkaline conditions), whereas weak bases are more soluble at lower pH (acidic conditions).
- **Site-Specific Absorption:** Understanding the pH solubility profile helps predict where in the GI tract a drug will dissolve and be absorbed. For instance, a drug that is more soluble in the acidic environment of the stomach may be absorbed better in the stomach, while a drug that is more soluble in the slightly alkaline environment of the intestine may be absorbed in the intestines.

3. Partition Coefficient (Log P)

Definition and Role

The **partition coefficient (Log P)** is a measure of a drug's lipophilicity, representing the ratio of its concentrations in a nonpolar solvent (usually octanol) and a polar solvent (usually water). It provides insights into the drug's ability to cross biological membranes, which is critical for its absorption and distribution.

Influence on Solubility

- **Balancing Solubility and Permeability:** A drug with a high partition coefficient (high Log P) is more lipophilic and tends to dissolve better in lipids but poorly in water. Conversely, a drug with a low partition coefficient (low Log P) is more hydrophilic and dissolves better in water but poorly in lipids. Optimal drug candidates often have a balanced Log P to ensure sufficient solubility in aqueous biological fluids and adequate permeability across lipid membranes.
- **Formulation Implications:** For drugs with high Log P (lipophilic), formulation strategies may include the use of surfactants, complexation,

or lipid-based delivery systems to enhance their solubility in aqueous environments. For drugs with low Log P (hydrophilic), strategies may involve using co-solvents or solid dispersions to improve their solubility in lipid membranes.

Interplay between pKa, pH, and Partition Coefficient

- **Ionization and Lipophilicity:** The ionization state of a drug (determined by its pKa and the pH of the environment) can affect its partition coefficient. Ionized forms of drugs are typically more soluble in water but less lipophilic, impacting their ability to permeate cell membranes. Non-ionized forms, on the other hand, are more lipophilic and can cross lipid membranes more easily but may have reduced aqueous solubility.
- **Optimizing Drug Formulation:** A comprehensive understanding of pKa, pH, and partition coefficient allows formulation scientists to predict and optimize the solubility and permeability of drugs. This knowledge is used to design formulations that maintain the drug in its optimal ionization state for maximum solubility and absorption at the site of administration.

Importance of Determining the Solubility Profile for Predicting Drug Absorption and Bioavailability

Determining the **solubility profile** of a drug substance is a crucial step in preformulation studies because it directly impacts the drug's absorption, bioavailability, and overall therapeutic effectiveness. Here's an in-depth explanation of why solubility profiles are essential for predicting these key aspects of drug performance:

1. Predicting Absorption

Dissolution and Absorption

The first step in the oral absorption of a drug is its dissolution in the gastrointestinal (GI) fluids. Only the dissolved drug can pass through the intestinal membrane into the bloodstream. Therefore, a drug's solubility in GI fluids is a critical determinant of its absorption. A comprehensive solubility profile helps predict how well a drug will dissolve in the varying pH environments of the GI tract, which is essential for designing effective formulations.

Site-Specific Absorption

The solubility profile indicates the solubility of the drug at different pH levels, corresponding to different parts of the GI tract. For example, the stomach has an acidic environment (low pH), while the intestines have a more neutral to slightly basic environment (higher pH). Understanding the solubility at these different pH levels helps in predicting where the drug will dissolve and be absorbed, aiding in the design of formulations that target specific absorption sites.

2. Enhancing Bioavailability

Solubility and Bioavailability

Bioavailability is the proportion of an administered dose of a drug that reaches the systemic circulation in an active form. Poorly soluble drugs often exhibit low bioavailability because they dissolve slowly and incompletely in the GI tract, limiting the amount available for absorption. By determining the solubility profile, formulation scientists can identify solubility-limiting steps and develop strategies to enhance dissolution, thereby improving bioavailability.

Formulation Strategies

A well-characterized solubility profile allows for the selection of appropriate formulation techniques to enhance solubility and bioavailability. For instance, techniques such as particle size reduction (micronization or nanonization), the use of solubilizing excipients, solid dispersions, or complexation with cyclodextrins can be employed based on the solubility data. These strategies increase the surface area available for dissolution, improve wettability, or alter the drug's crystalline form to enhance solubility and bioavailability.

3. Optimizing Dosage Forms

Designing Effective Dosage Forms

The solubility profile informs the design of various dosage forms, ensuring that the drug is delivered in a form that maximizes its dissolution and absorption. For instance, a drug with poor water solubility might be formulated as a lipid-based system, a self-emulsifying drug delivery system (SEDDS), or an amorphous solid dispersion to enhance its solubility. For highly soluble drugs, simpler dosage forms like tablets or capsules might be sufficient.

Controlled Release Formulations

For drugs that require controlled or sustained release, the solubility profile helps in designing formulations that release the drug at the desired rate and location in the GI tract. By understanding how the drug dissolves at different pH levels, scientists can develop matrix systems, coated beads, or osmotic pumps that provide a controlled release profile, maintaining therapeutic levels of the drug over an extended period.

4. Ensuring Stability and Efficacy

Preventing Precipitation

Some drugs may precipitate out of solution if their solubility is exceeded, leading to reduced absorption and bioavailability. Determining the solubility profile helps identify conditions under which precipitation may occur, allowing for the design of formulations that maintain the drug in a soluble state throughout its shelf life and during its passage through the GI tract.

Stability Considerations

The solubility profile also provides insights into the stability of the drug in different environments. Drugs that are highly soluble in water but unstable in solution may require special formulation techniques, such as lyophilization (freeze-drying) or the use of stabilizing agents, to ensure they remain effective until they reach the target site.

5. Regulatory Compliance and Drug Approval

Regulatory Requirements

Regulatory agencies require comprehensive solubility data to ensure the safety and efficacy of new drug products. A well-documented solubility profile supports regulatory submissions by providing evidence that the drug will dissolve and be absorbed adequately in the human body. This data is critical for gaining approval from regulatory bodies and bringing new drugs to market.

6. Reducing Development Costs and Time

Streamlining Development

Identifying and addressing solubility issues early in the drug development process can reduce development costs and time. By understanding the solubility profile, potential challenges can be anticipated and mitigated before they become significant obstacles. This proactive approach streamlines the development process, increases the likelihood of success in later stages, and accelerates the time to market.

Polymorphism

Definition and Impact on Drug Development

Polymorphism refers to the ability of a substance to exist in more than one crystalline form. These different forms, known as polymorphs, can have distinct physical and chemical properties despite being composed of the same molecules. Polymorphism is a critical concept in drug development because the polymorphic form of a drug substance can significantly impact its **solubility, stability, bioavailability,** and **manufacturability.** Understanding and controlling polymorphism is essential for ensuring the efficacy, safety, and quality of pharmaceutical products.

1. Solubility and Dissolution Rate

Impact on Solubility

Different polymorphic forms can exhibit markedly different solubility profiles. Generally, polymorphs with higher free energy, such as metastable forms, tend to be more soluble than their stable counterparts. This increased solubility can enhance the dissolution rate of the drug, potentially leading to improved bioavailability. For instance, a metastable polymorph of a poorly soluble drug might dissolve faster and to a greater extent in the gastrointestinal tract, improving its absorption and therapeutic effect.

Dissolution Rate

The rate at which a drug dissolves is critical for its absorption. Polymorphs with higher solubility will typically dissolve more rapidly, enhancing the drug's bioavailability. Conversely, a less soluble polymorph may dissolve slowly, limiting the amount of drug available for absorption and potentially reducing its effectiveness.

2. Stability and Shelf Life

Physical Stability

Polymorphic forms can differ significantly in their physical stability. The most stable polymorph will generally be less prone to transformation or degradation under varying environmental conditions such as temperature, humidity, and mechanical stress. Ensuring that the drug is in its most stable polymorphic form can help maintain its potency and efficacy throughout its shelf life.

Chemical Stability

Chemical stability can also be influenced by polymorphism. Some polymorphs may be more susceptible to chemical degradation than others. For example, a less stable polymorph might degrade faster under stress conditions, leading to reduced shelf life and potential safety concerns. Identifying the most chemically stable polymorph is crucial for developing a robust drug product.

3. Bioavailability
Enhanced Bioavailability

As mentioned, more soluble polymorphs can dissolve more readily in biological fluids, leading to higher concentrations of the drug in the bloodstream and thus improved bioavailability. This is particularly important for drugs with poor water solubility, as optimizing the polymorphic form can be a key strategy for enhancing their therapeutic efficacy.

Consistency in Bioavailability

Ensuring consistent bioavailability requires maintaining the drug in a specific polymorphic form throughout its shelf life and during administration. If a drug transforms into a less soluble polymorph during storage or upon administration, its bioavailability could decrease, leading to variable therapeutic outcomes.

4. Manufacturability
Processing and Formulation

Polymorphism can affect the mechanical properties of drug substances, such as compressibility and flowability, which are critical for the manufacturing process. For example, one polymorph may have better flow properties, making it easier to process and formulate into tablets or capsules. Conversely, a polymorph with poor mechanical properties could pose challenges during manufacturing, leading to issues like tablet capping or inconsistent dosing.

Scale-Up and Reproducibility

Reproducibility in producing a specific polymorph at a commercial scale can be challenging. Variations in manufacturing conditions, such as temperature, pressure, and solvent use, can influence the polymorphic outcome. Ensuring that the chosen polymorph can be reliably produced at scale is essential for consistent drug quality.

5. Regulatory and Intellectual Property Considerations
Regulatory Approval

Regulatory agencies require detailed characterization of the polymorphic forms of a drug substance. This includes data on the stability, solubility, and bioavailability of each polymorph. Ensuring that the drug product remains in the intended polymorphic form throughout its shelf life is critical for regulatory approval.

Intellectual Property

Polymorphs can be patented, providing a form of intellectual property protection. Discovering a new, more effective polymorph of an existing drug can extend the market exclusivity of a product. However, this also means that competitors may seek to develop alternative polymorphs to circumvent existing patents.

Examples of Polymorphism in Drug Development

A well-known example of polymorphism impacting drug development is **ritonavir**, an antiretroviral medication used to treat HIV/AIDS. Initially, ritonavir was marketed in a specific polymorphic form. However, a more stable but less soluble polymorph unexpectedly appeared, leading to formulation challenges and a temporary market withdrawal. This case underscores the importance of thorough polymorphic screening and control during drug development.

Another example is **carbamazepine**, an anticonvulsant drug that exhibits multiple polymorphic forms with different solubilities and stabilities. The choice of polymorph significantly influences the drug's formulation and therapeutic performance.

Impact of Different Polymorphic Forms on Therapeutic Efficacy and Stability

1. Therapeutic Efficacy

Solubility and Dissolution Rate

The solubility and dissolution rate of a drug are directly influenced by its polymorphic form, which in turn affects the drug's therapeutic efficacy. Different polymorphs can have varying degrees of solubility:

- **Higher Solubility:** Polymorphs with higher solubility dissolve more readily in biological fluids, leading to faster and more complete absorption. This can result in higher plasma drug concentrations, enhancing therapeutic efficacy. For example, a more soluble polymorph of a poorly water-soluble drug may achieve better bioavailability, resulting in more consistent and predictable therapeutic effects.

- **Lower Solubility:** Conversely, polymorphs with lower solubility dissolve more slowly, potentially limiting absorption and bioavailability. This can lead to suboptimal drug levels in the bloodstream and reduced therapeutic efficacy. For instance, if a drug predominantly exists in a less soluble polymorph, it might require higher doses to achieve the desired therapeutic effect, which could increase the risk of side effects.

Bioavailability

Bioavailability is a critical factor in determining the therapeutic efficacy of a drug. Polymorphs that exhibit better dissolution rates and solubility are likely to have higher bioavailability. This is particularly important for oral dosage forms where the drug must dissolve in the gastrointestinal fluids before being absorbed. A polymorph with poor bioavailability may necessitate more complex formulations or alternative administration routes to achieve effective plasma concentrations.

Onset of Action

The onset of action of a drug can also be influenced by its polymorphic form. More soluble polymorphs tend to dissolve and absorb faster, leading to a quicker onset of therapeutic effects. This can be crucial for drugs intended for acute conditions, where rapid relief is necessary. Conversely, a less soluble polymorph might delay the onset of action, which could be detrimental in urgent treatment scenarios.

2. Stability

Physical Stability

Polymorphic forms can exhibit different physical stabilities, which affect the shelf life and handling of the drug product:

- **Stable Polymorphs:** The most stable polymorph typically resists physical changes under varying environmental conditions such as temperature, humidity, and mechanical stress. Ensuring the drug is in its most stable polymorphic form helps maintain its integrity, potency, and safety throughout its shelf life.
- **Metastable Polymorphs:** Metastable polymorphs, while often more soluble, are less stable and may transform into more stable forms over time or under certain conditions. This transformation can result in changes in solubility, dissolution rate, and ultimately, therapeutic efficacy. For instance, a metastable polymorph might provide excellent initial bioavailability but could convert to a less soluble, stable polymorph during storage, reducing its effectiveness.

Chemical Stability

The chemical stability of different polymorphic forms can vary, impacting the degradation rate of the drug:

- **Stable Polymorphs:** These forms are generally more resistant to chemical degradation. Ensuring the drug is formulated in a chemically stable polymorph helps prevent degradation, maintaining its therapeutic efficacy and safety.
- **Less Stable Polymorphs:** Polymorphs that are less chemically stable might degrade faster, leading to a loss of potency and the formation of potentially harmful degradation products. This can compromise the drug's efficacy and safety, necessitating the use of stabilizers or protective packaging to extend shelf life.

Storage and Handling

Different polymorphs may have varying requirements for storage and handling:

- **Stable Polymorphs:** These are generally easier to store and handle, as they are less likely to undergo physical or chemical changes. This simplifies the logistics of drug distribution and storage.
- **Metastable Polymorphs:** These may require special storage conditions, such as controlled temperature and humidity, to prevent transformation into less desirable forms. This can complicate the supply chain and increase costs.

Examples in Drug Development
Ritonavir

Ritonavir, an antiretroviral drug, is a well-known example where polymorphism significantly impacted its therapeutic efficacy and stability. Initially, ritonavir was developed and marketed in a specific polymorphic form. However, a more stable but less soluble polymorph emerged during manufacturing, which led to reduced bioavailability and necessitated a reformulation of the drug. This case underscores the importance of thorough polymorphic screening and control in drug development.

Carbamazepine

Carbamazepine, an anticonvulsant, exhibits multiple polymorphic forms, each with different solubilities and stabilities. The different polymorphs of carbamazepine can affect its dissolution rate, bioavailability, and stability, influencing its therapeutic efficacy. Proper selection and control of the polymorphic form are essential to ensure consistent drug performance.

Techniques to Identify and Characterize Polymorphic Forms of Drugs

Identifying and characterizing the polymorphic forms of drug substances is critical in pharmaceutical development to ensure the drug's efficacy, stability, and manufacturability. Several advanced techniques are employed to analyze and differentiate between polymorphic forms, each offering unique insights into the structural and physical properties of the drug. Here are the key techniques used:

1. X-Ray Powder Diffraction (XRPD)

Principle and Application

X-Ray Powder Diffraction (XRPD) is the gold standard for identifying and characterizing polymorphic forms. It works on the principle that crystalline materials diffract X-rays at specific angles, producing a unique diffraction pattern that serves as a "fingerprint" for the crystalline structure.

Advantages

- **Distinctive Fingerprints:** Each polymorph produces a unique XRPD pattern, allowing for precise identification and differentiation between polymorphic forms.
- **Non-Destructive:** XRPD is a non-destructive technique, preserving the sample for further analysis.
- **Quantitative Analysis:** It can quantify the relative amounts of different polymorphs in a mixture, providing valuable information for quality control.

2. Differential Scanning Calorimetry (DSC)

Principle and Application

Differential Scanning Calorimetry (DSC) measures the heat flow associated with phase transitions in a material as a function of temperature. Different polymorphs exhibit distinct melting points and enthalpies of fusion, which can be detected and analyzed using DSC.

Advantages

- **Thermal Properties:** DSC provides information on the thermal properties of polymorphs, including melting points, crystallization, and phase transitions.

- **Quantitative:** It allows for the quantification of polymorphs based on their thermal transitions.
- **Compatibility Studies:** DSC can be used to study the compatibility of polymorphs with excipients.

3. Fourier-Transform Infrared Spectroscopy (FTIR)

Principle and Application

Fourier-Transform Infrared Spectroscopy (FTIR) measures the absorption of infrared light by a sample, producing a spectrum that represents the molecular vibrations within the sample. Different polymorphs may have distinct infrared absorption patterns due to variations in their molecular arrangements.

Advantages

- **Molecular Fingerprints:** FTIR provides detailed information on the molecular structure and chemical environment of polymorphs.
- **Rapid Analysis:** It is a quick and non-destructive technique that requires minimal sample preparation.
- **Compatibility Studies:** FTIR can be used to assess the compatibility of polymorphs with other formulation components.

4. Raman Spectroscopy

Principle and Application

Raman Spectroscopy measures the scattering of monochromatic light (usually from a laser) by a sample, producing a spectrum that provides information about the molecular vibrations. Different polymorphs can produce distinct Raman spectra.

Advantages

- **Complementary to FTIR:** Raman spectroscopy provides complementary information to FTIR, helping to confirm polymorphic forms.
- **Non-Destructive:** It is a non-destructive technique that requires little to no sample preparation.
- **High Spatial Resolution:** Raman spectroscopy offers high spatial resolution, making it useful for studying polymorphs in heterogeneous samples.

5. Solid-State Nuclear Magnetic Resonance (ssNMR) Spectroscopy

Principle and Application

Solid-State Nuclear Magnetic Resonance (ssNMR) Spectroscopy provides detailed information about the atomic environment and molecular dynamics in solid samples. Different polymorphs exhibit distinct ssNMR spectra due to variations in their crystalline structures.

Advantages

- **Detailed Structural Information:** ssNMR provides comprehensive information about the atomic and molecular structure of polymorphs.
- **Non-Destructive:** It is a non-destructive technique that preserves the sample.
- **Complex Systems:** ssNMR is particularly useful for studying complex systems, including amorphous and crystalline mixtures.

6. Thermogravimetric Analysis (TGA)

Principle and Application

Thermogravimetric Analysis (TGA) measures the change in weight of a sample as a function of temperature. Different polymorphs can exhibit distinct thermal degradation patterns, which can be used to identify and characterize them.

Advantages

- **Thermal Stability:** TGA provides information on the thermal stability and composition of polymorphs.
- **Quantitative:** It allows for the quantification of different components based on their thermal degradation profiles.

7. Hot-Stage Microscopy (HSM)

Principle and Application

Hot-Stage Microscopy (HSM) involves the observation of a sample under a microscope while it is heated. This technique allows for the direct visual observation of phase transitions, crystallization, and melting behavior of polymorphs.

Advantages

- **Visual Observation:** HSM provides direct visual evidence of phase transitions and morphological changes.

- **Qualitative Analysis:** It is useful for qualitative analysis and understanding the behavior of polymorphs under thermal stress.

8. Single-Crystal X-Ray Diffraction (SCXRD)
Principle and Application

Single-Crystal X-Ray Diffraction (SCXRD) provides detailed information about the three-dimensional atomic structure of a single crystal. It is used to determine the precise arrangement of atoms in a polymorphic form.
Advantages

- **Detailed Structural Information:** SCXRD provides the most detailed information about the atomic arrangement and molecular geometry of polymorphs.
- **High Resolution:** It offers high-resolution structural data, essential for understanding complex polymorphic systems.

9. Polarized Light Microscopy (PLM)
Principle and Application

Polarized Light Microscopy (PLM) uses polarized light to observe the birefringent properties of crystalline materials. Different polymorphs can exhibit distinct optical properties under polarized light.
Advantages

- **Morphological Information:** PLM provides valuable information on the morphology and birefringence of polymorphs.
- **Rapid Analysis:** It is a quick and straightforward technique for initial polymorphic screening.

1.2 Study of Physicochemical Characteristics of Drug Substances
1.2.2 Chemical Properties

Hydrolysis

Hydrolysis is a chemical reaction in which a compound reacts with water, resulting in the breakdown of the compound into smaller molecules. In the context of pharmaceuticals, hydrolysis typically involves the cleavage of chemical bonds such as esters, amides, lactones, and lactams, leading to the formation of acids, alcohols, or amines. This reaction is catalyzed by the presence of water and can be influenced by factors such as pH, temperature, and the presence of catalytic ions or enzymes.

Hydrolysis is a critical consideration in preformulation studies for several reasons:

1. **Drug Stability**: Many drug substances are susceptible to hydrolytic degradation, which can lead to a loss of potency and efficacy. Understanding the hydrolytic stability of a drug is essential to ensure that it remains effective throughout its shelf life.
2. **Formulation Design**: Knowledge of hydrolysis helps in designing appropriate formulations that protect the drug from water and moisture. This is particularly important for drugs that are highly susceptible to hydrolysis.
3. **Storage Conditions**: Identifying the hydrolytic properties of a drug aids in determining suitable storage conditions, such as controlling humidity and temperature, to prolong the drug's stability.
4. **Regulatory Compliance**: Regulatory agencies require stability data, including hydrolytic stability, to ensure the safety and efficacy of drug products. Comprehensive hydrolytic studies are necessary for regulatory submissions and approvals.

Impact of Hydrolysis on the Stability and Shelf Life of Drug Products
1. Degradation and Loss of Potency

Hydrolysis can lead to the chemical degradation of drug substances, resulting in a loss of potency. For instance, ester-containing drugs may hydrolyze into their corresponding acids and alcohols, which may not have the desired therapeutic activity. This degradation reduces the drug's effectiveness, potentially rendering it ineffective for its intended use.

2. Formation of Toxic or Inactive Metabolites

In some cases, hydrolysis can produce toxic or inactive metabolites that compromise the safety and efficacy of the drug. For example, the hydrolytic degradation of certain antibiotics can produce inactive metabolites that do not exhibit antimicrobial activity, reducing the drug's therapeutic effectiveness and potentially leading to treatment failure.

3. Reduced Shelf Life

The hydrolytic instability of a drug can significantly reduce its shelf life. Drugs that are prone to hydrolysis may require special packaging and storage conditions to prevent exposure to moisture. Without these precautions, the drug may degrade rapidly, leading to a shorter shelf life and increased costs due to the need for frequent replacements.

4. Impact on Drug Formulation

Hydrolysis can affect the physical and chemical properties of the drug formulation, such as pH, viscosity, and solubility. These changes can impact the drug's bioavailability and overall performance. For example, the hydrolytic degradation of a drug in a liquid formulation can alter the pH, affecting the solubility and stability of other components in the formulation.

Strategies to Minimize Hydrolytic Degradation of Pharmaceuticals

Several strategies can be employed to minimize hydrolytic degradation and enhance the stability of pharmaceutical products:

1. Use of Stabilizers

Incorporating stabilizers into the formulation can help protect the drug from hydrolysis. Stabilizers work by either complexing with the drug to form a more stable compound or by scavenging water to prevent it from reacting with the drug. For example, antioxidants and chelating agents can be used to inhibit hydrolytic reactions.

2. pH Adjustment

Adjusting the pH of the formulation to a range where the drug is less susceptible to hydrolysis can enhance stability. For example, buffering agents can be used to maintain the pH within a range that minimizes hydrolytic degradation. This approach requires a thorough understanding of the pH-stability profile of the drug.

3. Use of Anhydrous or Low-Moisture Formulations

Formulating the drug in an anhydrous (water-free) or low-moisture environment can significantly reduce the risk of hydrolysis. Solid dosage forms, such as tablets and capsules, are less prone to hydrolytic degradation compared to liquid formulations. Lyophilization (freeze-drying) can be used to produce stable, anhydrous formulations for drugs that are highly sensitive to moisture.

4. Protective Packaging

Packaging materials that provide a barrier to moisture can help protect the drug from hydrolytic degradation. Examples include blister packs with desiccants, moisture-impermeable containers, and vacuum-sealed packaging. These packaging solutions help maintain a dry environment around the drug, reducing the risk of hydrolysis.

5. Refrigeration and Controlled Storage Conditions

Storing the drug at lower temperatures can slow down the rate of hydrolytic reactions. Refrigeration and climate-controlled storage environments help maintain the stability of hydrolysis-sensitive drugs. Additionally, controlling humidity levels in storage areas can further reduce the risk of moisture-induced degradation.

6. Prodrug Approach

In some cases, designing a prodrug—a chemically modified version of the active drug—can enhance stability. Prodrugs are inactive derivatives that undergo bioconversion to the active form within the body. By modifying the chemical structure to resist hydrolysis, prodrugs can improve the stability and shelf life of the active drug.

7. Incorporation of Water-Resistant Excipients

Using excipients that are resistant to moisture can help protect the drug from hydrolysis. These excipients can form a protective matrix around the drug, reducing its exposure to water. Examples include certain polymers, lipids, and hydrophobic carriers.

1.2 Study of Physicochemical Characteristics of Drug Substances
1.2.2 Chemical Properties

Oxidation

Oxidation is a chemical reaction involving the transfer of electrons from a substance to an oxidizing agent, often resulting in the formation of free radicals and reactive oxygen species. This process can lead to the degradation of drug substances. Studying oxidation during preformulation is crucial for several reasons:

1. **Drug Stability**: Many drug substances are susceptible to oxidative degradation, which can lead to the formation of degradation products that affect the drug's stability, potency, and efficacy. Understanding the oxidative stability of a drug is essential to ensure that it remains effective throughout its shelf life.

2. **Safety and Efficacy**: Oxidative degradation can produce toxic or inactive metabolites that compromise the safety and efficacy of the drug. Identifying and mitigating oxidative pathways during preformulation helps in developing safe and effective pharmaceutical products.

3. **Formulation Development**: Knowledge of a drug's susceptibility to oxidation guides the selection of appropriate formulation strategies and excipients that protect the drug from oxidative degradation.

4. **Regulatory Compliance**: Regulatory agencies require comprehensive stability data, including the oxidative stability of drug substances. Conducting oxidation studies during preformulation supports regulatory submissions and approvals.

Impact of Oxidation Reactions on the Potency and Safety of Drug Substances

1. Degradation and Loss of Potency

Oxidation can lead to the chemical degradation of drug substances, resulting in the loss of potency. For example, drugs containing phenolic, alcoholic, or amine groups are particularly prone to oxidation. When these functional groups are oxidized, the drug's active form may be converted into inactive or less active forms, reducing its therapeutic efficacy.

2. Formation of Toxic Metabolites

Oxidative degradation can produce harmful or toxic metabolites that pose safety risks to patients. For instance, the oxidation of certain drugs can lead to the formation of reactive intermediates or peroxides, which can cause cellular damage and adverse effects.

3. Reduced Shelf Life

The oxidative instability of a drug can significantly shorten its shelf life. Drugs that are prone to oxidation may require special packaging and storage conditions to protect them from exposure to oxygen and light. Without these precautions, the drug may degrade rapidly, leading to a shorter shelf life and increased costs due to the need for frequent replacements.

4. Impact on Drug Formulation

Oxidation can affect the physical and chemical properties of the drug formulation, such as color, odor, and solubility. These changes can impact the drug's acceptability and performance. For example, the oxidation of certain drugs can lead to discoloration, making the product less appealing to patients.

Measures to Protect Drugs from Oxidative Degradation

Several strategies can be employed to protect drugs from oxidative degradation and enhance their stability:

1. Use of Antioxidants

Incorporating antioxidants into the formulation can help protect the drug from oxidation. Antioxidants work by scavenging free radicals and reactive oxygen species, preventing them from reacting with the drug. Common antioxidants used in pharmaceutical formulations include ascorbic acid (vitamin C), tocopherols (vitamin E), butylated hydroxytoluene (BHT), and butylated hydroxyanisole (BHA).

2. Exclusion of Oxygen

Removing oxygen from the formulation environment can significantly reduce the risk of oxidative degradation. This can be achieved through:

- **Nitrogen or Argon Purging:** Inert gases like nitrogen or argon can be used to purge oxygen from containers and packaging.
- **Vacuum Sealing:** Vacuum sealing removes air from the packaging, minimizing the presence of oxygen.
- **Controlled Atmosphere Packaging:** Packaging in a controlled atmosphere with reduced oxygen levels helps protect the drug from oxidation.

3. Use of Chelating Agents

Chelating agents can bind to metal ions that catalyze oxidative reactions, thereby inhibiting the oxidation process. Common chelating agents used in pharmaceuticals include ethylenediaminetetraacetic acid (EDTA) and citric acid.

4. pH Control

Maintaining the formulation at an optimal pH can reduce the rate of oxidative degradation. The pH can influence the ionization state of the drug and the reactivity of oxidizing agents. Buffering agents can be used to maintain the pH within a range that minimizes oxidative reactions.

5. Protective Packaging

Using packaging materials that provide a barrier to oxygen and light can help protect the drug from oxidative degradation. Examples include:

- **Amber Glass Bottles:** Amber glass provides protection from light, which can catalyze oxidative reactions.
- **Blister Packs with Foil Backing:** Foil-backed blister packs offer an effective barrier to both oxygen and moisture.
- **High-Barrier Plastics:** Certain plastics are designed to provide excellent oxygen barrier properties.

6. Refrigeration and Controlled Storage Conditions

Storing the drug at lower temperatures can slow down the rate of oxidative reactions. Refrigeration and climate-controlled storage environments help maintain the stability of oxidation-sensitive drugs. Additionally, controlling humidity levels in storage areas can further reduce the risk of oxidative degradation.

7. Prodrug Approach

Designing a prodrug—a chemically modified version of the active drug—can enhance stability. Prodrugs are inactive derivatives that undergo bioconversion to the active form within the body. By modifying the chemical structure to resist oxidation, prodrugs can improve the stability and shelf life of the active drug.

8. Incorporation of Oxygen Scavengers

Oxygen scavengers can be incorporated into the packaging to remove residual oxygen. These scavengers react with oxygen to form inert compounds, thereby protecting the drug from oxidation. Oxygen scavengers are often used in sachets or canisters placed within the packaging.

1.2 Study of Physicochemical Characteristics of Drug Substances

1.2.2 Chemical Properties

Reduction

Reduction is a chemical reaction in which a molecule gains electrons, resulting in a decrease in its oxidation state. This process is the opposite of **oxidation**, where a molecule loses electrons and increases its oxidation state. In the context of drug stability, reduction can lead to the conversion of drug molecules into different chemical forms, potentially affecting their efficacy, safety, and stability.

Differences Between Reduction and Oxidation:

- **Electron Transfer:** In reduction, a molecule gains electrons, whereas in oxidation, a molecule loses electrons.
- **Oxidation State:** Reduction decreases the oxidation state of a molecule, while oxidation increases it.
- **Reaction Types:** Reduction reactions often involve hydrogenation (addition of hydrogen) or the removal of oxygen, whereas oxidation reactions typically involve the addition of oxygen or removal of

hydrogen.

Examples of Drugs that Undergo Reduction Reactions and Their Implications

1. Nitro Compounds

Example: Nitrofurantoin

- **Reduction Reaction:** Nitrofurantoin undergoes reduction in the body, where its nitro group is reduced to an amine group.
- **Implications:** The reduction of nitrofurantoin is necessary for its antibacterial activity. However, in some cases, the reduction process can lead to the formation of toxic metabolites, which can cause adverse effects such as liver damage.

2. Quinones

Example: Doxorubicin

- **Reduction Reaction:** Doxorubicin, an anticancer drug, can undergo reduction to form hydroquinone derivatives.
- **Implications:** The reduction of doxorubicin can lead to the generation of reactive oxygen species (ROS), contributing to its cardiotoxicity. This highlights the importance of monitoring and controlling reduction reactions to mitigate side effects.

3. Azobenzene Compounds

Example: Prodrug Sulfasalazine

- **Reduction Reaction:** Sulfasalazine is reduced in the colon by bacterial azoreductases, splitting it into sulfapyridine and 5-aminosalicylic acid (5-ASA).
- **Implications:** This reduction is essential for the therapeutic action of sulfasalazine in treating inflammatory bowel disease, as 5-ASA is the active anti-inflammatory agent.

How Do Preformulation Studies Address the Challenges Posed by Reduction?

1. Identifying Reduction-Prone Functional Groups

Preformulation studies involve the identification of functional groups within drug molecules that are prone to reduction. By understanding the chemical structure and reactivity of the drug, scientists can predict potential reduction pathways and their implications. This knowledge helps in designing strategies to stabilize the drug against reduction.

2. Evaluating the Stability of Drug Substances

Preformulation studies include stability testing under various conditions to evaluate the susceptibility of the drug to reduction. These tests involve exposing the drug to reducing environments, such as the presence of reducing agents or specific pH conditions, and monitoring any chemical changes. Stability testing helps in understanding the conditions that promote reduction and designing formulations to mitigate these effects.

3. Use of Reducing Agent Inhibitors

To protect drugs from reduction, preformulation studies may explore the use of reducing agent inhibitors. These inhibitors can prevent or slow down the reduction process by reacting preferentially with the reducing agents or by stabilizing the drug molecule in its original oxidation state. For example, antioxidants can be used to scavenge free radicals and prevent unwanted reduction reactions.

4. Formulation Strategies

Formulation strategies play a crucial role in addressing reduction challenges:

- **Protective Coatings:** Applying protective coatings to drug particles can shield them from reducing environments. These coatings can be designed to dissolve only under specific conditions, such as in the stomach or intestines, ensuring that the drug remains stable until it reaches its target site.
- **Encapsulation:** Encapsulation techniques, such as using liposomes or microspheres, can protect the drug from reduction by creating a physical barrier between the drug and reducing agents.
- **Use of Stabilizing Excipients:** Incorporating stabilizing excipients into the formulation can enhance the drug's resistance to reduction. Excipients such as cyclodextrins can form inclusion complexes with the drug, protecting it from chemical reactions.

5. Optimizing Storage and Packaging Conditions

Preformulation studies help determine the optimal storage and packaging conditions to minimize reduction. These conditions include controlling temperature, humidity, and exposure to reducing agents. Packaging materials that provide an effective barrier against environmental factors are selected to enhance the stability of the drug.

6. Monitoring and Analytical Techniques

Advanced analytical techniques are employed in preformulation studies to monitor reduction reactions and identify degradation products. Techniques such as high-performance liquid chromatography (HPLC), mass spectrometry (MS), and nuclear magnetic resonance (NMR) spectroscopy are used to detect and quantify the extent of reduction. These techniques provide detailed insights into the drug's stability and guide the development of stabilization strategies.

7. Prodrug Approach

In some cases, designing prodrugs that are more resistant to reduction can enhance stability. Prodrugs are chemically modified versions of the active drug that undergo bioconversion to the active form within the body. By modifying the chemical structure to reduce susceptibility to reduction, prodrugs can improve stability and extend shelf life.

1.2 Study of Physicochemical Characteristics of Drug Substances

1.2.2 Chemical Properties

Racemisation

Racemisation is a chemical process in which an optically active chiral molecule is converted into a racemic mixture, containing equal amounts of both enantiomers (mirror-image isomers). This process results in the loss of chirality and optical activity of the original substance.

Relevance in Drug Substances

1. **Chirality and Drug Activity**: Many drugs are chiral, meaning they have molecules that can exist in two enantiomeric forms. These enantiomers often have different pharmacological activities. In some cases, one enantiomer is therapeutically active, while the other may be inactive or even harmful. Racemisation can convert the active enantiomer into its inactive or harmful counterpart, affecting the drug's efficacy and safety.

2. **Regulatory Requirements**: Regulatory agencies require comprehensive evaluation of the chiral properties of drugs. Understanding and

controlling racemisation is crucial for meeting regulatory standards and ensuring the consistency and quality of chiral drugs.

Impact of Racemisation on Efficacy and Safety of Chiral Drugs

1. **Loss of Efficacy**

   - **Active Enantiomer Conversion**: If the active enantiomer of a chiral drug racemises to its inactive form, the overall therapeutic effect of the drug can diminish. This loss of efficacy can lead to suboptimal treatment outcomes.
   - **Dose Adjustment**: Racemisation might necessitate higher doses to achieve the desired therapeutic effect, potentially increasing the risk of side effects and toxicity.

2. **Safety Concerns**

   - **Toxicity of Inactive Enantiomer**: The inactive enantiomer produced through racemisation may have adverse effects, causing toxicity or side effects not associated with the original active enantiomer.
   - **Unpredictable Behavior**: The presence of both enantiomers can lead to unpredictable pharmacokinetics and pharmacodynamics, complicating dosage and treatment regimens.

Methods to Detect and Prevent Racemisation During Drug Development

1. **Detection Methods**

   - **Chiral Chromatography**: High-performance liquid chromatography (HPLC) with chiral stationary phases is commonly used to separate and quantify enantiomers, allowing for the detection of racemisation.
   - **Nuclear Magnetic Resonance (NMR) Spectroscopy**: Chiral NMR spectroscopy can identify and quantify enantiomers, providing detailed information on the extent of racemisation.
   - **Optical Rotation**: Measuring the optical rotation of a solution can indicate changes in the enantiomeric composition, detecting racemisation.

2. Prevention Strategies

- **Optimal pH and Temperature Control**: Maintaining the drug in a pH and temperature range that minimizes racemisation can help preserve the enantiomeric purity.
- **Stabilizing Agents**: Adding excipients or stabilizers that inhibit racemisation can help maintain the chirality of the drug.
- **Prodrug Approach**: Designing prodrugs that are less susceptible to racemisation and convert to the active enantiomer in vivo can improve stability.

Polymerization

Polymerization is a chemical reaction in which small molecules, known as monomers, combine to form larger, more complex structures called polymers. In the context of pharmaceuticals, unintended polymerization can lead to the formation of unwanted high-molecular-weight compounds, potentially compromising the drug's quality and efficacy.

Concern in Pharmaceutical Preformulation

1. **Drug Purity**: Uncontrolled polymerization can lead to impurities that affect the purity of the drug substance, impacting its therapeutic effectiveness and safety.
2. **Stability Issues**: Polymers formed through unintended polymerization can alter the physical and chemical stability of the drug product, leading to degradation and reduced shelf life.
3. **Manufacturing Challenges**: Polymerized drug substances may have altered physical properties, such as increased viscosity, making them difficult to process and manufacture consistently.

Impact on the Stability and Performance of Drug Products

1. **Reduced Efficacy**

- **Active Ingredient Depletion**: Polymerization can reduce the concentration of the active drug substance, decreasing its efficacy.

- **Altered Drug Release**: Polymers can affect the dissolution and release profiles of the drug, leading to inconsistent therapeutic effects.

2. Increased Toxicity

- **Formation of Toxic Polymers**: Some polymers may be toxic or elicit adverse immune responses, compromising patient safety.
- **Unpredictable Pharmacokinetics**: Polymerization can alter the absorption, distribution, metabolism, and excretion (ADME) of the drug, leading to unpredictable pharmacokinetic profiles.

3. Physical and Chemical Instability

- **Changes in Physical Properties**: Increased viscosity, precipitation, or gel formation can occur, affecting the drug's handling and administration.
- **Chemical Degradation**: Polymers may interact with other formulation components, leading to chemical degradation and reduced stability.

Approaches to Prevent or Control Polymerization in Drug Substances

1. Use of Stabilizers

- **Antioxidants**: Adding antioxidants can prevent oxidative polymerization by scavenging free radicals that initiate the process.
- **Free Radical Scavengers**: Compounds that scavenge free radicals can inhibit the polymerization process and protect the drug substance.

2. Optimal Storage Conditions

- **Temperature Control**: Storing drugs at lower temperatures can slow down or prevent polymerization reactions.
- **Light Protection**: Using packaging that protects the drug from light can prevent photo-initiated polymerization.

3. Inhibitors

- ○ **Polymerization Inhibitors**: Specific inhibitors can be added to the formulation to prevent polymerization. These inhibitors work by reacting with the monomers or the active sites of the growing polymer chains.
- ○ **Metal Chelators**: Chelating agents that bind metal ions can prevent metal-catalyzed polymerization.

4. **Formulation Adjustments**

- ○ **pH Control**: Adjusting the pH of the formulation to a range that minimizes polymerization can enhance stability.
- ○ **Solvent Selection**: Using solvents that do not promote polymerization can help maintain the drug's stability.

5. **Analytical Monitoring**

- ○ **Regular Testing**: Implementing regular testing and monitoring for signs of polymerization during storage and throughout the shelf life can help detect early stages of polymerization.
- ○ **Advanced Analytical Techniques**: Techniques such as gel permeation chromatography (GPC) and mass spectrometry (MS) can be used to detect and characterize polymerization products.

1.3 Biopharmaceutics Classification System (BCS)

Classification of Drugs

The **Biopharmaceutics Classification System (BCS)** is a scientific framework that categorizes drugs based on their solubility and permeability characteristics. Developed by the U.S. Food and Drug Administration (FDA), the BCS helps in understanding the factors affecting drug absorption and bioavailability. The classification system divides drugs into four classes:

1. **Class I:** High Solubility, High Permeability
2. **Class II:** Low Solubility, High Permeability
3. **Class III:** High Solubility, Low Permeability
4. **Class IV:** Low Solubility, Low Permeability

Criteria for Classification

- **Solubility:** A drug is considered highly soluble if the highest dose strength is soluble in 250 mL or less of aqueous media over a pH range of 1 to 7.5.
- **Permeability:** A drug is considered highly permeable if the extent of absorption in humans is greater than 90% of the administered dose.

BCS Classification Influence on the Development and Regulatory Approval of Pharmaceuticals?

1. Guiding Formulation Strategies

The BCS classification provides critical insights that guide the formulation development process:

- **Class I Drugs:** These drugs typically do not face significant formulation challenges as they are both highly soluble and highly permeable. Formulators can focus on ensuring stability and patient compliance.
- **Class II Drugs:** The main challenge for these drugs is solubility. Formulation strategies such as particle size reduction, solid dispersions, and lipid-based formulations can be employed to enhance solubility and bioavailability.
- **Class III Drugs:** The primary challenge for these drugs is permeability. Formulation approaches might include the use of absorption enhancers, permeation enhancers, or alternative delivery routes to improve permeability.
- **Class IV Drugs:** These drugs present significant formulation challenges due to their poor solubility and permeability. Innovative formulation techniques and delivery systems are often required to enhance both solubility and permeability.

2. Streamlining Regulatory Approval

The BCS framework helps streamline the regulatory approval process by providing a scientific basis for waiving in vivo bioavailability and bioequivalence studies under certain conditions:

- **Biowaivers:** For BCS Class I drugs, regulatory agencies may grant biowaivers, allowing for the waiver of in vivo bioequivalence studies based on in vitro dissolution testing. This can expedite the approval process and reduce development costs.

- **Predictable Performance:** Understanding the BCS class helps predict the drug's in vivo performance, providing confidence in its bioavailability and therapeutic efficacy. This predictability supports more efficient regulatory submissions and approvals.

3. Facilitating Global Harmonization

The BCS classification is recognized by regulatory agencies worldwide, including the FDA, European Medicines Agency (EMA), and World Health Organization (WHO). This global acceptance facilitates harmonized regulatory requirements and smoother international drug development and approval processes.

Examples of Drugs from Each BCS Class and Their Significance in Preformulation

1. BCS Class I: High Solubility, High Permeability
Example: Metoprolol

- **Significance:** Metoprolol, a beta-blocker used to treat hypertension, is highly soluble and permeable, making it straightforward to formulate. The focus in preformulation is on ensuring stability and developing patient-friendly dosage forms, such as extended-release tablets.

2. BCS Class II: Low Solubility, High Permeability
Example: Ibuprofen

- **Significance:** Ibuprofen, a nonsteroidal anti-inflammatory drug (NSAID), has high permeability but low solubility. Preformulation efforts focus on enhancing solubility through techniques such as micronization, solid dispersions, and lipid-based formulations to improve its bioavailability and therapeutic efficacy.

3. BCS Class III: High Solubility, Low Permeability
Example: Cimetidine

- **Significance:** Cimetidine, used to treat gastrointestinal ulcers, has high solubility but low permeability. Preformulation strategies aim to enhance permeability using absorption enhancers, formulation of prodrugs, or employing drug delivery systems like nanoparticles to improve its absorption.

4. BCS Class IV: Low Solubility, Low Permeability
Example: Hydrochlorothiazide

- **Significance:** Hydrochlorothiazide, a diuretic used to treat hypertension, presents challenges in both solubility and permeability. Preformulation studies focus on innovative delivery systems, such as nanosuspensions, complexation with cyclodextrins, or the use of surfactants to enhance both solubility and permeability.

1.3 Biopharmaceutics Classification System (BCS)
Significance in Preformulation

The **Biopharmaceutics Classification System (BCS)** is crucial in preformulation studies for several reasons:

1. **Framework for Understanding Drug Behavior**: The BCS provides a scientific framework to understand the relationship between a drug's solubility, permeability, and its absorption in the body. This understanding is fundamental in predicting how a drug will behave in vivo, which is essential for effective drug development.
2. **Efficient Resource Allocation**: By classifying drugs into different BCS categories, researchers can prioritize resources and efforts. For instance, Class I drugs, being both highly soluble and permeable, typically require fewer resources to develop effective formulations compared to Class II or IV drugs.
3. **Risk Mitigation**: Early identification of potential issues related to solubility and permeability allows for proactive measures to be taken during the formulation process, thereby mitigating risks associated with poor bioavailability and ensuring the drug's therapeutic efficacy.

How Does the BCS Classification Guide the Selection of Formulation Strategies for New Drug Substances?

The BCS classification provides a clear direction for formulating new drug substances by highlighting the primary challenges that need to be addressed:

1. **Class I: High Solubility, High Permeability**

- ○ **Formulation Focus**: Stability and patient compliance. Since solubility and permeability are not major issues, efforts can be concentrated on ensuring chemical and physical stability, as well as optimizing the dosage form for ease of use.
- ○ **Example Strategies**: Simple solid or liquid formulations, controlled-release formulations to enhance patient adherence.

2. **Class II: Low Solubility, High Permeability**

- ○ **Formulation Focus**: Enhancing solubility. Given that these drugs are highly permeable, improving their solubility is crucial to ensure adequate absorption and bioavailability.
- ○ **Example Strategies**: Particle size reduction (micronization or nanonization), use of solubilizing excipients, solid dispersions, lipid-based formulations, and self-emulsifying drug delivery systems (SEDDS).

3. **Class III: High Solubility, Low Permeability**

- ○ **Formulation Focus**: Enhancing permeability. Since these drugs are highly soluble, the key challenge is to improve their permeability to ensure sufficient absorption.
- ○ **Example Strategies**: Use of absorption enhancers, permeation enhancers, formulation of prodrugs, and the development of advanced drug delivery systems such as nanoparticles or liposomes.

4. **Class IV: Low Solubility, Low Permeability**

- ○ **Formulation Focus**: Enhancing both solubility and permeability. These drugs present significant formulation challenges due to their poor solubility and permeability.
- ○ **Example Strategies**: Combination approaches that include solubilization techniques (such as solid dispersions and lipid-based systems) alongside permeability enhancement strategies (such as use of surfactants, absorption enhancers, and complexation with cyclodextrins).

Role of BCS in Predicting Drug Absorption and Bioavailability?

The BCS plays a critical role in predicting drug absorption and bioavailability by providing insights into the key factors that influence these processes:

1. **Solubility and Dissolution Rate**: The BCS classification helps predict the dissolution rate of the drug in the gastrointestinal tract. Drugs with high solubility (Classes I and III) are expected to dissolve readily, facilitating absorption. In contrast, drugs with low solubility (Classes II and IV) may require special formulation techniques to enhance dissolution.

2. **Permeability and Membrane Transport**: The BCS provides an understanding of a drug's ability to permeate biological membranes. High permeability drugs (Classes I and II) are likely to be absorbed efficiently once dissolved. Low permeability drugs (Classes III and IV) may need strategies to enhance membrane transport to improve bioavailability.

3. **Predicting In Vivo Performance**: By categorizing drugs based on their solubility and permeability, the BCS helps predict their in vivo performance, including the rate and extent of absorption. This predictive capability is crucial for designing formulations that achieve desired therapeutic outcomes.

4. **Regulatory Guidance and Biowaivers**: The BCS is recognized by regulatory agencies to streamline the drug approval process. For example, BCS Class I drugs may qualify for biowaivers, allowing for the waiver of in vivo bioequivalence studies based on in vitro dissolution testing. This facilitates faster and more cost-effective drug development.

Examples of BCS Impact in Preformulation

1. **Class I Example - Metoprolol**: Metoprolol is both highly soluble and permeable, making it easier to develop into a stable, effective formulation without complex solubilization techniques. The focus can be on optimizing the delivery form for patient compliance, such as extended-release tablets.

2. **Class II Example - Ibuprofen**: Ibuprofen's low solubility but high permeability necessitates formulation strategies to enhance its solubility, such as micronization or the use of solid dispersions. These techniques improve its dissolution rate and bioavailability.

3. **Class III Example - Cimetidine**: Cimetidine has high solubility but low permeability. Strategies such as the use of permeation enhancers or alternative delivery routes (e.g., buccal or nasal delivery) can improve its absorption.

4. **Class IV Example - Hydrochlorothiazide**: Hydrochlorothiazide's low solubility and permeability require innovative approaches like nanoparticles or lipid-based formulations to enhance both solubility and permeability, ensuring effective drug delivery.

1.4 Application of Preformulation Considerations
Development of Solid Dosage Forms

Preformulation studies are essential for the development of solid dosage forms such as tablets and capsules. These studies provide critical information about the physical, chemical, and mechanical properties of the drug substance, guiding formulation scientists in designing and optimizing the dosage form. Here's how preformulation studies inform this development:

1. **Characterization of Physicochemical Properties**: Preformulation studies characterize key physicochemical properties of the drug, including solubility, dissolution rate, stability, hygroscopicity, and melting point. Understanding these properties helps in selecting appropriate excipients, designing the formulation process, and predicting potential challenges.

2. **Compatibility Studies**: Preformulation studies involve compatibility testing between the drug substance and various excipients. Identifying compatible excipients ensures that the drug does not undergo unwanted chemical reactions or physical changes during formulation, storage, and administration.

3. **Particle Size and Shape Analysis**: The particle size and shape of the drug substance affect its flow properties, compressibility, dissolution rate, and bioavailability. Preformulation studies determine optimal particle size and shape, guiding milling, micronization, or other size reduction techniques to achieve the desired properties.

4. **Flow Properties and Compressibility**: Understanding the flow properties and compressibility of the drug substance is crucial for the manufacturing process. Good flow ensures uniform filling of tablet dies or capsule bodies, while appropriate compressibility ensures that tablets

have the right hardness and friability. Preformulation studies help in selecting excipients that improve these properties.

5. **Solubility and Dissolution Enhancement**: For drugs with poor solubility, preformulation studies explore various solubility enhancement techniques, such as the use of solubilizing agents, solid dispersions, or salt formation. This information guides the formulation of solid dosage forms to ensure adequate bioavailability.

Several preformulation parameters are critical for ensuring the quality and performance of solid dosage forms:

1. **Solubility and Dissolution Rate**

   ◦ **Importance**: Determines the rate and extent of drug release and absorption.
   ◦ **Assessment**: Solubility testing in various solvents and dissolution testing under simulated physiological conditions.

2. **Stability**

   ◦ **Importance**: Ensures the drug remains stable during formulation, storage, and administration.
   ◦ **Assessment**: Stability studies under different environmental conditions (temperature, humidity, light) to identify degradation pathways and shelf life.

3. **Hygroscopicity**

   ◦ **Importance**: Affects the handling, processing, and storage of the drug.
   ◦ **Assessment**: Hygroscopicity testing to determine the drug's affinity for moisture and the need for moisture-protective measures.

4. **Particle Size and Distribution**

   ◦ **Importance**: Influences flow properties, compressibility, dissolution rate, and uniformity.

- **Assessment**: Particle size analysis using techniques like laser diffraction, microscopy, and sieving.

5. **Flow Properties**

    - **Importance**: Essential for efficient manufacturing and uniform dosage form production.
    - **Assessment**: Flow property evaluation using methods such as angle of repose, Carr's index, and Hausner ratio.

6. **Compressibility**

    - **Importance**: Determines the ability to form tablets with adequate hardness and low friability.
    - **Assessment**: Compressibility testing using instruments like the Heckel plot, tablet press, and compaction simulators.

7. **Compatibility with Excipients**

    - **Importance**: Ensures the drug and excipients do not interact adversely.
    - **Assessment**: Compatibility studies using differential scanning calorimetry (DSC), thermogravimetric analysis (TGA), and chromatographic techniques.

Case Studies Where Preformulation Data Has Led to Successful Solid Dosage Form Development:
Case Study 1: Ibuprofen Tablets
Background: Ibuprofen, a Class II drug with poor water solubility, posed challenges in achieving sufficient bioavailability.
Preformulation Studies:

- **Solubility Enhancement**: Preformulation studies identified the need for solubility enhancement. Techniques such as micronization and the use of solubilizing excipients like sodium lauryl sulfate were explored.
- **Compatibility Testing**: Ibuprofen was tested with various excipients to ensure compatibility. Lactose, microcrystalline cellulose, and croscarmellose sodium were selected based on compatibility results.

- **Flow and Compressibility**: The flow properties of ibuprofen were improved using granulation techniques, and its compressibility was assessed to optimize tablet hardness and friability.

Outcome: The preformulation data guided the development of a robust formulation, resulting in tablets with improved dissolution rates and enhanced bioavailability. The product achieved commercial success with consistent therapeutic efficacy.

Case Study 2: Metformin Hydrochloride Extended-Release Tablets

Background: Metformin hydrochloride, a Class III drug with high solubility but low permeability, required a formulation that ensured sustained release and improved permeability.

Preformulation Studies:

- **Stability Testing**: Stability studies identified the optimal pH range to maintain drug stability. Buffering agents were incorporated into the formulation to ensure consistent pH.
- **Solubility and Permeability**: Preformulation studies explored the use of permeation enhancers and extended-release matrices to improve bioavailability. Hydroxypropyl methylcellulose (HPMC) was selected as the matrix-forming agent.
- **Particle Size Analysis**: The particle size of metformin was optimized to ensure uniformity and controlled release.

Outcome: The preformulation data facilitated the development of an extended-release tablet that provided consistent drug release over 24 hours, improving patient compliance and therapeutic outcomes.

Case Study 3: Amorphous Solid Dispersion of Ritonavir

Background: Ritonavir, an antiretroviral drug, faced solubility challenges due to its crystalline form.

Preformulation Studies:

- **Amorphous Formulation**: Preformulation studies focused on converting ritonavir to an amorphous form to enhance solubility. Techniques like hot melt extrusion and spray drying were evaluated.
- **Compatibility Testing**: Polymers such as polyvinylpyrrolidone (PVP) and hydroxypropyl cellulose (HPC) were tested for compatibility and their ability to stabilize the amorphous form.

- **Stability Testing**: The stability of the amorphous solid dispersion was assessed under various conditions to ensure long-term stability.

Outcome: The amorphous solid dispersion of ritonavir demonstrated significantly improved solubility and bioavailability. The formulation was successfully commercialized, providing effective treatment for HIV patients with enhanced therapeutic efficacy.

1.4 Application of Preformulation Considerations

Development of Liquid Oral Dosage Forms

Key Preformulation Considerations for Developing Liquid Oral Dosage Forms

1. **Solubility**: Determining the solubility of the drug substance in various solvents is crucial. The solubility data help in selecting suitable solvents or cosolvents to dissolve the drug effectively.
2. **Stability**: Evaluating the chemical and physical stability of the drug in solution under different conditions (temperature, light, pH) ensures the formulation's shelf life and efficacy.
3. **pH and Buffer Systems**: Identifying the optimal pH for stability and solubility. Buffer systems may be required to maintain this pH.
4. **Viscosity**: The viscosity of the formulation affects the ease of administration, particularly for pediatric and geriatric patients. Preformulation studies help in selecting appropriate viscosity modifiers.
5. **Preservatives**: Liquid formulations are prone to microbial contamination. Preformulation studies identify suitable preservatives that are compatible with the drug and effective at the desired pH and concentration.
6. **Taste and Flavor**: Since oral solutions are ingested, taste masking and flavoring agents are often necessary to enhance patient compliance.
7. **Compatibility with Container and Closure Systems**: Ensuring that the formulation does not interact with the packaging materials, which could affect the drug's stability and efficacy.

Influence of Solubility and Stability Data on the Formulation of Liquid Oral Drugs

1. **Solubility Enhancement**: Solubility data guide the choice of solubilizing agents, cosolvents, surfactants, or complexing agents to achieve the

desired drug concentration in the solution.

2. **Formulation Design**: Stability data determine the need for antioxidants, pH adjusters, and preservatives. It also influences the selection of buffer systems to maintain the drug in its most stable form.

3. **Shelf Life Prediction**: Stability studies under accelerated conditions help predict the shelf life of the product, ensuring it remains effective and safe throughout its intended use.

Challenges Commonly Encountered in the Development of Liquid Oral Dosage Forms

1. **Poor Solubility**: Many drugs have poor solubility in water. This is addressed by using solubilizing agents, cosolvents, surfactants, or forming soluble salts.

2. **Stability Issues**: Drugs may degrade in solution due to hydrolysis, oxidation, or photodegradation. Antioxidants, stabilizers, proper pH adjustments, and light-protective packaging can mitigate these issues.

3. **Taste Masking**: Unpleasant taste is a significant challenge. This can be addressed by using sweeteners, flavoring agents, and taste-masking techniques such as complexation with cyclodextrins.

4. **Microbial Contamination**: Preservatives are necessary to prevent microbial growth. Compatibility studies ensure that preservatives do not interact adversely with the drug or excipients.

Development of Parenteral Dosage Forms
Preformulation Studies Crucial for the Development of Parenteral Dosage Forms: Reasons

1. **Sterility and Safety**: Parenteral formulations must be sterile and free from contaminants. Preformulation studies help in selecting excipients and designing formulations that can withstand sterilization processes without degrading.

2. **Solubility and Compatibility**: Ensuring that the drug is soluble in the chosen solvent and compatible with excipients and packaging materials.

3. **Stability**: Parenteral formulations require a high degree of stability to maintain efficacy and safety. Preformulation studies identify stability issues and guide the use of stabilizers.

Preformulation Data Impact on the Design and Stability of Injectable Drug Products

1. **Solubility Optimization**: Preformulation studies identify solubilizing techniques to ensure the drug is in a suitable form for injection, whether as a solution, suspension, or emulsion.
2. **pH and Osmolarity Adjustment**: Ensuring that the formulation has an appropriate pH and osmolarity to match physiological conditions, reducing the risk of irritation or pain upon injection.
3. **Selection of Stabilizers**: Identifying suitable stabilizers to prevent degradation during storage and administration.

Important Preformulation Parameters for Ensuring the Safety and Efficacy of Parenteral Dosage Forms

1. **Sterility**: Ensuring that the formulation can be sterilized without losing efficacy or stability.
2. **Isotonicity**: Adjusting the formulation to be isotonic with blood to prevent irritation or damage at the injection site.
3. **pH**: Maintaining a pH close to physiological pH to reduce irritation and ensure stability.
4. **Stability**: Conducting extensive stability studies to ensure the drug remains effective throughout its shelf life.

Impact on Stability of Dosage Forms

1. **Identification of Degradation Pathways**: Preformulation studies identify how a drug degrades under various conditions (temperature, humidity, light), enabling the design of formulations that are more stable.
2. **Selection of Stabilizers**: Identifying suitable antioxidants, preservatives, and pH adjusters to enhance the stability of the drug.
3. **Packaging Compatibility**: Ensuring that the drug and its formulation are compatible with packaging materials to prevent interactions that could lead to degradation.

Common Stability Issues Identified During Preformulation

Hydrolysis: Mitigated by using anhydrous formulations, appropriate pH adjustments, and moisture-protective packaging.

1. **Oxidation**: Mitigated by using antioxidants, oxygen scavengers, and light-protective packaging.
2. **Photodegradation**: Mitigated by using light-protective packaging and incorporating UV absorbers.

Examples

Case Study: Amorphous Solid Dispersion of Ritonavir

- **Challenge**: Ritonavir was unstable in its crystalline form.
- **Preformulation Solution**: Conversion to an amorphous solid dispersion using a polymer carrier.
- **Outcome**: Improved solubility and stability, leading to enhanced bioavailability and a successful commercial product.

2. **Case Study: Stabilization of Vitamin C in Liquid Formulation**

- **Challenge**: Vitamin C is prone to oxidation.
- **Preformulation Solution**: Inclusion of antioxidants like ascorbic acid and packaging in amber glass bottles to protect from light.
- **Outcome**: Enhanced stability and extended shelf life.

CHAPTER TWO

Tablets

2.1 Introduction to Tablets

Ideal Characteristics

Tablets are a widely used dosage form in pharmaceuticals due to their convenience and precise dosing. The **ideal characteristics of tablets** encompass **physical, chemical, and pharmacological properties** that ensure their **quality and efficacy.** Physically, tablets should have a **uniform size, shape, and color**, which not only ensures patient acceptance but also confirms consistency in each dosage form. The tablets must be **sufficiently hard** to withstand handling but not so hard that they resist dissolution. **Friability**, or the tendency of tablets to crumble, should be minimal, with acceptable limits generally being less than 1% weight loss when tested. Chemically, the **active pharmaceutical ingredient (API)** and excipients in tablets should remain **stable** throughout the product's shelf life. This stability includes resistance to moisture, heat, and light. Pharmacologically, the **bioavailability** of the drug is crucial, meaning the **tablet should disintegrate and dissolve** in the gastrointestinal tract to release the active ingredient promptly and completely. The dissolution rate must align with pharmacokinetic requirements, ensuring the drug's therapeutic effect. Furthermore, **content uniformity** is vital, with regulatory guidelines often specifying that the API content should be within 85% to 115% of the labeled amount for 9 out of 10 tablets tested. Each of these characteristics ensures that the patient receives the intended therapeutic benefit without variability between doses, thus maintaining safety and efficacy.

Classification of Tablets

Tablets can be **classified** in various tways based on their **method of manufacture, route of administration, and purpose. Manufacturing**

methods include direct compression, wet granulation, and dry granulation, each chosen based on the properties of the API and the desired characteristics of the final product. For instance, **direct compression** is often used for APIs that are stable and free-flowing, while **wet granulation** is chosen for those requiring improved cohesiveness. **Dry granulation** is suitable for moisture-sensitive APIs.

By the **route of administration**, tablets are classified into oral tablets, buccal and sublingual tablets, effervescent tablets, and chewable tablets. **Oral tablets** are swallowed whole and include **immediate-release tablets**, which dissolve quickly to provide rapid drug action, and **extended-release tablets**, designed to release the drug over an extended period to maintain therapeutic levels. **Buccal and sublingual tablets** dissolve in the mouth, allowing the drug to be absorbed directly into the bloodstream, bypassing the gastrointestinal tract, which is beneficial for drugs that undergo extensive first-pass metabolism. **Effervescent tablets** dissolve in water before administration, often used for faster absorption and to improve palatability. **Chewable tablets** are formulated for ease of consumption, especially in children or patients with difficulty swallowing.

In terms of **purpose**, tablets can be **therapeutic, diagnostic, or cosmetic. Therapeutic tablets** are the most common, intended to treat or prevent disease. **Diagnostic tablets** might contain substances that help diagnose conditions, such as glucose tablets used in glucose tolerance tests. **Cosmetic tablets** include products like breath fresheners that do not have a therapeutic effect but provide a benefit.

2.2 Excipients in Tablet Formulation

Types and Roles

Excipients are crucial components in tablet formulation, playing various roles that ensure the tablet's functionality, stability, and manufacturability. The primary types of excipients include **binders, disintegrants, fillers, lubricants, and glidants.** Each type serves a specific purpose, contributing to the overall quality of the tablet.

Binders are substances that help hold the ingredients of a tablet together, providing the necessary mechanical strength. Common binders include **starch, gelatin, and polyvinylpyrrolidone (PVP).** These agents promote adhesion between powder particles during granulation and compression, ensuring that the tablet remains intact until it reaches the gastrointestinal tract. Binders can be added in dry form or as a solution, depending on the granulation process used.

Disintegrants are added to tablets to facilitate their breakup and dissolution after ingestion. This ensures that the active pharmaceutical ingredient (API) is released promptly for absorption. Common disintegrants include **sodium starch glycolate, croscarmellose sodium, and crospovidone**. These substances absorb water rapidly, swelling and creating a force that disintegrates the tablet matrix, thus aiding in the quick release of the drug.

Fillers, also known as **diluents**, add bulk to the tablet, ensuring that it is of a manageable size for handling and consumption. Fillers are particularly important when the dosage of the API is very small. Common fillers include **lactose, microcrystalline cellulose, and mannitol**. These substances not only increase the tablet's weight but also help in the uniform distribution of the API within the tablet, contributing to content uniformity.

Lubricants are essential to prevent tablet ingredients from sticking to the equipment during manufacturing. They reduce friction between the tablet material and the die wall during compression and ejection, ensuring smooth tablet production. **Magnesium stearate, stearic acid, and talc** are commonly used lubricants. Proper use of lubricants is crucial as insufficient lubrication can lead to sticking, while excessive lubrication can affect tablet hardness and disintegration.

Glidants improve the flow properties of the powder mixture during the tablet manufacturing process. They ensure that the powder or granules move smoothly and uniformly into the tablet die, which is vital for consistent tablet weight and content. **Colloidal silicon dioxide and talc** are examples of glidants. These agents reduce interparticle friction, thus enhancing the flowability of the powder mixture.

Each of these excipients plays a vital role in the tablet formulation process. **Binders** ensure the tablet's integrity, **disintegrants** facilitate rapid dissolution, **fillers** add necessary bulk, **lubricants** prevent manufacturing issues, and **glidants** ensure uniform flow. Together, they contribute to the **quality, efficacy, and manufacturability** of the final tablet product, ensuring that patients receive consistent and effective doses of their medication. Proper selection and optimization of these excipients are critical to developing a robust tablet formulation.

2.3 Granulation Methods

Wet Granulation

Wet granulation is a widely used method in tablet manufacturing that involves the agglomeration of powder particles using a liquid binder solution to form granules. This process improves the flowability, compressibility, and uniformity of the tablet formulation. The wet granulation process consists of several key steps:

1. **Mixing of Dry Ingredients**: The first step involves mixing the active pharmaceutical ingredient (API) with excipients like binders, fillers, disintegrants, and other additives in a blender to ensure uniform distribution.

2. **Preparation of Binder Solution**: A binder, such as polyvinylpyrrolidone (PVP), starch paste, or cellulose derivatives, is dissolved in a suitable solvent, usually water or ethanol, to prepare the binder solution.

3. **Addition of Binder Solution**: The binder solution is added to the dry powder mixture slowly while mixing continuously. This step can be performed in equipment like a high-shear granulator or a planetary mixer. The binder solution causes the powder particles to adhere to each other, forming wet granules.

4. **Wet Massing**: The wet mass is mixed until the desired granule size and consistency are achieved. The end point of wet massing is usually determined by visual inspection or by measuring the granule's moisture content.

5. **Screening/Wet Sieving**: The wet mass is then passed through a sieve to break down large lumps and to achieve uniform granule size. This step ensures that the granules are of consistent size for subsequent drying.

6. **Drying**: The wet granules are dried using methods such as tray drying, fluid bed drying, or vacuum drying to remove excess moisture. The drying process is critical as it affects the granules' hardness, compressibility, and stability.

7. **Dry Screening**: After drying, the granules are passed through a sieve again to eliminate oversized particles and to obtain a uniform granule size.

8. **Blending with Lubricants and Glidants**: The dried granules are mixed with lubricants like magnesium stearate and glidants like colloidal silicon dioxide to improve the flow properties and prevent sticking during tablet

compression.

Advantages of Wet Granulation:

- **Improved Flowability**: Wet granulation enhances the flow properties of powders, making them easier to handle and process.
- **Better Compressibility**: The formation of granules improves the compressibility of the mixture, resulting in tablets with uniform hardness.
- **Homogeneous Distribution**: Ensures a more uniform distribution of the API within the granules, reducing content variability.
- **Reduced Dust**: The granulation process minimizes dust generation, improving the working environment and reducing the risk of cross-contamination.

Disadvantages of Wet Granulation:

- **Complex and Time-Consuming**: Wet granulation involves multiple steps, making it more complex and time-consuming compared to direct compression.
- **Higher Costs**: The process requires additional equipment and energy, increasing manufacturing costs.
- **Moisture Sensitivity**: Not suitable for moisture-sensitive APIs, as exposure to liquid can cause degradation.
- **Solvent Handling**: Requires handling of solvents, which may pose safety and environmental concerns.

Equipment Used in Wet Granulation:

- **High-Shear Granulator**: Utilized for rapid and efficient mixing and granulation, producing dense and uniform granules.
- **Fluid Bed Granulator**: Combines mixing, granulation, and drying in one unit, using a fluidized bed of particles.
- **Planetary Mixer**: Used for the initial mixing of powders and binder addition, providing thorough mixing.
- **Tray Dryers**: Used for drying granules spread on trays in a heated chamber.

- **Fluid Bed Dryers**: Utilizes hot air to fluidize and dry granules, offering faster drying times and uniform drying.

Preferred Conditions for Wet Granulation: Wet granulation is preferred when the API has poor flowability and compressibility, or when uniform distribution of a low-dose API is critical. It is also chosen when the formulation contains hygroscopic materials that need to be agglomerated to prevent caking and improve stability. Additionally, wet granulation is ideal when the tablet requires a specific dissolution profile that can be controlled through the granulation process.

2.3 Granulation Methods

Dry Granulation

Dry granulation is a method used to form granules without the use of any liquid solution. This technique is particularly suitable for moisture-sensitive and heat-sensitive APIs. Dry granulation involves compacting powder particles into larger aggregates, which are then broken down into granules. The process includes several key steps:

1. **Blending**: The active pharmaceutical ingredient (API) is blended with excipients such as fillers, binders, and disintegrants. This ensures a uniform distribution of all ingredients.
2. **Compaction**: The blended mixture is compressed to form large, dense compacts known as slugs (slugging) or ribbons (roller compaction). The compaction process increases the bulk density of the material and improves its flow properties.
3. **Size Reduction**: The slugs or ribbons are then broken down into granules using milling or sieving. This step ensures that the granules are of the desired size and consistency.
4. **Final Blending**: The granules are blended with additional excipients, such as lubricants and glidants, to improve flowability and prevent sticking during the tablet compression process.

Advantages of Dry Granulation:

- **No Need for Liquids**: Ideal for moisture-sensitive APIs as no liquid is used in the process, eliminating the risk of hydrolysis.

- **Thermal Stability**: Suitable for heat-sensitive APIs since the process does not involve drying at high temperatures.
- **Simple and Cost-Effective**: The process is simpler and less time-consuming compared to wet granulation, leading to cost savings.
- **Improved Flowability and Compressibility**: The compaction process enhances the flow and compressibility of the powder blend, resulting in uniform tablets.

Disadvantages of Dry Granulation:

- **Dust Generation**: The process can generate a significant amount of dust, requiring proper dust handling and containment systems.
- **Limited Uniformity**: Achieving uniform distribution of low-dose APIs can be challenging, leading to content uniformity issues.
- **High Mechanical Stress**: The compaction process may subject the API and excipients to high mechanical stress, potentially affecting their stability.

Equipment Used in Dry Granulation:

- **Slugging**: Involves the use of a tablet press to produce large, flat tablets called slugs. These slugs are then broken down into granules using a mill.
- **Roller Compaction**: Utilizes a roller compactor, where the powder blend is fed between two counter-rotating rollers, forming a dense ribbon or sheet. The ribbons are then milled to produce granules.

Preferred Conditions for Dry Granulation: Dry granulation is preferred when the API or excipients are sensitive to moisture and heat. It is also suitable for formulations where improving the bulk density and flow properties of the powder blend is necessary. This method is often chosen for high-dose APIs where wet granulation might not be feasible due to the large quantity of binder required.

Dry granulation is an efficient and effective method for granule formation, particularly for sensitive APIs. It offers several advantages, including simplicity, cost-effectiveness, and suitability for moisture and heat-sensitive materials. Despite its limitations, dry granulation remains a valuable technique in tablet manufacturing, providing a viable alternative to wet granulation for specific formulations.

2.3 Granulation Methods

Direct Compression

Direct compression is a straightforward and efficient method for tablet manufacturing where powders are compressed directly into tablets without the need for any granulation step. This process relies on the free-flowing and compressible nature of the powder blend to form cohesive tablets under pressure. Direct compression is increasingly popular due to its simplicity and cost-effectiveness.

Process Description: The process involves the following steps:

1. **Blending**: The active pharmaceutical ingredient (API) is blended with excipients to ensure a uniform distribution of all components.
2. **Compression**: The blended powder is fed into a tablet press where it is compressed into tablets using punches and dies. The pressure applied causes the particles to bond together, forming a solid tablet.

Advantages of Direct Compression:

- **Simplicity**: The process eliminates the need for wet or dry granulation steps, reducing the complexity of tablet production.
- **Cost-Effective**: Fewer processing steps translate to lower manufacturing costs and shorter production times.
- **Stability**: Suitable for moisture-sensitive and heat-sensitive APIs as there is no exposure to solvents or heat during the process.
- **High Efficiency**: Direct compression requires less equipment and fewer processing steps, leading to higher productivity and throughput.
- **Enhanced Tablet Properties**: Provides good control over tablet hardness and disintegration time, ensuring consistent product quality.

Limitations of Direct Compression:

- **Flowability Issues**: Requires excipients and APIs with excellent flow properties to ensure uniform filling of the tablet dies.
- **Segregation**: The tendency of powder blends to segregate due to differences in particle size and density, leading to content uniformity issues.

- **Limited API Load**: High doses of API may be challenging to process due to poor compressibility and flow properties.
- **Excipient Dependency**: Relies heavily on the properties of excipients to achieve acceptable tablet characteristics, which may limit formulation flexibility.

Types of Excipients Suitable for Direct Compression: The success of direct compression depends on the selection of suitable excipients, which must exhibit good flowability and compressibility. Commonly used direct compression excipients include:

- **Microcrystalline Cellulose (MCC)**: A widely used filler and binder known for its excellent compressibility and ability to form hard tablets with low friability. MCC is available in various grades, such as Avicel PH 101 and Avicel PH 102, which differ in particle size and flow properties.
- **Dicalcium Phosphate (DCP)**: Used as a filler and binder, DCP provides good flow properties and high density, which is beneficial for forming robust tablets. However, it may require additional lubricants due to its abrasive nature.
- **Lactose**: A commonly used filler that provides good compressibility and compatibility with many APIs. Anhydrous lactose is particularly suitable for direct compression due to its free-flowing nature.
- **Starch**: Modified starches, such as pregelatinized starch, act as fillers and binders, offering good compressibility and flow properties. Starch can also serve as a disintegrant, aiding tablet dissolution.
- **Mannitol**: A filler and binder with excellent flow properties and a pleasant taste, making it ideal for chewable tablets. Mannitol also provides a cooling sensation in the mouth, enhancing patient compliance.

Criteria for Selecting Excipients: When selecting excipients for direct compression, several factors must be considered:

- **Flowability**: The excipient must flow freely to ensure uniform die filling and consistent tablet weight.
- **Compressibility**: The ability of the excipient to form a cohesive compact under pressure is crucial for producing tablets with adequate hardness and low friability.

- **Compatibility**: The excipient should be compatible with the API and other formulation components, without causing chemical or physical instability.
- **Particle Size and Distribution**: Uniform particle size and distribution minimize segregation and ensure content uniformity.
- **Moisture Sensitivity**: Excipients should be chosen based on their stability in the presence of moisture, particularly for moisture-sensitive APIs.

Direct compression offers a simple and efficient method for tablet manufacturing, with significant advantages in terms of cost, stability, and productivity. The selection of suitable excipients is critical to the success of this method, requiring careful consideration of their flowability, compressibility, and compatibility with the API. By leveraging the properties of appropriate excipients, manufacturers can produce high-quality tablets that meet stringent regulatory standards and patient needs.

2.4 Tablet Compression and Processing Problems

Common Issues and Solutions

Tablet compression is a critical step in the manufacturing process, where powder blends are transformed into solid dosage forms. However, various issues can arise during this process, affecting the quality and efficacy of the final product. Some common problems include **capping, lamination, sticking, and picking**. Each issue has distinct causes and requires specific solutions and preventive measures to ensure smooth production.

Capping

Capping occurs when the upper or lower part of the tablet separates horizontally, resulting in a cap-like structure. This defect can be caused by several factors, including air entrapment, insufficient binder, excessive compression force, and worn tooling.

Solutions and Preventive Measures:

- **Reduce Compression Speed**: Lowering the speed allows more time for air to escape, reducing the likelihood of capping.
- **Optimize Binder Levels**: Ensure the binder is present in the appropriate quantity to provide adequate cohesion without causing excessive brittleness.

- **Adjust Compression Force**: Use the minimum compression force necessary to achieve the desired tablet hardness, avoiding over-compression.
- **Tooling Maintenance**: Regularly inspect and maintain punches and dies to ensure they are in good condition and replace them when necessary.

Lamination

Lamination is similar to capping but involves the separation of the tablet into multiple horizontal layers. It can result from excessive fines in the powder blend, over-lubrication, or improper granulation.

Solutions and Preventive Measures:

- **Granulation Optimization**: Ensure the granulation process produces uniform granules with minimal fines to improve compressibility.
- **Control Lubricant Levels**: Avoid over-lubrication, as excess lubricant can reduce the bonding strength between particles. Use only the necessary amount of lubricant.
- **Compression Force Adjustment**: Similar to capping, adjust the compression force to the optimal level to prevent lamination.

Sticking

Sticking occurs when the tablet material adheres to the punch faces, leading to defective tablets with rough surfaces. This problem is often due to inadequate lubrication, excessive moisture, or unsuitable formulation properties.

Solutions and Preventive Measures:

- **Increase Lubricant**: Adding more lubricant to the formulation can reduce sticking. Ensure that the lubricant is evenly distributed throughout the powder blend.
- **Control Moisture Content**: Maintain the moisture content of the powder blend within optimal limits. Dry the granules adequately if necessary.
- **Punch Coatings**: Use punches with special coatings, such as Teflon or chromium, to reduce adhesion.

Picking

Picking involves small amounts of material sticking to the punch tips, especially in the engraving or embossing areas, causing defects in the tablet surface. It can be caused by insufficient drying, inadequate lubrication, or improper punch design.

Solutions and Preventive Measures:

- **Proper Drying**: Ensure the granules are dried to the appropriate moisture content to reduce the tendency of picking.
- **Increase Lubricant**: Similar to sticking, increasing the lubricant can help minimize picking. Ensure thorough mixing of the lubricant with the powder blend.
- **Punch Design**: Use punch designs with smooth, polished surfaces and avoid intricate engravings that are prone to picking.

General Preventive Measures for Tablet Compression Problems:

- **Blend Uniformity**: Ensure uniform mixing of the API and excipients to achieve consistent powder flow and compressibility.
- **Environmental Control**: Maintain optimal temperature and humidity conditions in the manufacturing area to prevent moisture-related issues.
- **Regular Tooling Inspection**: Conduct regular inspections and maintenance of punches and dies to ensure they are free from wear and damage.
- **Process Optimization**: Continuously monitor and optimize the compression parameters, such as speed, force, and dwell time, to achieve the best results.

2.4 Tablet Compression and Processing Problems

Equipment Used

The equipment used in tablet compression is critical to the successful production of high-quality tablets. The main types of equipment include **tablet presses and tooling**. Understanding their working principles and specifications is essential for optimal tablet manufacturing.

Tablet Presses

Tablet presses are machines designed to compress powder blends into tablets. They can be categorized into two main types: **single-station (eccentric) presses** and **rotary presses**.

Single-Station Presses

Single-station presses, also known as **eccentric presses**, operate with a single pair of punches and a die. They are typically used for small-scale production and research and development.

Working Principle:

- The powder blend is fed into the die cavity.
- The upper punch descends to compress the powder within the die.
- After compression, the upper punch retracts, and the lower punch rises to eject the formed tablet.

Specifications:

- **Compression Force**: Typically ranges from 5 to 50 kN.
- **Output**: Up to 100 tablets per minute.
- **Applications**: Suitable for small batches and laboratory-scale production.

Rotary Presses

Rotary presses are the most commonly used type in large-scale tablet manufacturing. They feature multiple sets of punches and dies mounted on a rotating turret.

Working Principle:

- The powder blend is fed continuously into the dies via a feed frame.
- As the turret rotates, each set of punches compresses the powder into tablets.
- The compressed tablets are ejected as the punches rise from the dies, and the cycle repeats.

Specifications:

- **Compression Force**: Can exceed 100 kN, depending on the model.
- **Output**: Ranges from 5,000 to over 1,000,000 tablets per hour, depending on the number of stations and speed of rotation.
- **Stations**: Typically range from 5 to 75 stations.
- **Applications**: Ideal for high-volume production, ensuring consistent quality and high throughput.

Tooling

Tooling in tablet compression refers to the punches and dies used to shape and form the tablets. The design and quality of tooling are crucial for achieving the desired tablet specifications.

Punches

Punches are cylindrical tools with a flat or shaped end used to compress the powder blend in the die. They are classified into two types: **upper punches** and **lower punches**.

Specifications:

- **Material**: Typically made from hardened steel or other durable materials to withstand high compression forces.
- **Shapes**: Can be flat, concave, beveled, or multi-tipped, depending on the desired tablet shape and design.
- **Coatings**: Some punches have coatings like chromium or Teflon to reduce sticking and improve wear resistance.

Dies

Dies are cylindrical components with a cavity that determines the size and shape of the tablet. The punches compress the powder blend within this cavity.

Specifications:

- **Material**: Made from high-strength steel to resist wear and deformation.
- **Cavity Design**: Can be customized to produce tablets of various shapes and sizes, including round, oval, and unique designs.
- **Dimensions**: The diameter and depth of the die cavity must match the specifications of the tablet.

Tablet Compression Equipment Overview:
Feed Frame:

- Ensures consistent feeding of the powder blend into the dies.
- Can be single or double-sided, depending on the press design.

Pre-Compression Rollers:

- Apply an initial compression force to remove air and pre-consolidate the powder before the main compression.

Main Compression Rollers:

- Apply the primary compression force to form the tablet.
- The force is adjustable to achieve the desired tablet hardness and density.

Ejection Mechanism:

- Ejects the formed tablet from the die after compression.
- Includes scrapers and brushes to ensure complete removal of tablets.

Control Systems:

- Modern tablet presses are equipped with advanced control systems for precise regulation of compression force, turret speed, and tablet weight.
- Include sensors and software for real-time monitoring and quality control.

2.4 Tablet Compression and Processing Problems

Tablet Tooling

Tablet Tooling refers to the punches and dies used in tablet compression machines to shape and form tablets. The precision and quality of tooling are critical in ensuring the uniformity, appearance, and overall quality of the final product. Tooling consists of **punches (upper and lower)** and **dies**, which come in various designs and materials to accommodate different tablet specifications.

Types of Punches

Upper Punches and **Lower Punches** work together to compress the powder blend within the die cavity. Each type of punch has specific roles and characteristics:

- **Upper Punch**: The upper punch descends to apply pressure on the powder blend inside the die cavity. It usually has a shorter stem compared to the lower punch.

- **Lower Punch**: The lower punch remains stationary during powder filling and rises to meet the upper punch during compression, finally ejecting the tablet from the die cavity.

Punches are available in different shapes to produce tablets with various profiles:

- **Flat-Faced Punches**: Used to create tablets with flat surfaces.
- **Concave-Faced Punches**: Produce tablets with a concave shape, which can enhance tablet strength and aesthetics.
- **Beveled-Edge Punches**: Provide tablets with beveled edges, reducing chipping and improving appearance.
- **Multi-Tip Punches**: Contain multiple tips on a single punch, allowing the production of several tablets per compression cycle, thus increasing output.

Types of Dies

Dies are cylindrical components with a cavity that determines the tablet's shape and size. They work in conjunction with punches to form tablets:

- **Standard Dies**: These dies have simple round cavities for producing circular tablets.
- **Shaped Dies**: Used to produce tablets in various shapes, such as oval, triangular, or custom designs, to differentiate products and improve patient compliance.
- **Embossed Dies**: Feature engravings that imprint logos, dosage information, or other identifiers on the tablet surface during compression.

Importance of Proper Tooling Maintenance

Proper maintenance of tooling is vital for several reasons:

- **Consistency and Quality**: Well-maintained punches and dies ensure that each tablet produced meets the desired specifications for weight, hardness, and dimensions, leading to consistent quality.
- **Reduced Downtime**: Regular inspection and maintenance of tooling help identify wear and damage early, reducing the risk of unexpected

machine downtime due to tooling failures.

- **Extended Tooling Life**: Proper care, including cleaning, lubrication, and storage, extends the lifespan of punches and dies, reducing replacement costs.
- **Prevention of Contamination**: Clean and well-maintained tooling prevents contamination of the tablet product, which is crucial for maintaining product safety and efficacy.

Impact of Tooling on Tablet Quality

The quality of the tooling directly impacts the quality of the tablets produced. Several factors illustrate this impact:

- **Dimensional Accuracy**: Accurate and precise tooling ensures that tablets have consistent dimensions, which is crucial for uniform dosage and patient compliance.
- **Surface Finish**: The surface finish of punches and dies affects the tablet's appearance and texture. Smooth, polished surfaces prevent sticking and picking, leading to tablets with clean, defect-free surfaces.
- **Compression Efficiency**: High-quality tooling allows for efficient compression cycles, producing tablets with the desired hardness and friability. Poor tooling can lead to problems such as capping, lamination, and uneven tablet weight.
- **Productivity**: Efficient and well-designed tooling can increase the production rate by reducing downtime and ensuring smooth operation. Multi-tip punches, for example, enhance productivity by producing multiple tablets per compression cycle.

2.5 Tablet Coating

Types of Coating (Sugar, Film, Enteric)

Tablet coatings are applied to enhance the properties of tablets, such as their appearance, stability, and ease of swallowing. The three main types of tablet coatings are **sugar coating, film coating, and enteric coating**. Each type has distinct characteristics, purposes, and benefits.

Sugar Coating

Sugar coating is one of the oldest and most traditional methods of coating tablets. It involves the application of multiple layers of sugar-based solutions, which are colored and polished to achieve a glossy finish.

Characteristics:

- **Multiple Layers**: Typically involves 30-50 layers, including sealing, subcoating, smoothing, coloring, and polishing layers.
- **Thicker Coating**: Results in a relatively thick and smooth coat.

Purposes and Benefits:

- **Taste Masking**: Effectively masks the bitter taste of the active pharmaceutical ingredient (API), improving patient compliance.
- **Appearance**: Enhances the visual appeal of the tablets with bright, glossy colors.
- **Protection**: Provides a protective barrier against moisture, light, and air, improving the stability of the tablet.

Drawbacks:

- **Time-Consuming**: The process is labor-intensive and time-consuming, requiring skilled operators.
- **Increased Size and Weight**: Adds significant bulk to the tablet, which can be a disadvantage for large-dose medications.

Film Coating

Film coating is a more modern and widely used method compared to sugar coating. It involves the application of a thin polymer-based layer over the tablet core.

Characteristics:

- **Thin and Uniform Layer**: Provides a smooth, thin coat that does not significantly increase the tablet's size or weight.
- **Faster Process**: Generally quicker and more efficient than sugar coating.

Purposes and Benefits:

- **Protection**: Shields the tablet from environmental factors like moisture, light, and air, thereby enhancing stability.
- **Taste Masking**: Can mask unpleasant tastes and odors of the API.
- **Ease of Swallowing**: Improves the tablet's surface smoothness, making it easier to swallow.
- **Identification**: Allows for easy printing of logos or identification marks on the tablet surface.

Drawbacks:

- **Potential for Coating Defects**: May develop defects like peeling or cracking if not applied properly.

Enteric Coating

Enteric coating is a specialized type of film coating designed to withstand the acidic environment of the stomach and dissolve in the more neutral or alkaline environment of the intestine.

Characteristics:

- **Acid-Resistant Polymers**: Uses polymers like cellulose acetate phthalate (CAP) or methacrylic acid copolymers that resist stomach acid.

Purposes and Benefits:

- **Protection of API**: Protects acid-sensitive APIs from degradation in the stomach.
- **Targeted Release**: Ensures the release of the API in the intestine, which is beneficial for drugs intended for intestinal absorption or local action in the gut.
- **Reduced Gastric Irritation**: Minimizes irritation of the gastric mucosa by preventing the release of the API in the stomach.

Drawbacks:

- **Complex Formulation**: Requires precise formulation and process control to achieve the desired enteric properties.

- **Cost**: Generally more expensive than regular film coating due to the specialized materials and processes involved.

Comparison:

1. **Thickness and Appearance:**

   - **Sugar Coating**: Thick, glossy, and colorful.
   - **Film Coating**: Thin, smooth, can be transparent or colored.
   - **Enteric Coating**: Thin, usually opaque, designed for delayed release.

2. **Processing Time:**

   - **Sugar Coating**: Long, due to multiple layers.
   - **Film Coating**: Shorter, more efficient.
   - **Enteric Coating**: Similar to film coating but requires additional control measures.

3. **Functionality:**

   - **Sugar Coating**: Primarily for taste masking and appearance.
   - **Film Coating**: Versatile for protection, taste masking, and identification.
   - **Enteric Coating**: Specifically for targeted release in the intestine and protection of the API from stomach acid.

4. **Impact on Tablet Size:**

   - **Sugar Coating**: Increases size and weight significantly.
   - **Film Coating**: Minimal impact on size and weight.
   - **Enteric Coating**: Minimal impact but adds functional benefits.

2.5 Tablet Coating

Coating Materials

Tablet coatings utilize various materials, each contributing specific properties to the coating process and the final product. These materials include polymers, plasticizers, colorants, and solvents, which collectively influence the functionality, appearance, and stability of the coated tablets.

Polymers

Polymers are the primary components of tablet coatings, forming the film that envelops the tablet. The choice of polymer affects the coating's properties, such as its dissolution profile, mechanical strength, and protective capabilities.

- **Hydroxypropyl Methylcellulose (HPMC):** A widely used film-forming polymer known for its excellent film-forming properties and stability. HPMC dissolves readily in water, providing a clear, smooth, and flexible film. It is used in both immediate-release and controlled-release coatings.
- **Ethylcellulose:** An insoluble polymer often used in controlled-release formulations. Ethylcellulose forms a barrier that regulates the release of the API, making it suitable for sustained-release and enteric coatings. It is typically used in combination with other polymers to achieve the desired release profile.
- **Methacrylic Acid Copolymers:** Commonly used in enteric coatings, these polymers resist dissolution in acidic environments but dissolve in the more neutral pH of the intestine. Examples include Eudragit L and Eudragit S, which provide targeted release in the duodenum and colon, respectively.
- **Polyvinyl Alcohol (PVA):** Known for its good film-forming properties, PVA is used in immediate-release coatings. It provides a glossy finish and protects the tablet from moisture and mechanical damage.

Plasticizers

Plasticizers are added to coating formulations to enhance the flexibility and workability of the polymer films. They reduce brittleness and improve the mechanical properties of the coating.

- **Polyethylene Glycol (PEG):** A commonly used plasticizer that imparts flexibility and reduces the brittleness of the coating. PEG is compatible with many polymers and enhances the film's smoothness and durability.
- **Triethyl Citrate:** A non-toxic plasticizer often used in combination with enteric polymers. It improves the film's flexibility and reduces the risk of cracking during storage and handling.

- **Glycerin**: Another widely used plasticizer, glycerin enhances the flexibility and tensile strength of the coating, making it suitable for various types of polymer films.

Colorants

Colorants are added to tablet coatings to improve the appearance and facilitate identification. They can be natural or synthetic and must be safe for consumption.

- **Titanium Dioxide**: A white pigment used to provide opacity and brightness to the coating. It also acts as a UV protectant, enhancing the stability of light-sensitive APIs.
- **Iron Oxides**: These colorants provide a range of colors, including red, yellow, and brown. They are stable and non-toxic, making them suitable for pharmaceutical applications.
- **FD&C and D&C Dyes**: Synthetic dyes approved for use in food and drugs. They offer a wide spectrum of colors and are used in combination with other colorants to achieve the desired shade.

Solvents

Solvents are used to dissolve polymers and other coating materials, facilitating the application process. The choice of solvent affects the drying time, film formation, and overall efficiency of the coating process.

- **Water**: The most commonly used solvent due to its safety, cost-effectiveness, and environmental friendliness. Aqueous coatings are preferred for their reduced toxicity and ease of handling.
- **Ethanol**: An organic solvent used when water-sensitive materials are involved. Ethanol evaporates quickly, reducing the drying time and enhancing the efficiency of the coating process.
- **Isopropanol**: Another organic solvent with fast evaporation properties. It is often used in combination with water or ethanol to improve the solubility of certain polymers.

Properties and Impact on Coating Process and Final Product

The properties of these materials significantly impact the coating process and the quality of the final product:

- **Film Formation**: Polymers and plasticizers work together to create a uniform, flexible film that adheres well to the tablet surface. The choice of polymer determines the film's dissolution behavior, while plasticizers ensure that the film remains intact without cracking.
- **Mechanical Strength**: Plasticizers enhance the mechanical properties of the coating, preventing brittleness and ensuring the tablets can withstand handling and transportation without damage.
- **Appearance**: Colorants improve the aesthetic appeal of the tablets, making them more attractive and easier to identify. The uniform distribution of colorants ensures consistent appearance across batches.
- **Stability**: Solvents play a crucial role in the coating process, affecting the drying time and film formation. Proper solvent selection ensures efficient coating application and reduces the risk of defects like peeling or cracking.
- **Protection and Release Profile**: Polymers like HPMC, ethylcellulose, and methacrylic acid copolymers determine the protective properties of the coating and the release profile of the API. Enteric coatings ensure that the API is released in the intestine, while sustained-release coatings regulate the drug's release over time.

2.5 Tablet Coating

Formulation of Coating Composition

The formulation of a tablet coating composition involves selecting appropriate materials and optimizing various coating parameters to achieve the desired properties and performance of the coated tablets. The process includes choosing the right polymers, plasticizers, colorants, and solvents, as well as adjusting the formulation parameters to ensure efficient coating application and high-quality final products.

Selection of Materials

1. **Polymers**: The choice of polymer depends on the desired properties of the coating, such as immediate-release, controlled-release, or enteric protection.

    ◦ **Immediate-Release Coatings**: Hydroxypropyl methylcellulose (HPMC), polyvinyl alcohol (PVA).

- **Controlled-Release Coatings**: Ethylcellulose, methylcellulose.
- **Enteric Coatings**: Methacrylic acid copolymers (e.g., Eudragit L, Eudragit S), cellulose acetate phthalate (CAP).

2. **Plasticizers**: Selected to enhance the flexibility and durability of the coating film.

   - Common plasticizers: Polyethylene glycol (PEG), triethyl citrate, glycerin.

3. **Colorants**: Used to improve the appearance and identification of the tablets.

   - Common colorants: Titanium dioxide (white), iron oxides (various colors), FD&C and D&C dyes (synthetic colors).

4. **Solvents**: Chosen based on the solubility of the coating materials and the desired drying properties.

   - Aqueous coatings: Water.
   - Organic solvents: Ethanol, isopropanol, or a mixture of solvents.

Optimization of Coating Parameters

1. **Concentration of Coating Solution**: The concentration of polymers and other materials in the coating solution affects the viscosity, sprayability, and final film thickness. Typically, a concentration of 5-20% (w/w) is used, depending on the specific materials and desired properties.
2. **Spray Rate**: The rate at which the coating solution is sprayed onto the tablets should be optimized to ensure uniform application without causing over-wetting or surface defects. A controlled spray rate helps achieve consistent coating thickness.
3. **Atomization Air Pressure**: This parameter affects the droplet size of the sprayed coating solution. Optimal atomization ensures fine droplets, resulting in a smooth and uniform coating. Typical atomization pressures range from 1-3 bar, depending on the equipment and formulation.

4. **Inlet Air Temperature**: The temperature of the air entering the coating chamber influences the drying rate of the coating. Higher temperatures accelerate drying but must be balanced to prevent thermal degradation of the coating materials. Inlet air temperatures usually range from 40-80°C, depending on the solvent used and the thermal stability of the ingredients.

5. **Tablet Bed Temperature**: The temperature of the tablets during coating should be monitored to ensure proper drying without causing defects like sticking or cracking. Tablet bed temperatures typically range from 30-50°C.

6. **Pan Speed**: The rotation speed of the coating pan affects the mixing and tumbling of the tablets, ensuring even coating application. Optimal pan speeds vary but generally fall between 5-25 rpm.

Factors Influencing the Formulation

1. **Physical and Chemical Properties of the API**: The nature of the active pharmaceutical ingredient (API) influences the choice of coating materials and process parameters. For example, moisture-sensitive APIs require non-aqueous coating systems, and heat-sensitive APIs necessitate lower drying temperatures.

2. **Desired Release Profile**: The target release characteristics of the tablet determine the type of polymer and plasticizer used. Immediate-release coatings require water-soluble polymers, while controlled-release and enteric coatings use polymers that dissolve or degrade under specific conditions.

3. **Tablet Core Properties**: The hardness, porosity, and surface roughness of the tablet core affect the adhesion and uniformity of the coating. Tablets with smooth, non-porous surfaces generally require less coating material for uniform coverage.

4. **Environmental Conditions**: Humidity and temperature in the coating environment can impact the drying rate and final quality of the coating. Controlled environmental conditions are essential for consistent results.

5. **Equipment Capabilities**: The design and capabilities of the coating equipment, such as spray guns, atomization systems, and drying mechanisms, influence the formulation and process parameters. Compatibility between the coating formulation and equipment is critical for efficient operation.

Formulation Process

1. **Preparation of Coating Solution**: The selected polymers, plasticizers, colorants, and solvents are mixed to form a homogeneous coating solution. The solution is typically prepared by dissolving or dispersing the materials in the solvent under continuous stirring.
2. **Screening and Filtering**: The coating solution is screened and filtered to remove any undissolved particles or contaminants that could cause nozzle blockages or coating defects.
3. **Spraying**: The coating solution is sprayed onto the tablet cores using a coating pan or fluidized bed coater. The parameters, such as spray rate, atomization air pressure, and inlet air temperature, are adjusted to achieve uniform coating.
4. **Drying**: The tablets are dried continuously as the coating solution is applied, ensuring that each layer is properly dried before the next application. This step is critical to prevent defects like sticking or peeling.
5. **Final Polishing**: If necessary, the coated tablets are polished to enhance their appearance and reduce surface tackiness.

2.5 Tablet Coating

Methods of Coating

Pan Coating

Principles: Pan coating involves the application of a coating solution to tablets in a rotating drum or pan. Tablets are tumbled in the pan while the coating solution is sprayed onto their surface. The process includes drying the tablets to ensure a uniform coat.

Advantages:

- **Versatility**: Suitable for various types of coatings, including sugar, film, and enteric.
- **Scalability**: Easily scaled from laboratory to production-scale operations.
- **Cost-Effective**: Generally less expensive equipment and lower operational costs compared to other methods.

Limitations:

- **Manual Labor**: Often requires more manual intervention and supervision.
- **Time-Consuming**: Can be slower than other coating methods, especially for multiple-layer coatings.
- **Uniformity**: Achieving uniform coating can be challenging with high-volume batches.

Fluidized Bed Coating

Principles: In fluidized bed coating, tablets are suspended in an upward stream of air, creating a fluidized state. The coating solution is sprayed onto the fluidized tablets, and the solvent is rapidly evaporated by the heated air.

Advantages:

- **Efficiency**: Faster coating process due to efficient drying and uniform application.
- **Uniformity**: Provides excellent coating uniformity and control over coating thickness.
- **Versatility**: Suitable for various types of coatings and can handle heat-sensitive APIs due to rapid drying.

Limitations:

- **Complexity**: More complex equipment and process control compared to pan coating.
- **Cost**: Higher initial investment and operational costs.
- **Maintenance**: Requires regular maintenance to ensure optimal performance.

Spray Coating

Principles: Spray coating involves the application of a coating solution through a spray nozzle onto tablets that are continuously moved in a coating drum or pan. This method ensures a fine, even coating on each tablet.

Advantages:

- **Precision**: Offers precise control over coating thickness and uniformity.
- **Flexibility**: Suitable for a wide range of tablet sizes and shapes.
- **Speed**: Generally faster than traditional pan coating.

Limitations:

- **Equipment Requirements:** Requires sophisticated spray systems and precise control of spray parameters.
- **Initial Cost:** Higher initial cost due to advanced equipment and technology.
- **Skill-Intensive:** Requires skilled operators for optimal performance and troubleshooting.

Equipment Employed

Coating Pans

Working Principles: Coating pans consist of a rotating drum or pan where tablets are placed. The coating solution is sprayed onto the tablets as they tumble in the pan, ensuring even distribution.

Key Features:

- **Variable Speed Control:** Allows adjustment of pan speed to optimize coating uniformity.
- **Spray Nozzles:** Precisely control the application of the coating solution.
- **Heating Systems:** Integrated heaters or external hot air sources to facilitate drying.

Maintenance Requirements:

- **Regular Cleaning:** To prevent cross-contamination and ensure proper functioning.
- **Inspection of Spray Nozzles:** Regular checks to avoid clogging and ensure even spray distribution.
- **Lubrication:** Periodic lubrication of moving parts to reduce wear and tear.

Fluidized Bed Coaters

Working Principles: Tablets are suspended in a fluidized state using an upward stream of heated air. The coating solution is sprayed onto the tablets, and the solvent evaporates quickly due to the hot air.

Key Features:

- **Air Flow Control**: Precise control of air velocity and temperature for optimal fluidization and drying.
- **Spray System**: Fine mist spray system to ensure uniform coating application.
- **Multi-Functional**: Can be used for granulation, drying, and coating processes.

Maintenance Requirements:

- **Filter Replacement**: Regular replacement of air filters to maintain air quality and prevent contamination.
- **Spray Nozzle Cleaning**: Frequent cleaning to prevent clogging and ensure consistent spray patterns.
- **System Calibration**: Periodic calibration of air flow and spray systems to maintain process accuracy.

Spray Coaters

Working Principles: Spray coaters apply a coating solution to tablets using a controlled spray system. Tablets are continuously moved in a drum or pan to ensure even coating application.

Key Features:

- **Automated Control**: Advanced control systems for precise regulation of spray rate, air pressure, and tablet movement.
- **Multiple Nozzles**: Multiple spray nozzles for uniform coating application.
- **Real-Time Monitoring**: Sensors and monitoring systems to track coating parameters and ensure consistent quality.

Maintenance Requirements:

- **Nozzle Inspection**: Regular inspection and cleaning of spray nozzles to prevent blockages.
- **System Checks**: Routine checks of the automated control systems to ensure accurate operation.
- **Preventive Maintenance**: Scheduled maintenance of moving parts and electrical components to prevent breakdowns.

2.5 Tablet Coating

Defects in Coating

Tablet coating is a complex process that can sometimes result in defects affecting the quality and efficacy of the final product. Common defects include **cracking, peeling, and color variation**. Understanding the causes of these defects and implementing preventive and corrective strategies is crucial for maintaining high-quality coated tablets.

Cracking

Causes:

- **Overdrying**: Excessive drying can make the coating brittle, leading to cracks.
- **High Tablet Hardness**: Extremely hard tablets may not compress adequately, causing the coating to crack under stress.
- **Inappropriate Plasticizer Levels**: Insufficient plasticizers in the coating formulation can reduce flexibility, making the film more prone to cracking.

Prevention and Rectification:

- **Optimize Drying Conditions**: Control drying parameters to avoid excessive heat and prolonged drying times. Adjust inlet air temperature and drying time to ensure a balance between drying efficiency and coating flexibility.
- **Adjust Tablet Hardness**: Optimize the compression force during tablet production to achieve the right balance between hardness and compressibility.
- **Use Appropriate Plasticizers**: Ensure the coating formulation includes sufficient plasticizers to enhance film flexibility. Common plasticizers include polyethylene glycol (PEG) and triethyl citrate.

Peeling

Causes:

- **Poor Adhesion**: Lack of proper adhesion between the coating and tablet core, often due to inadequate surface preparation or incompatible materials.

- **Excessive Coating Thickness**: Applying too thick a coating layer can lead to peeling as the outer layers may not adhere well to the inner layers.
- **Improper Drying**: Insufficient drying can cause the coating to peel off as the solvent is not fully evaporated.

Prevention and Rectification:

- **Improve Surface Preparation**: Ensure that the tablet cores are clean and dry before coating. Consider pre-treating the surface to enhance adhesion.
- **Optimize Coating Thickness**: Apply multiple thin layers rather than one thick layer to ensure better adhesion and flexibility. Monitor the spray rate and coating solution concentration.
- **Ensure Proper Drying**: Adjust drying parameters to ensure complete solvent evaporation. Use controlled drying conditions to prevent under-drying or over-drying.

Color Variation
Causes:

- **Inconsistent Mixing**: Inadequate mixing of the coating solution can result in uneven color distribution.
- **Spray Pattern Issues**: Irregular spray patterns or fluctuating spray rates can cause color variations.
- **Batch-to-Batch Variability**: Differences in raw material quality or process parameters between batches can lead to color inconsistency.

Prevention and Rectification:

- **Ensure Homogeneous Mixing**: Use high-shear mixers or homogenizers to achieve a uniform coating solution. Verify the consistency of the mixture before application.
- **Control Spray Parameters**: Maintain consistent spray patterns and rates by regularly inspecting and calibrating spray nozzles. Use automated systems to control spray parameters precisely.
- **Standardize Processes**: Implement standard operating procedures (SOPs) to maintain consistent raw material quality and process

conditions across batches. Conduct regular quality checks to ensure batch-to-batch uniformity.

Additional Common Defects
Picking and Sticking
Causes:

- **Overwetting:** Excessive application of the coating solution can lead to tablets sticking together.
- **Improper Drying:** Insufficient drying between layers can cause tablets to stick to each other or to the coating equipment.

Prevention and Rectification:

- **Control Spray Rate:** Adjust the spray rate to ensure even application without overwetting. Monitor the application closely to prevent excess solution buildup.
- **Optimize Drying:** Ensure adequate drying between layers. Use intermittent drying if necessary to prevent sticking and ensure layer integrity.

Roughness
Causes:

- **High Spray Rate:** Excessive spray rates can lead to uneven application and a rough surface.
- **Inappropriate Atomization:** Poor atomization of the coating solution can result in large droplets and a rough coating texture.

Prevention and Rectification:

- **Adjust Spray Rate:** Optimize the spray rate to achieve a smooth, even coating. Use lower spray rates if necessary to improve surface finish.
- **Enhance Atomization:** Use appropriate atomization air pressure to create fine droplets. Regularly inspect and clean spray nozzles to ensure proper functioning.

Blistering

Causes:

- **Rapid Drying**: Fast evaporation of the solvent can trap air or solvent vapors within the coating, causing blisters.
- **High Temperature**: Excessive drying temperatures can cause blistering by creating a temperature gradient across the coating layer.

Prevention and Rectification:

- **Control Drying Rate**: Use controlled drying conditions to prevent rapid solvent evaporation. Gradually increase the drying temperature to ensure even drying.
- **Monitor Temperature**: Avoid using excessively high temperatures. Use step-wise drying profiles to maintain uniform drying.

2.6 Quality Control Tests

In-Process Tests

In-process tests are performed during the tablet manufacturing process to ensure that the production parameters are within acceptable limits and that the tablets being produced meet quality standards. These tests are crucial for maintaining the consistency, safety, and efficacy of the tablets.

1. **Weight Variation Test:**

    - **Description**: Measures the weight of individual tablets at regular intervals during production to ensure uniformity.
    - **Significance**: Ensures that each tablet contains the intended amount of active pharmaceutical ingredient (API) and excipients. Consistent tablet weight is crucial for accurate dosing.
    - **Procedure**: Tablets are randomly selected and weighed individually. The average weight and the variation from this average are calculated. Regulatory guidelines typically allow a small percentage deviation from the average weight, depending on the tablet size.

2. **Thickness Test:**

- ◦ **Description:** Measures the thickness of tablets to ensure uniformity.
- ◦ **Significance:** Consistent thickness is important for uniform packaging and handling. It also affects the tablet's dissolution rate.
- ◦ **Procedure:** Tablets are measured using a micrometer or vernier caliper. The thickness should be consistent within a specified range.

3. **Hardness Test:**

- ◦ **Description:** Measures the force required to break a tablet.
- ◦ **Significance:** Ensures that tablets are strong enough to withstand mechanical stress during packaging, shipping, and handling, but also not too hard to affect dissolution.
- ◦ **Procedure:** A hardness tester applies force to the tablet until it breaks. The force required is measured in kiloponds (kp) or newtons (N).

4. **Friability Test:**

- ◦ **Description:** Assesses the tablet's ability to resist abrasion and chipping.
- ◦ **Significance:** Ensures that tablets can withstand handling without significant weight loss due to abrasion.
- ◦ **Procedure:** Tablets are placed in a friabilator, which rotates and subjects them to impact. The tablets are weighed before and after the test, and the percentage weight loss is calculated. The acceptable limit is typically less than 1%.

5. **Disintegration Test:**

- ◦ **Description:** Determines the time it takes for a tablet to break down into smaller particles in a specified liquid.
- ◦ **Significance:** Ensures that tablets disintegrate within a specified time frame to allow the API to be available for absorption.
- ◦ **Procedure:** Tablets are placed in a disintegration tester containing a specified fluid at 37°C. The time taken for all tablets to disintegrate is recorded. Regulatory guidelines specify the maximum allowable disintegration time.

Finished Product Tests

Finished product tests are conducted on completed tablets to ensure they meet the required specifications for quality, safety, and efficacy. These tests are essential for verifying that the tablets are suitable for patient use.

1. **Hardness Test:**

    ○ **Description**: Measures the force required to break a tablet.
    ○ **Purpose**: Ensures tablets are strong enough to withstand mechanical stress during packaging, shipping, and handling.
    ○ **Standards**: Typically, a hardness of 4-10 kp is acceptable, but the exact range depends on the tablet formulation and intended use.

2. **Friability Test:**

    ○ **Description**: Assesses the tablet's ability to resist abrasion and chipping.
    ○ **Purpose**: Ensures tablets can withstand handling without significant weight loss.
    ○ **Standards**: An acceptable weight loss is usually less than 1%. Tablets are subjected to a friabilator, and the percentage weight loss is measured after a specified number of rotations.

3. **Dissolution Test:**

    ○ **Description**: Measures the rate and extent of drug release from the tablet in a specified liquid medium over time.
    ○ **Purpose**: Ensures that the API is released at the correct rate for proper absorption and therapeutic effect.
    ○ **Standards**: The dissolution profile must meet specified criteria for the amount of API dissolved at various time points. This is typically compared against a reference standard or pharmacopeial requirements.

4. **Content Uniformity Test:**

    ○ **Description**: Assesses whether individual tablets contain the intended amount of API within a specified range.

- ○ **Purpose**: Ensures that each tablet contains a consistent dose of the API.
- ○ **Standards**: Typically, 10 tablets are randomly selected, and the amount of API in each tablet is measured. The content should be within 85-115% of the label claim for 9 out of 10 tablets tested, and no tablet should be outside 75-125%.

5. **Assay Test:**

- ○ **Description**: Quantifies the exact amount of API in the tablet.
- ○ **Purpose**: Confirms that the correct amount of API is present in the tablet.
- ○ **Standards**: The assay result should be within 95-105% of the labeled amount for most tablets, though exact limits can vary based on regulatory requirements.

6. **Disintegration Test:**

- ○ **Description**: Determines the time it takes for a tablet to break down into smaller particles in a specified liquid.
- ○ **Purpose**: Ensures that tablets disintegrate within a specified time to allow the API to be available for absorption.
- ○ **Standards**: Tablets must disintegrate within a specified time frame as outlined in pharmacopeial standards (e.g., USP, BP).

7. **Appearance and Organoleptic Properties:**

- ○ **Description**: Visual inspection for color, shape, size, and any physical defects; taste and odor for certain formulations.
- ○ **Purpose**: Ensures the tablets are visually consistent and acceptable to patients.
- ○ **Standards**: Tablets should be free from defects like cracks, chips, or discoloration, and should have a uniform appearance.

Liquid Orals

3.1 Introduction and Formulation Considerations

Syrups and Elixirs

Syrups are concentrated, aqueous preparations that contain one or more active pharmaceutical ingredients (APIs) dissolved in a solution of sugar. The primary **solvent** in syrups is purified water. **Sweeteners** like sucrose are used not only to mask the bitter taste of the API but also to provide the necessary viscosity and mouthfeel. The concentration of sucrose in syrups typically ranges from 60% to 85%. High concentrations of sucrose act as a natural **preservative** by creating an environment that is inhospitable for microbial growth. However, additional preservatives like methylparaben or sodium benzoate might be included to enhance the antimicrobial properties. **Flavoring agents** such as vanilla, cherry, or orange are added to improve palatability, especially for pediatric formulations.

Formulating a syrup involves ensuring that the API is completely soluble in the aqueous medium. The use of **viscosity enhancers** like glycerin or sorbitol can further improve the texture and stability of the syrup. The viscosity of the syrup is crucial as it affects the pourability and the uniformity of dosing. The pH of the syrup is also adjusted using buffers like citric acid or sodium citrate to enhance the stability of the API and the overall product.

Elixirs, on the other hand, are clear, sweetened hydroalcoholic solutions intended for oral use. The primary **solvents** in elixirs are a mixture of alcohol and water. The alcohol content typically ranges from 5% to 40%, depending on the solubility of the API and the desired preservation effect. The alcohol not only helps in dissolving the API but also acts as a **preservative. Sweeteners** such as sucrose, glycerin, or artificial sweeteners like saccharin sodium are used to enhance the taste.

In elixirs, **flavoring agents** are crucial due to the presence of alcohol, which can impart a strong taste. Common flavors include peppermint, orange, and lemon. The formulation of an elixir must consider the balance between the alcohol and water content to ensure the stability and solubility of the API. The viscosity of elixirs is generally lower than that of syrups, making them easier to pour and measure.

Differences between Syrups and Elixirs: The key difference lies in their solvent systems and their resulting properties. Syrups are purely aqueous solutions, making them ideal for APIs that are water-soluble. Their high sugar content also means they are viscous and have a pleasant taste, which is particularly advantageous for pediatric and geriatric patients. Elixirs, with their hydroalcoholic base, are suitable for APIs that are alcohol-soluble or require alcohol for stability. They are less viscous than syrups and often used when a rapid onset of action is desired, as the alcohol can enhance the absorption of the API.

Advantages: Syrups are advantageous for masking the taste of bitter APIs and providing a palatable dosage form for children and the elderly. Their high viscosity also ensures that the dose remains uniform. Elixirs, due to their alcohol content, have better solubility for certain APIs and offer improved stability and preservation. They are also less likely to support microbial growth compared to syrups.

Common Therapeutic Uses: Syrups are commonly used for **cough and cold remedies**, antipyretics, and vitamins. For example, cough syrups often contain APIs like dextromethorphan or guaifenesin. Elixirs are frequently used for **antihistamines**, sedatives, and bronchodilators. For instance, diphenhydramine elixir is used as an antihistamine for allergic reactions.

Examples of Commonly Used Ingredients:

- **Syrups:** Sucrose (sweetener), methylparaben (preservative), citric acid (buffer), glycerin (viscosity enhancer), cherry flavor (flavoring agent).
- **Elixirs:** Ethanol (solvent), glycerin (sweetener and viscosity enhancer), saccharin sodium (sweetener), propylene glycol (co-solvent), peppermint oil (flavoring agent).

Suspensions

Pharmaceutical suspensions are liquid dosage forms that contain finely divided, insoluble drug particles dispersed in a liquid medium. The formulation of suspensions involves several critical considerations to ensure stability, uniformity, and efficacy of the product. These considerations include the selection of **suspending agents, wetting agents, preservatives, and flavoring agents**. Additionally, challenges such as **sedimentation and particle size distribution** must be addressed to maintain the quality of the suspension.

Suspending Agents

Suspending agents are crucial in suspensions as they increase the viscosity of the liquid medium, preventing the sedimentation of dispersed particles. Common suspending agents include:

- **Methylcellulose**: A cellulose derivative that provides high viscosity and good stability. It is commonly used due to its non-toxic nature and compatibility with various APIs.
- **Sodium Carboxymethylcellulose (CMC)**: Known for its excellent suspending properties and stability over a wide pH range. It is often used in concentrations of 0.5-2%.
- **Xanthan Gum**: A natural polysaccharide that offers high viscosity at low concentrations and excellent stability. It is effective in both acidic and alkaline environments.
- **Carbomers**: Synthetic high molecular weight polymers that provide high viscosity and are used in concentrations of 0.1-0.5%.

Wetting Agents

Wetting agents are added to reduce the surface tension between the drug particles and the liquid medium, ensuring uniform dispersion of the particles. These agents help prevent the particles from clumping together and settling too quickly. Common wetting agents include:

- **Polysorbates (e.g., Tween 80)**: Non-ionic surfactants that enhance the wetting of hydrophobic drug particles.
- **Sodium Lauryl Sulfate**: An anionic surfactant that effectively lowers surface tension and improves wetting.
- **Lecithin**: A natural surfactant derived from soy or egg yolk, used for its biocompatibility and effectiveness in wetting.

Preservatives

Preservatives are necessary to prevent microbial growth in aqueous suspensions. Common preservatives include:

- **Methylparaben and Propylparaben**: Often used in combination to provide broad-spectrum antimicrobial activity.
- **Sodium Benzoate**: Effective against fungi and bacteria, commonly used in concentrations of 0.1-0.2%.
- **Benzalkonium Chloride**: A quaternary ammonium compound with broad-spectrum antimicrobial properties, used in low concentrations.

Flavoring Agents

Flavoring agents are added to improve the taste and palatability of the suspension, especially important for pediatric and geriatric patients. Common flavoring agents include:

- **Fruit Flavors**: Such as cherry, orange, and grape, which are popular choices for masking unpleasant tastes.
- **Sweeteners**: Such as sucrose, sorbitol, and aspartame, which enhance the overall flavor profile.

Challenges and Solutions

Sedimentation: One of the primary challenges in suspensions is sedimentation, where dispersed particles settle over time, leading to a non-uniform distribution of the drug. This can be addressed by:

- **Optimizing Viscosity**: Using appropriate concentrations of suspending agents to increase the viscosity of the suspension, thereby reducing the rate of sedimentation.
- **Particle Size Reduction**: Reducing the particle size of the drug to a fine and uniform distribution. Techniques such as milling and homogenization are used to achieve the desired particle size.

Particle Size Distribution: Uniform particle size distribution is critical for the stability and efficacy of suspensions. Inconsistent particle sizes can lead to rapid sedimentation and variable dosing. This can be managed by:

- **Controlled Milling**: Using processes like ball milling or high-pressure homogenization to achieve consistent particle size.
- **Stabilizers**: Adding stabilizers such as surfactants or polymers to prevent aggregation and ensure uniform dispersion of particles.

Formulation Process

1. **Selection of Excipients**: Choose appropriate suspending agents, wetting agents, preservatives, and flavoring agents based on the properties of the API and the desired characteristics of the suspension.
2. **Preparation of Suspension**: Disperse the drug particles in the liquid medium using high-shear mixing or homogenization. Add the suspending agent to increase viscosity and prevent sedimentation. Incorporate wetting agents to ensure uniform dispersion of particles.
3. **Addition of Preservatives and Flavoring Agents**: Add preservatives to inhibit microbial growth and flavoring agents to enhance taste.
4. **Particle Size Reduction**: Utilize milling or homogenization techniques to achieve the desired particle size distribution, ensuring stability and uniformity.
5. **Quality Control**: Conduct tests such as sedimentation rate, particle size analysis, viscosity measurement, and microbial testing to ensure the suspension meets quality standards.

Emulsions

Pharmaceutical emulsions are biphasic liquid systems in which one liquid is dispersed in another in the form of small droplets. They are classified into **oil-in-water (O/W) emulsions** and **water-in-oil (W/O) emulsions**. Formulating emulsions involves selecting appropriate **emulsifying agents, stabilizers, preservatives, and flavoring agents** to ensure stability and efficacy. Understanding the differences between O/W and W/O emulsions, as well as the stability issues and strategies to enhance stability, is crucial for successful emulsion formulation.

Selection of Emulsifying Agents

Emulsifying agents are critical in emulsions as they reduce the interfacial tension between the oil and water phases, enabling the formation and stabilization of small droplets. Common emulsifying agents include:

- **Surfactants**: Molecules with both hydrophilic and lipophilic ends that stabilize emulsions by forming a protective layer around the droplets. Examples include polysorbates (Tween), sorbitan esters (Span), and lecithin.
- **Hydrophilic-Lipophilic Balance (HLB)**: Surfactants are chosen based on their HLB value. For O/W emulsions, surfactants with HLB values between 8 and 18 are preferred, while for W/O emulsions, those with HLB values between 3 and 6 are more suitable.

Stabilizers

Stabilizers are added to emulsions to prevent droplet coalescence and improve stability. They enhance the viscosity of the continuous phase, reducing the movement of droplets and thereby preventing separation. Common stabilizers include:

- **Polymers**: Such as carbomers and cellulose derivatives, which increase the viscosity of the emulsion and stabilize the droplets.
- **Proteins**: Like gelatin and casein, which adsorb at the oil-water interface and stabilize the emulsion.

Preservatives

Preservatives are essential in emulsions to prevent microbial growth, as the presence of water in O/W emulsions provides a medium for microbes. Common preservatives include:

- **Parabens**: Methylparaben and propylparaben, used in combination for broad-spectrum antimicrobial activity.
- **Benzalkonium Chloride**: A quaternary ammonium compound with effective antimicrobial properties.
- **Phenoxyethanol**: A preservative with broad-spectrum activity, often used in concentrations of 0.5-1%.

Flavoring Agents

Flavoring agents improve the taste and palatability of oral emulsions, making them more acceptable to patients. Common flavoring agents include:

- **Fruit Flavors**: Such as orange, lemon, and cherry, which mask the taste of the oil phase.
- **Sweeteners**: Such as sucrose, sorbitol, and aspartame, which enhance the overall flavor profile.

Differences between O/W and W/O Emulsions

Oil-in-Water (O/W) Emulsions: In O/W emulsions, oil droplets are dispersed in the aqueous phase. These emulsions are commonly used for oral and topical formulations due to their ease of application and absorption. O/W emulsions are less greasy and more easily washable compared to W/O emulsions.

Water-in-Oil (W/O) Emulsions: In W/O emulsions, water droplets are dispersed in the oil phase. These emulsions are typically used for topical formulations where an occlusive and moisturizing effect is desired. W/O emulsions are more emollient and provide a longer-lasting moisturizing effect than O/W emulsions.

Stability Issues and Strategies to Enhance Emulsion Stability

Stability Issues:

- **Creaming**: The upward or downward movement of dispersed droplets, leading to concentration gradients. Creaming is reversible but can lead to phase separation if not addressed.
- **Coalescence**: The merging of droplets to form larger droplets, leading to phase separation. Coalescence is irreversible and detrimental to emulsion stability.
- **Phase Inversion**: A change from O/W to W/O or vice versa, often caused by changes in temperature or the addition of electrolytes.

Strategies to Enhance Emulsion Stability:

- **Optimize Emulsifier Concentration**: Use an appropriate concentration of emulsifying agents to ensure complete coverage of the droplets and prevent coalescence.
- **Control Droplet Size**: Use high-shear mixing or homogenization to produce small and uniform droplets, which are more stable.
- **Increase Viscosity**: Add stabilizers to increase the viscosity of the continuous phase, reducing droplet movement and preventing creaming.

- **Avoid Phase Inversion**: Maintain consistent formulation conditions and avoid drastic changes in temperature or pH. Use emulsifiers with a suitable HLB value for the desired emulsion type.
- **Use Antioxidants**: Add antioxidants like tocopherols or ascorbic acid to prevent oxidation of the oil phase, which can destabilize the emulsion.

Formulation Process

1. **Selection of Excipients**: Choose suitable emulsifying agents, stabilizers, preservatives, and flavoring agents based on the properties of the API and the desired characteristics of the emulsion.
2. **Preparation of Emulsion**: Disperse the oil phase in the aqueous phase (for O/W emulsions) or vice versa (for W/O emulsions) using high-shear mixing or homogenization. Ensure uniform dispersion of droplets.
3. **Addition of Stabilizers and Preservatives**: Add stabilizers to increase viscosity and preservatives to prevent microbial growth.
4. **Flavoring and Sweetening**: Incorporate flavoring agents and sweeteners to improve the taste and palatability.
5. **Quality Control**: Conduct tests such as droplet size analysis, viscosity measurement, pH, and microbial testing to ensure the emulsion meets quality standards.

3.2 Manufacturing Considerations

Equipment Used

The manufacturing of liquid oral formulations involves various types of equipment to ensure proper mixing, homogenization, particle size reduction, and filtration. Each type of equipment has specific working principles and specifications that make it suitable for different formulation types. Understanding these principles and criteria for equipment selection is crucial for optimizing the manufacturing process.

Mixers

Mixers are essential for blending ingredients uniformly in liquid oral formulations. They ensure that active pharmaceutical ingredients (APIs), excipients, and other additives are evenly distributed throughout the formulation.

Working Principles:

- **Propeller Mixers**: Use a rotating propeller to create flow patterns that circulate the liquid and mix the ingredients.
- **Turbine Mixers**: Feature a turbine blade that generates radial and axial flow, providing efficient mixing for low to medium viscosity liquids.
- **High-Shear Mixers**: Utilize a high-speed rotor-stator assembly to create intense shear forces, breaking down particles and ensuring uniform dispersion.

Specifications:

- **Speed Range**: Variable speed control, typically ranging from 100 to 10,000 rpm, depending on the type of mixer.
- **Capacity**: Varies from small laboratory-scale units (1-10 liters) to large industrial-scale mixers (up to several thousand liters).

Selection Criteria:

- **Viscosity of the Formulation**: High-shear mixers are preferred for high-viscosity formulations, while propeller or turbine mixers are suitable for low to medium viscosity liquids.
- **Homogeneity Requirements**: High-shear mixers provide better particle size reduction and uniform dispersion for suspensions and emulsions.

Homogenizers

Homogenizers are used to reduce particle size and ensure uniform distribution of particles within the liquid formulation, enhancing stability and bioavailability.

Working Principles:

- **High-Pressure Homogenizers**: Force the liquid through a narrow orifice at high pressure (up to 30,000 psi), causing intense shear, cavitation, and turbulence that break down particles.
- **Ultrasonic Homogenizers**: Use ultrasonic waves to create cavitation bubbles in the liquid, which collapse and produce shock waves that disrupt particles.

Specifications:

- **Pressure Range:** High-pressure homogenizers typically operate between 5,000 and 30,000 psi.
- **Frequency Range:** Ultrasonic homogenizers operate at frequencies between 20 kHz and 40 kHz.

Selection Criteria:

- **Particle Size Reduction:** High-pressure homogenizers are effective for achieving very fine particle sizes, making them ideal for emulsions and suspensions.
- **Formulation Sensitivity:** Ultrasonic homogenizers are suitable for sensitive formulations where excessive heat generation needs to be avoided.

Colloid Mills

Colloid Mills are used for reducing particle size and achieving fine dispersions and emulsions by applying shear forces through a rotating stator and rotor.

Working Principles:

- The liquid formulation is fed between a rotating stator and rotor, where it is subjected to high shear forces that reduce particle size and create a uniform dispersion.

Specifications:

- **Speed Range:** Rotational speeds typically range from 1,000 to 20,000 rpm.
- **Gap Adjustment:** The gap between the stator and rotor can be adjusted to control the shear force and particle size reduction.

Selection Criteria:

- **Desired Particle Size:** Colloid mills are suitable for achieving very fine particle sizes and uniform dispersions in emulsions and suspensions.
- **Viscosity of the Formulation:** Effective for high-viscosity formulations that require intense shear forces for particle size reduction.

Filtration Systems

Filtration Systems are used to remove particulate matter, microorganisms, and other impurities from liquid formulations, ensuring clarity and sterility.

Working Principles:

- **Depth Filtration**: Uses thick filter media to trap particles throughout the depth of the filter.
- **Membrane Filtration**: Employs a thin membrane with specific pore sizes to retain particles and microorganisms on the surface.

Specifications:

- **Pore Size**: Membrane filters are available with pore sizes ranging from 0.1 to 10 micrometers, depending on the filtration requirements.
- **Flow Rate**: The flow rate depends on the filter area and the viscosity of the liquid, typically ranging from a few milliliters per minute to several liters per minute.

Selection Criteria:

- **Filtration Requirements**: Depth filters are suitable for bulk filtration of large particles, while membrane filters are ideal for fine filtration and sterilization.
- **Formulation Sensitivity**: Consider the chemical compatibility of the filter material with the formulation components to avoid contamination or degradation.

3.2 Manufacturing Considerations

Process Parameters

The manufacturing of liquid oral formulations involves several critical process parameters that significantly affect the quality and stability of the final product. These parameters include **temperature, mixing speed, homogenization pressure, and pH**. Each parameter must be carefully controlled and optimized to ensure consistent production of high-quality liquid orals.

Temperature

Temperature plays a crucial role in the manufacturing of liquid oral formulations, affecting the solubility of ingredients, viscosity of the formulation, and stability of the final product.

- **Effect on Quality and Stability**: Elevated temperatures can increase the solubility of certain APIs and excipients, facilitating better mixing and dissolution. However, excessive heat can degrade temperature-sensitive APIs and excipients, leading to loss of potency and stability.
- **Optimal Conditions**:

  - For syrups: Typically maintained at 60-70°C during the preparation to ensure complete dissolution of sucrose and other ingredients without causing degradation.
  - For suspensions: Temperature is often kept below 40°C to prevent degradation of heat-sensitive components while ensuring adequate mixing and dispersion of particles.

Mixing Speed

Mixing speed is a critical parameter in ensuring the uniform distribution of APIs and excipients within the liquid formulation.

- **Effect on Quality and Stability**: Inadequate mixing can lead to poor homogeneity, resulting in dose variability and inconsistent therapeutic effects. Conversely, excessive mixing speeds can introduce air bubbles, leading to foaming and potential oxidation of sensitive APIs.
- **Optimal Conditions**:

  - For emulsions: A moderate mixing speed of 500-1500 rpm is typically used during the initial blending phase to ensure proper dispersion of the oil and water phases.
  - For syrups: Lower mixing speeds (200-500 rpm) are used to prevent excessive air incorporation while ensuring complete dissolution of ingredients.

Homogenization Pressure

Homogenization pressure is critical for achieving the desired particle size and uniform distribution in emulsions and suspensions.

- **Effect on Quality and Stability**: High homogenization pressures create intense shear forces that reduce particle size, enhancing the stability and bioavailability of the formulation. However, excessive pressure can lead to the degradation of sensitive APIs and increased temperature, which may affect stability.
- **Optimal Conditions**:

  - For emulsions: Homogenization pressures of 10,000-20,000 psi are typically used to achieve fine and stable emulsions.
  - For suspensions: Lower pressures (5,000-10,000 psi) are sufficient to ensure uniform dispersion without degrading the API.

pH

pH is a vital parameter that affects the solubility, stability, and overall effectiveness of the liquid oral formulation.

- **Effect on Quality and Stability**: The pH of the formulation must be within a range that ensures the stability of the API and excipients while maintaining compatibility with the gastrointestinal environment. Deviations from the optimal pH can lead to precipitation, degradation, or reduced efficacy of the API.
- **Optimal Conditions**:

  - For syrups: The pH is typically adjusted to 4.5-6.5 using buffers like citric acid or sodium citrate to ensure the stability of the API and prevent microbial growth.
  - For suspensions: The pH range of 3.0-7.0 is commonly maintained, depending on the API's stability and solubility profile. Buffer systems like phosphate or acetate buffers are used to maintain the desired pH.

Examples of Optimal Process Conditions for Different Types of Liquid Orals

1. **Syrups:**

   - **Temperature**: Maintain at 60-70°C during preparation to ensure complete dissolution of sucrose and other soluble ingredients.

- **Mixing Speed**: 200-500 rpm to ensure proper mixing without incorporating excessive air.
- **pH**: Adjust to 4.5-6.5 using appropriate buffer systems.

2. **Suspensions**:

- **Temperature**: Keep below 40°C to prevent degradation of heat-sensitive components.
- **Mixing Speed**: 300-600 rpm to achieve uniform dispersion of particles.
- **Homogenization Pressure**: 5,000-10,000 psi to ensure uniform particle size without degrading the API.
- **pH**: Adjust to 3.0-7.0 based on the API's stability profile using suitable buffers.

3. **Emulsions**:

- **Temperature**: Maintain at 30-40°C during emulsification to ensure stability and prevent phase separation.
- **Mixing Speed**: 500-1500 rpm during initial blending to ensure proper dispersion.
- **Homogenization Pressure**: 10,000-20,000 psi to achieve fine and stable emulsions.
- **pH**: Adjust based on the type of emulsion (O/W or W/O) and the stability requirements of the API.

3.3 Filling and Packaging
Techniques and Equipment

Filling and packaging are critical steps in the manufacturing of liquid oral formulations. The choice of filling techniques and equipment, as well as the selection of appropriate packaging materials, directly affects the product's stability, safety, and ease of use. There are several methods used for filling liquid orals, each with its unique advantages and suitability depending on the formulation type.

Volumetric Filling

Volumetric filling involves dispensing a precise volume of liquid into each container. This method relies on piston fillers, diaphragm fillers, or time/pressure fillers.

- **Piston Fillers**: Use a piston to draw a specific volume of liquid into a cylinder and then dispense it into the container. They are accurate and suitable for viscous and non-viscous liquids.
- **Diaphragm Fillers**: Utilize a flexible diaphragm to draw and dispense liquid. They are ideal for small volume fills and sensitive formulations.
- **Time/Pressure Fillers**: Control the filling time and pressure to achieve the desired volume. These are versatile and can handle a wide range of viscosities.

Advantages:

- High accuracy and consistency.
- Suitable for a wide range of viscosities.
- Minimal product waste.

Limitations:

- Equipment complexity and maintenance requirements.
- Calibration needed for different volumes and viscosities.

Gravimetric Filling

Gravimetric filling is based on the weight of the liquid being dispensed. This method uses load cells and weighing systems to ensure each container receives the correct amount of liquid.

- **Load Cell-Based Fillers**: Weigh the container before and after filling to ensure precise dosing. These systems are highly accurate and suitable for high-value or sensitive formulations.

Advantages:

- High precision and accuracy.
- Ideal for expensive or potent formulations where exact dosing is critical.
- Suitable for various liquid viscosities.

Limitations:

- Slower compared to volumetric filling due to weighing process.

- Higher initial cost for equipment.

Peristaltic Filling

Peristaltic filling uses a peristaltic pump to move liquid through a flexible tube by compressing and releasing it. This method is often used for sterile or sensitive formulations.

- **Peristaltic Pumps**: Gently move liquid without exposing it to the pump mechanism, reducing the risk of contamination.

Advantages:

- Excellent for sterile or aseptic filling due to minimal product contact.
- Easy to clean and sterilize.
- Suitable for low to medium viscosity liquids.

Limitations:

- Limited to lower viscosity formulations.
- Potential for tubing wear and tear.

Packaging Materials and Types

The selection of appropriate packaging materials is crucial for maintaining the stability, safety, and efficacy of liquid oral formulations. The choice depends on the formulation's properties, including its chemical stability, sensitivity to light and oxygen, and required shelf life.

Glass Bottles

Glass bottles are commonly used for liquid oral formulations due to their excellent chemical resistance and barrier properties.

- **Advantages:**

  - Inert and non-reactive with most formulations.
  - Excellent barrier against moisture, oxygen, and light.
  - Suitable for both acidic and alkaline formulations.

- **Disadvantages:**

- ◦ Breakable and heavier than plastic.
- ◦ Higher shipping costs due to weight and fragility.

Plastic Bottles

Plastic bottles are widely used for their lightweight, durability, and versatility. Common plastics include polyethylene (PE), polypropylene (PP), and polyethylene terephthalate (PET).

- **Advantages**:

  - ◦ Lightweight and shatterproof.
  - ◦ Flexible design options.
  - ◦ Lower shipping costs.

- **Disadvantages**:

  - ◦ Potential for chemical interactions with the formulation.
  - ◦ Permeability to gases and moisture, depending on the plastic type.
  - ◦ Not suitable for all types of formulations, especially those sensitive to oxygen and light.

Selection Criteria

1. **Chemical Compatibility**: Ensure that the packaging material does not interact with the formulation. Glass is highly inert, while certain plastics might react with or absorb components of the formulation.
2. **Barrier Properties**: Consider the formulation's sensitivity to light, moisture, and oxygen. Amber glass provides excellent protection against light, while certain plastics can be coated or treated to improve barrier properties.
3. **Stability and Shelf Life**: Choose materials that maintain the formulation's stability throughout its intended shelf life. Glass is preferred for long-term stability, whereas high-barrier plastics like PET can be used for products with shorter shelf lives.
4. **Patient Safety and Convenience**: Select packaging that ensures ease of use and safety for patients. Plastic bottles are lighter and less likely to break, making them more convenient for everyday use.

Filling and Packaging Process

1. **Preparation of Formulation**: Ensure the liquid oral formulation is homogeneously mixed and meets all quality specifications before filling.
2. **Filling**: Use the selected filling method (volumetric, gravimetric, or peristaltic) to dispense the formulation into containers accurately.
3. **Capping and Sealing**: Secure the containers with appropriate caps and seals to prevent leakage and contamination.
4. **Labeling and Packaging**: Apply labels with necessary information, including dosage instructions and expiration dates. Package the filled containers in secondary packaging for protection during transport and storage.

3.4 Evaluation of Liquid Orals

Quality Control Tests

Ensuring the quality and consistency of liquid oral formulations involves conducting a series of quality control tests. These tests are critical for verifying that the formulations meet the required specifications and are safe and effective for patient use. Key quality control tests include those for **viscosity, pH, specific gravity, microbial contamination, and content uniformity**. Each test has its own significance in maintaining the overall quality of the product.

Viscosity

Description: Viscosity measures the resistance of a liquid to flow. It is a critical parameter for liquid oral formulations, especially for suspensions and emulsions.

Significance:

- Ensures that the formulation is easy to pour and administer.
- Helps in maintaining the stability of suspensions and emulsions by preventing sedimentation or phase separation.
- Affects the mouthfeel and acceptability of the product to patients.

Procedure: Viscosity is measured using viscometers or rheometers, which determine the flow characteristics of the liquid under specified conditions. The results are typically expressed in centipoises (cP) or milliPascal-seconds (mPa·s).

pH

Description: pH measures the acidity or alkalinity of the formulation. It is crucial for the stability and solubility of the active pharmaceutical ingredient (API) and excipients.

Significance:

- Ensures the chemical stability of the API and excipients.
- Influences the taste and safety of the product.
- Ensures compatibility with the gastrointestinal environment.

Procedure: pH is measured using a calibrated pH meter. The sample is prepared according to the product specifications, and the pH electrode is immersed in the liquid to obtain a reading.

Specific Gravity

Description: Specific gravity is the ratio of the density of the liquid formulation to the density of water. It indicates the concentration of the formulation.

Significance:

- Ensures the consistency and uniformity of the formulation.
- Verifies the correct concentration of ingredients.
- Affects the dosing accuracy and efficacy of the product.

Procedure: Specific gravity is measured using a hydrometer, pycnometer, or digital density meter. The liquid is compared to the density of water at a specified temperature.

Microbial Contamination

Description: Tests for microbial contamination ensure that the formulation is free from harmful microorganisms such as bacteria, fungi, and yeasts.

Significance:

- Ensures the safety and sterility of the product, particularly for formulations with a long shelf life.
- Prevents infections or adverse reactions in patients.
- Complies with regulatory standards for microbial limits.

Procedure: Microbial contamination is assessed using methods such as total aerobic microbial count (TAMC), total combined yeasts and molds count (TYMC), and specific pathogen testing (e.g., for E. coli, Salmonella). Samples are cultured on appropriate media, and colony-forming units (CFUs) are counted.

Content Uniformity

Description: Content uniformity tests ensure that each dose of the liquid formulation contains the intended amount of API within specified limits.

Significance:

- Ensures consistent therapeutic effect and safety.
- Verifies the accuracy and precision of the manufacturing process.
- Complies with regulatory requirements for dosage uniformity.

Procedure: Content uniformity is assessed by taking multiple samples from a batch and analyzing the API content using techniques like high-performance liquid chromatography (HPLC) or ultraviolet-visible (UV-Vis) spectroscopy. The results are compared to the labeled claim, and acceptance criteria are based on pharmacopeial standards.

Additional Quality Control Tests

Appearance and Clarity

Description: Visual inspection of the formulation to check for any particulate matter, color consistency, and overall clarity.

Significance:

- Ensures the aesthetic quality and acceptability of the product.
- Detects any visible contamination or formulation issues.
- Helps in identifying phase separation in emulsions or sedimentation in suspensions.

Procedure: The formulation is examined under suitable lighting conditions, and any deviations from the expected appearance are recorded.

Assay of Active Ingredient

Description: Quantitative determination of the API content to ensure it is within the specified range.

Significance:

- Verifies the correct dosage of the API in each unit of the product.

- Ensures the efficacy and safety of the formulation.
- Complies with pharmacopeial standards for API content.

Procedure: The assay is typically performed using analytical techniques such as HPLC, UV-Vis spectroscopy, or titration, depending on the nature of the API.

Stability Testing

Description: Stability testing evaluates how the quality of a liquid oral formulation changes over time under various environmental conditions.

Significance:

- Ensures the product remains effective and safe throughout its shelf life.
- Identifies potential degradation products and their impact on safety and efficacy.
- Provides data for determining the expiration date and storage conditions.

Procedure: Stability tests are conducted under accelerated (e.g., 40°C and 75% RH) and long-term (e.g., 25°C and 60% RH) conditions. The formulation is periodically tested for physical, chemical, and microbiological parameters.

3.4 Evaluation of Liquid Orals

Stability Testing

Importance of Stability Testing

Stability testing is a critical aspect of pharmaceutical development and quality control. It ensures that liquid oral formulations maintain their intended physical, chemical, microbiological, and therapeutic properties throughout their shelf life. Stability testing provides data to determine the expiration date, storage conditions, and packaging requirements for the product. It helps to identify potential degradation pathways and the impact of environmental factors such as temperature, humidity, and light on the product. By conducting stability testing, manufacturers can ensure the safety, efficacy, and quality of their liquid oral formulations for the duration of their use.

Types of Stability Tests

Accelerated Stability Testing

Accelerated stability testing involves subjecting the liquid oral formulation to elevated stress conditions, typically higher temperatures and humidity, to predict the product's shelf life in a shorter period. This type of testing is useful for identifying potential degradation products and their impact on the formulation.

- **Conditions**: Common conditions include 40°C ± 2°C and 75% ± 5% relative humidity (RH) for six months.
- **Purpose**: To accelerate the chemical degradation and physical changes that the product may undergo, providing an early indication of its stability profile.
- **Parameters Monitored**: Physical appearance, pH, assay, degradation products, viscosity, and microbial contamination.

Long-Term Stability Testing

Long-term stability testing is conducted under recommended storage conditions to evaluate the stability of the liquid oral formulation over its intended shelf life. This testing provides the most accurate assessment of the product's stability.

- **Conditions**: Typical conditions are 25°C ± 2°C and 60% ± 5% RH for at least 12 months or longer, depending on the regulatory requirements.
- **Purpose**: To confirm the stability and shelf life of the product under normal storage conditions.
- **Parameters Monitored**: Physical appearance, pH, assay, degradation products, viscosity, and microbial contamination.

Intermediate Stability Testing

Intermediate stability testing is performed at conditions between accelerated and long-term storage to provide additional data on the stability of the formulation.

- **Conditions**: Common conditions are 30°C ± 2°C and 65% ± 5% RH for six months.
- **Purpose**: To evaluate the stability of the product under moderate stress conditions.
- **Parameters Monitored**: Physical appearance, pH, assay, degradation products, viscosity, and microbial contamination.

Parameters Monitored During Stability Testing

Physical Appearance: Visual inspection for changes in color, clarity, precipitation, phase separation, or any other visible changes. Any alteration in appearance can indicate chemical or physical instability.

pH: Measurement of the pH to detect any significant changes that could affect the stability, solubility, and effectiveness of the API and excipients.

Assay: Quantification of the active ingredient to ensure it remains within the specified potency range throughout the shelf life. Deviation from the specified range indicates degradation or loss of potency.

Degradation Products: Identification and quantification of degradation products to ensure they remain within acceptable limits. Degradation products can affect the safety and efficacy of the formulation.

Viscosity: Measurement of viscosity to detect any changes that could impact the pourability, dosing accuracy, and patient acceptability of the product.

Microbial Contamination: Assessment of microbial load to ensure the product remains free from harmful microorganisms, which is critical for patient safety.

Stability-Indicating Methods

High-Performance Liquid Chromatography (HPLC): A widely used analytical technique for quantifying the API and identifying degradation products. HPLC provides high sensitivity, specificity, and accuracy in detecting changes in the formulation.

Ultraviolet-Visible (UV-Vis) Spectroscopy: A common method for assessing the assay and degradation of the API. It is less specific than HPLC but useful for routine stability testing.

Mass Spectrometry (MS): Often coupled with HPLC, MS provides detailed information on the molecular weight and structure of degradation products, helping to identify and quantify impurities.

Infrared (IR) Spectroscopy: Used to detect changes in the chemical structure of the API and excipients. It can identify specific functional groups affected by degradation.

Microbial Testing Methods: Methods such as total aerobic microbial count (TAMC) and total combined yeasts and molds count (TYMC) are used to monitor microbial contamination. Specific pathogen tests are also conducted as part of stability testing.

Examples of Stability-Indicating Methods

1. **HPLC-UV**: Combines high-performance liquid chromatography with ultraviolet detection to quantify the API and detect degradation products. It is commonly used for stability testing due to its precision and reliability.
2. **HPLC-MS**: Integrates HPLC with mass spectrometry for detailed analysis of degradation products, providing both quantitative and qualitative data.
3. **UV-Vis Spectroscopy**: Measures the absorbance of the API at specific wavelengths to monitor its concentration and detect degradation.
4. **Fourier Transform Infrared (FTIR) Spectroscopy**: Analyzes the IR spectrum of the formulation to identify chemical changes in the API and excipients.
5. **Microbial Limit Tests**: Uses methods like membrane filtration or plate count to assess the microbial load and ensure the formulation meets safety standards.

CHAPTER FOUR

Capsules

4.1 Hard Gelatin Capsules

4.1.1 Introduction and Production

Composition and Properties of Hard Gelatin Capsules

Hard gelatin capsules are composed primarily of **gelatin**, a protein derived from the collagen of animal bones and skins. Gelatin used for pharmaceutical capsules is generally obtained from bovine or porcine sources. The composition typically includes **12-16% moisture**, which helps maintain the flexibility of the capsule shells, and small amounts of colorants and opacifying agents to provide the desired appearance and protect light-sensitive contents. Gelatin is preferred because it forms a strong, flexible, and digestible material that dissolves quickly in the gastrointestinal tract, allowing for rapid release of the capsule's contents.

Production Process

The production of hard gelatin capsules involves several key steps, including the **preparation of the gelatin solution, molding, drying, and trimming.**

Preparation of Gelatin Solution: The process begins with the preparation of the gelatin solution. Gelatin is dissolved in hot water, typically at temperatures between 60-70°C, along with plasticizers like glycerin or sorbitol to enhance flexibility. The solution is then deaerated under vacuum to remove any entrapped air bubbles, which can cause defects in the final product.

Molding: The deaerated gelatin solution is used to form the capsule shells. This is done using stainless steel **pins or pegs** that are dipped into the gelatin solution. The pins are maintained at a temperature slightly below the gelatin gelling point to ensure proper coating. As the pins are withdrawn, a thin layer of gelatin adheres to them, forming the capsule halves (body and cap).

Drying: The freshly molded capsule shells are dried under controlled conditions to remove excess moisture and to set the gelatin. The drying process is critical and typically occurs in stages, with an initial drying phase at higher temperatures (around 25-30°C) followed by a secondary drying phase at lower temperatures (around 20-25°C) to achieve the desired moisture content. Proper drying ensures the capsules have the right mechanical properties and stability.

Trimming: Once dried, the capsule halves are stripped from the pins and trimmed to the desired length. This is done using precision cutting machines that ensure uniform capsule dimensions. The trimmed capsule bodies and caps are then joined together and sorted for further processing or filling.

Advantages and Disadvantages of Hard Gelatin Capsules
Advantages:

- **Versatility**: Hard gelatin capsules can accommodate a wide range of formulations, including powders, granules, pellets, and even certain liquids. This versatility makes them suitable for various types of pharmaceutical applications.
- **Ease of Production**: The production process for hard gelatin capsules is relatively straightforward and well-established, allowing for efficient large-scale manufacturing.
- **Patient Compliance**: Capsules are easy to swallow and can mask the taste and odor of the drug, improving patient compliance. The smooth surface and shape of capsules facilitate ease of swallowing.
- **Rapid Drug Release**: Upon ingestion, the gelatin shell dissolves quickly in the stomach, allowing for rapid release and absorption of the drug.

Disadvantages:

- **Moisture Sensitivity**: Hard gelatin capsules can be sensitive to moisture. High humidity can cause the capsules to become too soft and sticky, while low humidity can make them brittle and prone to cracking. Proper storage conditions are essential to maintain capsule integrity.
- **Animal Origin**: The use of gelatin derived from animal sources may raise concerns among certain patient groups, including vegetarians, vegans,

and individuals with religious dietary restrictions.

- **Limited Protection**: While gelatin capsules can mask the taste and odor of the drug, they provide limited protection against light and oxygen. This can be a disadvantage for drugs that are sensitive to these environmental factors.

4.1 Hard Gelatin Capsules
4.1.2 Size and Filling
Different Sizes of Hard Gelatin Capsules and Their Capacity Ranges

Hard gelatin capsules come in various sizes, each designed to hold different quantities of medication. The sizes are standardized and typically range from **size 000** (the largest) to **size 5** (the smallest). The capacity of these capsules varies depending on the density and compressibility of the formulation being filled.

- **Size 000**: The largest capsule, holding approximately 950 mg to 1,350 mg of powder, depending on its density.
- **Size 00**: Holds about 650 mg to 1,000 mg.
- **Size 0**: Holds approximately 450 mg to 680 mg.
- **Size 1**: Holds about 300 mg to 600 mg.
- **Size 2**: Holds around 250 mg to 450 mg.
- **Size 3**: Holds approximately 200 mg to 300 mg.
- **Size 4**: Holds about 150 mg to 250 mg.
- **Size 5**: The smallest capsule, holding approximately 100 mg to 130 mg.

The selection of capsule size depends on the dose of the active pharmaceutical ingredient (API), the bulk density of the fill material, and the desired ease of swallowing.

Methods of Filling Capsules

Filling hard gelatin capsules can be performed using various methods, including **manual, semi-automatic, and automatic filling machines**. Each method has its advantages and is chosen based on the scale of production and the specific requirements of the formulation.

Manual Filling:

- **Description**: Manual filling involves using a capsule filler tray where empty capsules are placed and manually filled with the formulation using a spatula or other device. The filled capsules are then manually capped.

- **Advantages**: Suitable for small-scale production and laboratory settings. It is cost-effective and requires minimal equipment.
- **Limitations**: Labor-intensive and time-consuming, making it impractical for large-scale production. Variability in fill weight can be higher compared to automated methods.
- **Example**: Often used in compounding pharmacies or small-scale production of specialized formulations.

Semi-Automatic Filling Machines:

- **Description**: Semi-automatic machines automate some steps of the filling process. Typically, the machine separates the capsule body and cap, fills the body with the formulation, and then manually caps the filled capsules.
- **Advantages**: Increased efficiency and consistency compared to manual filling. Suitable for medium-scale production.
- **Limitations**: Requires manual intervention, particularly for capping, which can limit production speed. More expensive than manual methods.
- **Example**: Used in mid-sized pharmaceutical manufacturing units for regular production runs.

Automatic Filling Machines:

- **Description**: Automatic filling machines handle the entire filling process, including capsule separation, filling, and capping. These machines can fill hundreds to thousands of capsules per minute.
- **Advantages**: High efficiency and consistency in fill weight. Ideal for large-scale production with minimal manual intervention. Offers precise control over the filling process.
- **Limitations**: High initial cost and maintenance requirements. Requires trained personnel to operate and maintain.
- **Example**: Used in large pharmaceutical manufacturing plants for mass production of capsules.

Types of Formulations That Can Be Filled into Hard Gelatin Capsules

Hard gelatin capsules can accommodate a wide variety of formulations, making them versatile for different therapeutic needs.

Powders:

- **Description**: Dry powder formulations are the most common type filled into hard gelatin capsules. The powders can be single APIs or a blend of APIs and excipients.
- **Example**: Commonly used for antibiotics, vitamins, and dietary supplements.

Granules:

- **Description**: Granules are larger, more uniform particles that can improve flow properties and reduce dust generation during filling.
- **Example**: Extended-release formulations where granules contain the API coated with polymers to control release.

Pellets:

- **Description**: Pellets are small, spherical particles that provide controlled or extended release of the API. They can be filled as single pellets or mixed with other excipients.
- **Example**: Used for medications requiring sustained release, such **as proton pump inhibitors (PPIs) and certain antihypertensives.**

Mini-Tablets:

- **Description**: Mini-tablets are small compressed tablets that can be filled into capsules. They allow for precise dosing and can combine multiple mini-tablets with different release profiles.
- **Example**: Used for combination therapies where different APIs are formulated in separate mini-tablets within the same capsule.

Liquids and Semi-Solids:

- **Description**: Some hard gelatin capsules can be filled with liquids or semi-solid formulations using specialized equipment and sealing techniques. These formulations often require additional sealing to

prevent leakage.
- **Example**: Liquid-filled capsules are used for poorly soluble drugs, enhancing their bioavailability through lipid-based formulations.

Multiparticulates:

- **Description**: Multiparticulate formulations, such as beads or coated particles, offer controlled release and improved stability. They can be individually coated to achieve different release profiles within a single capsule.
- **Example**: Used for controlled-release drugs, allowing for a single daily dose of medications that require multiple release phases.

Selection Criteria for Filling Method
Production Scale:

- **Small-Scale Production**: Manual filling is suitable for small batches, research, and development, or custom formulations.
- **Medium-Scale Production**: Semi-automatic machines provide a balance between efficiency and cost, making them ideal for mid-sized production runs.
- **Large-Scale Production**: Automatic filling machines are necessary for high-volume manufacturing, offering speed, consistency, and efficiency.

Formulation Type:

- **Powders and Granules**: Both manual and automatic filling methods can handle these formulations, but automatic machines provide better accuracy and efficiency for large batches.
- **Liquids and Semi-Solids**: Require specialized automatic filling machines with sealing capabilities to prevent leakage and ensure stability.
- **Multiparticulates and Pellets**: Automatic filling machines with precise dosing capabilities are preferred to ensure uniform distribution of multiparticulates within the capsule.

4.1 Hard Gelatin Capsules
4.1.3 Finishing and Special Techniques
Finishing Processes for Hard Gelatin Capsules

Polishing

Polishing is a crucial finishing process for hard gelatin capsules. After filling and capping, capsules often have powder residues or marks that need to be removed to improve their appearance and ensure they are free from contaminants.

- **Description**: The polishing process involves tumbling the capsules in a rotating drum lined with soft brushes or cloth. This action removes any dust or powder adhering to the surface of the capsules.
- **Equipment**: Capsule polishing machines typically consist of a rotating drum, an airflow system to remove dust, and soft brushes to gently clean the capsules.
- **Outcome**: The result is a clean, glossy capsule that is visually appealing and ready for packaging.

Inspection

Inspection is another vital finishing process to ensure that the capsules meet the required quality standards.

- **Manual Inspection**: Capsules are manually inspected by operators who visually examine them for defects such as cracks, holes, or improper sealing.
- **Automated Inspection**: Automated systems use cameras and sensors to detect defects. These systems can quickly and accurately identify capsules that do not meet quality standards and remove them from the production line.
- **Outcome**: Ensures that only capsules meeting the stringent quality criteria are packaged and distributed, reducing the risk of defective products reaching the market.

Special Techniques to Improve Capsule Integrity and Prevent Tampering

Banding

Banding is a technique used to enhance the integrity of hard gelatin capsules by applying a band of gelatin or polymer around the joint where the cap and body meet.

- **Description**: A banding machine applies a thin layer of gelatin or a similar substance around the seam of the capsule. This band forms a tight seal, reducing the risk of capsule separation and preventing tampering.
- **Benefits**: Banding provides an additional layer of security, making it difficult to open the capsule without damaging it. This improves the tamper-evidence of the product.
- **Outcome**: Enhances the mechanical strength of the capsule, reducing the likelihood of separation during handling and transportation.

Sealing

Sealing involves permanently closing the cap and body of the capsule using various methods.

- **Liquid Sealing**: A liquid gelatin solution is applied at the junction of the cap and body. The capsules are then passed through a drying tunnel to solidify the gelatin, creating a sealed unit.
- **Thermal Sealing**: Heat is applied to fuse the cap and body together. This method is often used with capsules made from materials other than gelatin, such as hydroxypropyl methylcellulose (HPMC).
- **Ultrasonic Sealing**: High-frequency ultrasonic waves generate heat at the interface of the cap and body, creating a weld that seals the capsule.
- **Benefits**: Sealing prevents the capsule from being opened without visible damage, providing tamper evidence. It also improves the stability of the contents by reducing exposure to environmental factors like moisture and oxygen.
- **Outcome**: Enhances the overall quality and safety of the capsules, ensuring that the product remains intact and secure from the point of manufacture to consumption.

Enhancement of Quality and Stability

The finishing processes and special techniques employed for hard gelatin capsules significantly enhance their quality and stability.

- **Improved Appearance**: Polishing ensures that the capsules are clean and visually appealing, which is important for consumer acceptance and compliance.
- **Quality Assurance**: Rigorous inspection processes, both manual and automated, ensure that only capsules meeting the required standards are

released for packaging, reducing the incidence of defective products.

- **Increased Integrity and Security**: Banding and sealing techniques improve the structural integrity of the capsules, preventing accidental opening and tampering. These techniques also enhance the barrier properties of the capsules, protecting the contents from environmental factors.
- **Extended Shelf Life**: By preventing exposure to moisture, oxygen, and contaminants, banding and sealing contribute to the stability and shelf life of the product, ensuring that the active ingredients remain effective over time.

4.1 Hard Gelatin Capsules
4.1.4 Manufacturing Defects
Common Manufacturing Defects in Hard Gelatin Capsules
Size Variation
Size variation is a defect where capsules do not conform to the specified dimensions, leading to inconsistencies in dosage and packaging issues.
Causes:

- **Variations in Gelatin Solution**: Inconsistent preparation of the gelatin solution, including improper mixing or variations in gelatin concentration, can lead to differences in capsule wall thickness and size.
- **Improper Molding Conditions**: Variations in temperature, humidity, or dip speed during the molding process can result in non-uniform capsule sizes.
- **Wear and Tear of Equipment**: Worn-out or improperly maintained pins and molds can produce capsules of inconsistent size.

Prevention and Rectification:

- **Standardize Gelatin Solution Preparation**: Ensure strict adherence to the formulation and preparation protocols for the gelatin solution.
- **Control Molding Conditions**: Maintain consistent temperature and humidity levels during the molding process and calibrate the equipment regularly.
- **Regular Equipment Maintenance**: Inspect and replace worn-out pins and molds to ensure uniformity in capsule production.

Deformation

Deformation refers to capsules that are misshapen or have irregular surfaces, affecting their appearance and functionality.

Causes:

- **High Moisture Content**: Excess moisture in the gelatin solution or during drying can cause capsules to become soft and deformed.
- **Inadequate Drying**: Insufficient drying time or improper drying conditions can lead to capsules that are not fully set, resulting in deformation.
- **Mechanical Stress**: Excessive mechanical stress during handling, filling, or transportation can deform the capsules.

Prevention and Rectification:

- **Optimize Moisture Levels**: Monitor and control the moisture content in the gelatin solution and ensure proper drying conditions.
- **Adequate Drying Time**: Implement a controlled drying process with adequate time and conditions to ensure the capsules are fully set.
- **Gentle Handling**: Minimize mechanical stress during processing by using appropriate equipment and handling techniques.

Brittleness

Brittleness occurs when capsules become too dry and fragile, making them prone to cracking and breaking.

Causes:

- **Low Moisture Content**: Over-drying during the drying process or storage in low-humidity environments can reduce the moisture content of the capsules, making them brittle.
- **Inappropriate Storage Conditions**: Exposure to low humidity or high temperatures can cause capsules to lose moisture and become brittle.
- **Aging**: Over time, capsules can naturally lose moisture, especially if not stored properly, leading to brittleness.

Prevention and Rectification:

- **Controlled Drying**: Ensure the drying process maintains optimal moisture levels within the capsules.
- **Proper Storage**: Store capsules in controlled environments with appropriate humidity levels (typically around 30-50% RH) and temperatures (15-25°C).
- **Use of Humectants**: Incorporate humectants like glycerin or sorbitol into the gelatin formulation to retain moisture and prevent brittleness.

Additional Manufacturing Defects and Solutions
Color Variation

Color variation refers to inconsistencies in the color of the capsules, which can affect their appearance and perceived quality.

Causes:

- **Inconsistent Dye Distribution**: Uneven mixing of colorants in the gelatin solution can lead to color variation.
- **Temperature Fluctuations**: Variations in temperature during the drying process can cause uneven color development.
- **Batch-to-Batch Variability**: Differences in dye concentration or formulation between batches can result in color inconsistencies.

Prevention and Rectification:

- **Uniform Mixing**: Ensure thorough mixing of colorants in the gelatin solution to achieve consistent color distribution.
- **Stable Drying Conditions**: Maintain consistent drying temperatures to prevent color variations.
- **Standardize Formulation**: Use precise measurements and control processes to maintain consistent dye concentration across batches.

Air Bubbles and Voids

Air bubbles and voids are defects where small air pockets are trapped within the capsule shell, affecting its strength and integrity.

Causes:

- **Inadequate Deaeration**: Insufficient removal of air from the gelatin solution before molding can lead to trapped air bubbles.

- **High Viscosity**: A highly viscous gelatin solution can trap air bubbles more easily during the molding process.
- **Improper Molding Technique**: Rapid dipping and withdrawal of pins can create air pockets in the gelatin layer.

Prevention and Rectification:

- **Effective Deaeration**: Implement thorough deaeration processes to remove air from the gelatin solution before molding.
- **Control Viscosity**: Adjust the viscosity of the gelatin solution to optimal levels for molding.
- **Refined Molding Technique**: Use controlled dipping and withdrawal techniques to minimize air entrapment.

4.1 Hard Gelatin Capsules
4.1.5 Quality Control Tests

Quality control tests for hard gelatin capsules are essential to ensure that they meet the required standards for safety, efficacy, and consistency. These tests include **weight variation, disintegration, dissolution, and content uniformity**. Each test plays a crucial role in verifying different aspects of the capsules' quality.

Weight Variation

Description: The weight variation test measures the uniformity of weight among individual capsules within a batch. This test is particularly important for capsules containing a single active ingredient without excipients.

Procedure:

- Select a sample of 20 capsules randomly from a batch.
- Weigh each capsule individually and determine the average weight.
- Compare the individual weights to the average weight.

Acceptance Criteria:

- The individual weights should not deviate from the average weight by more than ±10% for capsules weighing less than 300 mg or ±7.5% for capsules weighing 300 mg or more.

Significance:

- Ensures uniformity in the amount of the active pharmaceutical ingredient (API) delivered to the patient.
- Verifies the consistency of the manufacturing process, helping to detect any issues with filling or formulation.

Disintegration

Description: The disintegration test determines the time it takes for a capsule to break down into smaller particles in a specified medium, ensuring that the API is released promptly.

Procedure:

- Place the capsules in a basket rack assembly that is immersed in a liquid medium at 37°C.
- The basket rack assembly is mechanically agitated to simulate the conditions in the gastrointestinal tract.
- Record the time taken for the capsules to disintegrate completely.

Acceptance Criteria:

- Capsules should disintegrate within the time specified in the pharmacopeial monograph, typically within 30 minutes for standard capsules.

Significance:

- Ensures that the capsules will break down appropriately in the gastrointestinal tract, allowing for the timely release and absorption of the API.
- Helps to verify the performance of the capsule shell and its compatibility with the formulation.

Dissolution

Description: The dissolution test measures the rate and extent of the API released from the capsule in a specified liquid medium over time.

Procedure:

- Capsules are placed in a dissolution apparatus containing a liquid medium (usually a buffer) at 37°C.
- The medium is agitated, and samples are taken at predetermined intervals.
- The concentration of the API in the samples is measured using analytical techniques such as high-performance liquid chromatography (HPLC).

Acceptance Criteria:

- The amount of API dissolved at each time point should meet the specifications outlined in the pharmacopeial monograph, typically expressed as a percentage of the labeled claim.

Significance:

- Ensures that the API is released at the appropriate rate and to the extent required for therapeutic efficacy.
- Helps to confirm the consistency and predictability of the capsule's performance in vivo.

Content Uniformity

Description: The content uniformity test measures the uniformity of the API content among individual capsules within a batch, ensuring that each capsule contains the correct dosage.

Procedure:

- Select a sample of 10 capsules randomly from a batch.
- Each capsule is assayed individually to determine the amount of API it contains.
- The results are compared to the labeled claim.

Acceptance Criteria:

- The content of the API in each capsule should be within 85-115% of the labeled claim for 9 out of 10 capsules, and none should fall outside the range of 75-125%.

Significance:

- Ensures the accuracy and consistency of the dosage in each capsule, which is critical for patient safety and therapeutic efficacy.
- Verifies the precision of the manufacturing and filling processes.

Additional Quality Control Tests
Moisture Content
Description: The moisture content test measures the amount of moisture present in the capsule shells.
Procedure:

- Capsules are tested using techniques such as loss on drying or Karl Fischer titration.
- The results are expressed as a percentage of the total weight.

Acceptance Criteria:

- The moisture content should be within the specified range, typically 12-16% for hard gelatin capsules.

Significance:

- Ensures the capsules have the right balance of flexibility and strength.
- Prevents issues such as brittleness or microbial growth due to improper moisture levels.

Microbial Limits
Description: The microbial limits test assesses the presence of microbial contamination in the capsules.
Procedure:

- Capsules are tested for total aerobic microbial count (TAMC) and total combined yeasts and molds count (TYMC), as well as specific pathogens like E. coli, Salmonella, and Staphylococcus aureus.
- Samples are cultured on appropriate media, and colony-forming units (CFUs) are counted.

Acceptance Criteria:

- The microbial counts should be within the limits specified in the pharmacopeial standards, typically less than 1000 CFU/g for TAMC and less than 100 CFU/g for TYMC.

Significance:

- Ensures the capsules are safe for consumption and free from harmful microorganisms.
- Verifies the effectiveness of the manufacturing process in preventing contamination.

4.2 Soft Gelatin Capsules

4.2.1 Nature of Shell and Capsule Content

Composition and Properties of Soft Gelatin Capsule Shells

Soft gelatin capsules are composed of a gelatin shell that is more flexible and elastic than hard gelatin capsules. The gelatin used in soft gelatin capsules is similar to that in hard gelatin capsules but includes additional components to enhance its softness and pliability. The primary components of soft gelatin capsule shells are:

- **Gelatin:** Derived from collagen, typically from bovine or porcine sources, providing the basic structure of the capsule.
- **Plasticizers:** Such as glycerin, sorbitol, or propylene glycol, which are added to increase the flexibility and reduce brittleness of the gelatin shell. The ratio of plasticizer to gelatin is usually between 0.3 to 0.6.
- **Water:** Used to dissolve gelatin and plasticizers, making up about 30-40% of the wet gel mass. The final moisture content of the dried capsule is typically around 5-8%.
- **Colorants and Opacifiers:** Such as titanium dioxide for opacity and various dyes to provide the desired color, enhancing product identification and aesthetics.
- **Preservatives:** Occasionally added to prevent microbial growth during manufacturing and storage.

The resulting capsule shell is smooth, flexible, and capable of sealing liquids, semi-solids, and suspensions, which provides versatility in encapsulating different types of formulations.

Types of Fill Materials Encapsulated

Soft gelatin capsules are particularly suitable for a variety of fill materials due to their ability to form a hermetic seal and protect the contents. Common types of fill materials include:

- **Oils**: Liquid or semi-liquid formulations, such as vegetable oils (e.g., olive oil, soybean oil), fish oils, and medium-chain triglycerides (MCTs). These are commonly used for fat-soluble vitamins (e.g., vitamins A, D, E, K) and essential fatty acids.
- **Suspensions**: Homogeneous mixtures of solid particles dispersed in a liquid medium. These can include APIs suspended in oils or other suitable liquids, allowing for the encapsulation of poorly soluble drugs.
- **Pastes**: Semi-solid formulations that are too thick for liquid encapsulation but can still flow. Pastes often contain high concentrations of APIs and excipients to create a stable and bioavailable formulation.
- **Self-Emulsifying Drug Delivery Systems (SEDDS)**: Formulations that form emulsions when in contact with gastrointestinal fluids, enhancing the bioavailability of poorly water-soluble drugs. These typically include a combination of oils, surfactants, and co-solvents.
- **Microemulsions and Nanoemulsions**: Thermodynamically stable dispersions of oil and water stabilized by surfactants, providing improved drug solubility and absorption.

Advantages of Soft Gelatin Capsules

Soft gelatin capsules offer several advantages for different types of formulations:

- **Improved Bioavailability**: The encapsulation of oils and lipophilic substances can enhance the bioavailability of poorly water-soluble drugs by promoting better dissolution and absorption.
- **Protection of Contents**: The hermetic seal of soft gelatin capsules protects sensitive ingredients from oxidation, moisture, and light, ensuring stability and prolonging shelf life.
- **Patient Compliance**: Soft gelatin capsules are easy to swallow, tasteless, and can mask the unpleasant taste and odor of the fill materials, improving patient compliance.

- **Versatility**: Capable of encapsulating a wide range of liquids, semi-solids, and suspensions, providing flexibility in formulation design.
- **Uniform Dosage**: The encapsulation process ensures precise and uniform dosing, which is critical for maintaining consistent therapeutic effects.

Limitations of Soft Gelatin Capsules

Despite their advantages, soft gelatin capsules also have some limitations:

- **Moisture Sensitivity**: Soft gelatin capsules are sensitive to moisture and require controlled storage conditions to maintain their integrity. High humidity can cause the capsules to become sticky, while low humidity can make them brittle.
- **Temperature Sensitivity**: Extreme temperatures can affect the physical properties of the gelatin shell, leading to deformation or leakage.
- **Limited Compatibility**: Some fill materials, especially those that are highly hygroscopic or have strong solvent properties, can interact with the gelatin shell, leading to potential stability issues.
- **Higher Production Costs**: The production of soft gelatin capsules is more complex and costly compared to hard gelatin capsules, requiring specialized equipment and stringent process controls.

4.2 Soft Gelatin Capsules

4.2.2 Production Techniques

Production Techniques for Soft Gelatin Capsules

Rotary Die Process

The **rotary die process** is the most widely used method for manufacturing soft gelatin capsules. This continuous process ensures high efficiency and consistent quality.

Key Steps:

1. **Gelatin Preparation**: Gelatin is dissolved in hot water along with plasticizers, such as glycerin or sorbitol, to create a homogenous, molten gelatin mass.
2. **Encapsulation**: The molten gelatin is fed into two rotating die rolls, which have recesses in the shape of the desired capsules. The fill material is simultaneously injected between the two ribbons of gelatin.

3. **Sealing and Cutting**: The die rolls come together, encapsulating the fill material and forming the capsule. The capsules are then sealed by the pressure and heat generated between the die rolls.

4. **Drying**: The formed capsules are transferred to drying tunnels where they undergo initial drying. They are then moved to drying trays for further drying under controlled temperature and humidity conditions to reach the desired moisture content.

Equipment Used: Rotary die machines consist of gelatin melting tanks, pumps, die rolls, fill injectors, and drying tunnels. Examples include the Roto-Fill machine and the Accura-Rotary die encapsulation system.

Plate Process

The **plate process** is an older method that is less common today but still used for specific applications and smaller-scale productions.

Key Steps:

1. **Gelatin Preparation**: Similar to the rotary die process, the gelatin mass is prepared with plasticizers.

2. **Encapsulation**: A sheet of the gelatin mass is spread on a bottom plate that contains cavities. The fill material is then deposited into these cavities.

3. **Sealing**: A second sheet of gelatin is placed over the filled cavities, and the two sheets are sealed together by applying pressure and heat using a top plate.

4. **Cutting**: The sealed capsules are cut out from the gelatin sheets and shaped.

5. **Drying**: The capsules are dried under controlled conditions to achieve the desired moisture content.

Equipment Used: Plate process equipment includes heated plates for spreading gelatin, molds with cavities, filling machines, and drying chambers.

Bubble Method

The **bubble method** is used to create seamless, spherical soft gelatin capsules. This method is particularly suited for encapsulating liquids and oils.

Key Steps:

1. **Gelatin Preparation**: The gelatin mass is prepared with plasticizers and maintained at a molten state.
2. **Encapsulation**: The fill material and molten gelatin are simultaneously extruded through concentric tubes. The gelatin forms a bubble around the fill material as it drops into a cooled liquid bath (usually oil).
3. **Sealing**: The gelatin bubble solidifies upon contact with the cooled liquid, forming a seamless capsule.
4. **Drying**: The capsules are collected from the liquid bath and dried under controlled conditions.

Equipment Used: Bubble method equipment includes concentric nozzles, cooling baths, and drying chambers. An example is the Seamless Capsule Machine.

Importance of Temperature and Humidity Control

Temperature and humidity control are critical factors in the production of soft gelatin capsules. Proper control ensures the quality and stability of both the gelatin shell and the encapsulated material.

- **Gelatin Preparation**: The temperature must be precisely controlled to ensure the gelatin remains molten and homogeneous. Typical temperatures range from 60-70°C.
- **Encapsulation**: During the encapsulation process, maintaining the right temperature ensures that the gelatin sheets or bubbles are pliable and can form proper seals.
- **Drying**: Controlled drying conditions (temperature around 20-25°C and humidity around 20-30% RH) are essential to remove excess moisture without causing brittleness or deformation. Gradual drying prevents the formation of cracks and ensures the capsules maintain their integrity.

4.2.3 Quality Control Tests

Quality Control Tests for Soft Gelatin Capsules

Weight Variation

Description: The weight variation test measures the uniformity of the capsule's weight to ensure consistent dosing.

Procedure:

- Randomly select 20 capsules from a batch.
- Weigh each capsule individually.

- Calculate the average weight and compare the individual weights to the average.

Acceptance Criteria:

- The individual weights should not deviate from the average weight by more than ±10%.

Significance: Ensures that each capsule contains the correct amount of active ingredient, providing consistent dosing and efficacy.

Leakage

Description: The leakage test checks for any leaks in the capsule that could lead to loss of the encapsulated material.

Procedure:

- Capsules are subjected to a pressure or vacuum test.
- Capsules are immersed in a dye solution and inspected for any dye ingress.

Acceptance Criteria:

- Capsules should show no signs of leakage or dye ingress.

Significance: Ensures the integrity of the capsule seal and prevents contamination and loss of the encapsulated material.

Disintegration

Description: The disintegration test determines the time it takes for a capsule to break down into smaller particles in a specified medium.

Procedure:

- Place the capsules in a basket rack assembly immersed in a liquid medium at 37°C.
- The basket rack assembly is mechanically agitated.
- Record the time taken for the capsules to disintegrate completely.

Acceptance Criteria:

- Capsules should disintegrate within the time specified in the pharmacopeial monograph, typically within 30 minutes.

Significance: Ensures that the capsules will break down appropriately in the gastrointestinal tract, allowing for the timely release and absorption of the active ingredient.

Dissolution

Description: The dissolution test measures the rate and extent of the active ingredient released from the capsule in a specified liquid medium over time.

Procedure:

- Capsules are placed in a dissolution apparatus containing a liquid medium (usually a buffer) at 37°C.
- The medium is agitated, and samples are taken at predetermined intervals.
- The concentration of the active ingredient in the samples is measured using analytical techniques such as high-performance liquid chromatography (HPLC).

Acceptance Criteria:

- The amount of active ingredient dissolved at each time point should meet the specifications outlined in the pharmacopeial monograph, typically expressed as a percentage of the labeled claim.

Significance: Ensures that the active ingredient is released at the appropriate rate and extent for therapeutic efficacy. Helps to confirm the consistency and predictability of the capsule's performance in vivo.

Additional Quality Control Tests

Moisture Content

Description: The moisture content test measures the amount of moisture present in the capsule shells and the fill material.

Procedure:

- Capsules are tested using techniques such as loss on drying or Karl Fischer titration.
- The results are expressed as a percentage of the total weight.

Acceptance Criteria:

- The moisture content should be within the specified range, typically around 5-8% for soft gelatin capsules.

Significance: Ensures the capsules have the right balance of flexibility and strength. Prevents issues such as brittleness or microbial growth due to improper moisture levels.

Microbial Limits

Description: The microbial limits test assesses the presence of microbial contamination in the capsules.

Procedure:

- Capsules are tested for total aerobic microbial count (TAMC) and total combined yeasts and molds count (TYMC), as well as specific pathogens like E. coli, Salmonella, and Staphylococcus aureus.
- Samples are cultured on appropriate media, and colony-forming units (CFUs) are counted.

Acceptance Criteria:

- The microbial counts should be within the limits specified in the pharmacopeial standards, typically less than 1000 CFU/g for TAMC and less than 100 CFU/g for TYMC.

Significance: Ensures the capsules are safe for consumption and free from harmful microorganisms. Verifies the effectiveness of the manufacturing process in preventing contamination.

4.2 Soft Gelatin Capsules

4.2.4 Packing and Storage

Packaging Requirements for Soft Gelatin Capsules

Soft gelatin capsules require carefully designed packaging to ensure their stability, integrity, and efficacy throughout their shelf life. The primary concerns in packaging these capsules include protection from moisture, light, and oxygen, which can affect the gelatin shell and the encapsulated contents.

Types of Containers and Packaging Materials

Blister Packs:

- **Description**: Blister packs consist of cavities or pockets made from formable material, usually a thermoformed plastic, with a foil or plastic backing. Each cavity holds a single capsule.
- **Materials Used**: Polyvinyl chloride (PVC), polyvinylidene chloride (PVDC), aluminum foil, and other barrier films.
- **Advantages**: Provide individual protection for each capsule, minimizing the risk of cross-contamination and mechanical damage. Easy to use and convenient for dosing.

Bottles:

- **Description**: Capsules are packaged in bottles, typically made of plastic or glass, which are sealed with a cap to protect the contents.
- **Materials Used**: High-density polyethylene (HDPE), polyethylene terephthalate (PET), and glass.
- **Advantages**: Suitable for bulk packaging, easy to handle, and cost-effective. Bottles can be equipped with desiccants to control moisture.

Importance of Protection from Moisture, Light, and Oxygen
Moisture:

- **Impact**: Excessive moisture can cause the gelatin shell to become soft, sticky, and prone to microbial growth, while low humidity can make the shell brittle and prone to cracking.
- **Protection Strategies**: Use moisture-resistant packaging materials, include desiccants within bottles, and ensure tight seals to prevent moisture ingress.

Light:

- **Impact**: Exposure to light, particularly UV light, can degrade both the gelatin shell and the encapsulated contents, leading to loss of potency and efficacy.
- **Protection Strategies**: Use opaque or amber-colored bottles, incorporate UV-blocking agents in blister packs, and store products in dark environments.

Oxygen:

- **Impact**: Oxygen can oxidize both the gelatin shell and the active ingredients, leading to degradation and reduced shelf life.
- **Protection Strategies**: Use oxygen-impermeable packaging materials, flush bottles with inert gases (e.g., nitrogen) before sealing, and ensure airtight seals.

Guidelines for Proper Storage Conditions

To maintain the stability and efficacy of soft gelatin capsules, it is essential to adhere to proper storage conditions:

- **Temperature**: Store capsules at controlled room temperatures, typically between 15-25°C. Avoid exposure to high temperatures that can accelerate degradation.
- **Humidity**: Maintain a relative humidity of around 30-50%. Use air conditioning or dehumidifiers in storage areas to control humidity levels.
- **Light**: Store capsules in a dark place, away from direct sunlight or other sources of UV light. Use packaging that protects against light exposure.
- **Handling**: Minimize mechanical stress and handle capsules gently to avoid damage to the gelatin shell.

4.2.5 Stability Testing

Importance of Stability Testing for Soft Gelatin Capsules

Stability testing is crucial to ensure that soft gelatin capsules maintain their quality, efficacy, and safety throughout their shelf life. Stability testing provides data to establish the product's expiration date, determine appropriate storage conditions, and identify any potential degradation pathways.

Types of Stability Tests
Accelerated Stability Testing:

- **Description**: Accelerated stability testing involves storing the capsules at elevated temperatures and humidity levels to simulate long-term storage conditions in a shorter time frame.
- **Conditions**: Common conditions include 40°C ± 2°C and 75% ± 5% relative humidity (RH) for six months.
- **Purpose**: To predict the shelf life and identify potential degradation products more quickly.

Long-Term Stability Testing:

- **Description:** Long-term stability testing is conducted under recommended storage conditions over the product's intended shelf life.
- **Conditions:** Typical conditions are 25°C ± 2°C and 60% ± 5% RH for at least 12 months or longer, depending on regulatory requirements.
- **Purpose:** To confirm the product's stability under normal storage conditions and ensure it remains within specifications for the duration of its shelf life.

Parameters Monitored During Stability Tests
Physical Appearance:

- **What is Monitored:** Changes in color, opacity, shape, and presence of any physical defects such as cracks or stickiness.
- **Significance:** Ensures the capsules maintain their intended appearance and physical integrity.

Leakage:

- **What is Monitored:** Any leakage of the encapsulated material from the gelatin shell.
- **Significance:** Ensures the integrity of the capsule seal and prevents loss of the active ingredient and contamination.

Assay:

- **What is Monitored:** The concentration of the active pharmaceutical ingredient (API) within the capsule.
- **Significance:** Ensures the potency of the API remains within specified limits, confirming the efficacy of the product.

Degradation Products:

- **What is Monitored:** Identification and quantification of any degradation products formed over time.
- **Significance:** Ensures that any degradation products remain within acceptable limits, maintaining the safety and efficacy of the capsules.

Dissolution:

- **What is Monitored**: The rate and extent of API release from the capsule in a specified liquid medium.
- **Significance**: Confirms that the release profile of the API remains consistent, ensuring therapeutic efficacy.

Examples of Stability-Indicating Methods
High-Performance Liquid Chromatography (HPLC):

- **Usage**: Quantifies the API and identifies degradation products. Highly sensitive and accurate, making it a standard method for stability testing.

Gas Chromatography (GC):

- **Usage**: Suitable for volatile compounds and detecting impurities. Provides detailed analysis of the chemical composition.

Mass Spectrometry (MS):

- **Usage**: Often coupled with HPLC or GC, MS provides detailed information on the molecular weight and structure of degradation products, helping to identify and quantify impurities.

Infrared (IR) Spectroscopy:

- **Usage**: Detects changes in the chemical structure of the API and excipients. Useful for identifying specific functional groups affected by degradation.

Karl Fischer Titration:

- **Usage**: Measures the moisture content in the capsules, ensuring it remains within acceptable limits to prevent brittleness or microbial growth.

Microbial Testing:

- **Usage**: Assesses the presence of microbial contamination, ensuring the capsules remain safe for consumption throughout their shelf life.

4.3 Pellets

4.3.1 Formulation Requirements

Formulation Requirements for Pellets

Pellets are small, free-flowing, spherical or semi-spherical solid dosage forms that offer several advantages over traditional tablets and capsules. The formulation of pellets involves the careful selection of excipients, binders, and coatings to achieve the desired properties and release characteristics.

Choice of Excipients

Excipients are inactive substances used as carriers for the active ingredients of a medication. In pellet formulation, excipients play critical roles in ensuring the stability, bioavailability, and manufacturability of the pellets.

- **Fillers**: These provide bulk to the pellet formulation. Common fillers include lactose, microcrystalline cellulose (MCC), and dibasic calcium phosphate.
- **Disintegrants**: Used to promote the breakup of pellets into smaller fragments to facilitate drug release. Examples include croscarmellose sodium and sodium starch glycolate.
- **Lubricants**: Reduce friction during the pelletization process and prevent sticking. Magnesium stearate and talc are commonly used lubricants.

Binders

Binders are essential for pellet formulation as they help in the agglomeration of powder particles to form pellets. The choice of binder affects the mechanical strength, size, and shape of the pellets.

- **Types of Binders:**

  - **Solution Binders:** Polyvinylpyrrolidone (PVP), hydroxypropyl methylcellulose (HPMC), and starch paste are dissolved in a solvent and sprayed onto the powder blend during granulation.

- ◦ **Dry Binders**: These are blended with the powder mix before the addition of granulating fluid. Examples include microcrystalline cellulose and cross-linked PVP.

Coatings

Coatings are applied to pellets to control the release of the active ingredient, protect the drug from degradation, and mask the taste.

- **Types of Coatings:**

  - ◦ **Immediate-Release Coatings**: Provide a protective layer without affecting the release rate. Examples include hydroxypropyl cellulose (HPC) and HPMC.
  - ◦ **Controlled-Release Coatings**: Used to modify the release rate of the drug. Polymers such as ethyl cellulose, Eudragit® (acrylate polymers), and cellulose acetate are commonly used.
  - ◦ **Enteric Coatings**: Prevent the release of the drug in the acidic environment of the stomach. Common enteric coating materials include cellulose acetate phthalate (CAP) and methacrylic acid copolymers.

Factors Influencing Size, Shape, and Release Characteristics of Pellets
Size and Shape:

- **Formulation Variables**: The type and amount of binder, filler, and the method of pelletization impact the size and shape of pellets.
- **Process Variables**: Parameters such as extrusion speed, spheronization time, and the type of spheronizer used can influence the uniformity and roundness of pellets.

Release Characteristics:

- **Excipients and Binders**: The choice of excipients and binders can affect the porosity and density of pellets, influencing the drug release profile.
- **Coating**: The thickness and composition of the coating layer can be adjusted to achieve the desired release rate, such as immediate, sustained, or delayed release.

- **Drug Loading**: The amount and distribution of the drug within the pellet matrix can impact the dissolution rate and bioavailability.

Advantages of Pellet Formulations
Uniformity:

- Pellets provide a high degree of dose uniformity and precision, ensuring consistent therapeutic effects.

Flexible Release Profiles:

- By varying the composition and thickness of coatings, pellets can be designed for immediate, sustained, or controlled release, offering flexibility in drug delivery.

Reduced Irritation:

- Pellets distribute the drug more evenly in the gastrointestinal tract, reducing the risk of localized irritation compared to single-unit dosage forms.

Improved Stability:

- Pellets can protect sensitive drugs from environmental factors such as light, moisture, and oxygen, enhancing the stability and shelf life of the product.

4.3.2 Pelletization Process
Pelletization Process
Extrusion-Spheronization
Extrusion-Spheronization is a widely used technique to produce uniform, spherical pellets.
Key Steps:

1. **Mixing**: The dry ingredients, including the API, fillers, and binders, are mixed to form a homogeneous powder blend.
2. **Granulation**: A granulating liquid (often water or a binder solution) is added to the powder blend to form a wet mass.

3. **Extrusion**: The wet mass is extruded through a die to produce cylindrical extrudates.
4. **Spheronization**: The extrudates are placed in a spheronizer, where they are broken into smaller segments and rounded into spherical pellets.
5. **Drying**: The formed pellets are dried to remove any residual moisture.

Equipment Used:

- **Mixer/Granulator**: High-shear mixers or planetary mixers.
- **Extruder**: Single-screw or twin-screw extruders with specific die configurations.
- **Spheronizer**: Rotating friction plates with a grooved surface.
- **Dryer**: Fluid bed dryers or tray dryers.

Layering

Layering involves depositing successive layers of drug and excipients onto inert cores or seed pellets.

Key Steps:

1. **Core Preparation**: Inert cores (e.g., sugar beads, MCC pellets) are prepared or selected.
2. **Solution/Suspension Spraying**: A solution or suspension containing the drug and binder is sprayed onto the cores.
3. **Drying**: Each layer is dried before applying the next layer to ensure adhesion and uniformity.
4. **Coating**: The final pellets may be coated to modify the release profile.

Equipment Used:

- **Coating Pan**: Used for small-scale production.
- **Fluid Bed Coater**: Preferred for large-scale production, providing uniform coating and efficient drying.

Agglomeration

Agglomeration is the process of forming larger particles from finer ones by the addition of a binder solution.

Key Steps:

1. **Mixing**: Dry powders are mixed to form a homogeneous blend.
2. **Agglomeration**: A binder solution is added to the powder blend, causing the particles to adhere and form larger aggregates.
3. **Drying**: The agglomerates are dried to remove moisture and stabilize the pellets.
4. **Sizing**: The dried agglomerates are passed through a screen to achieve the desired size distribution.

Equipment Used:

- **High-Shear Granulator**: Provides intense mixing and agglomeration.
- **Fluid Bed Granulator**: Combines mixing, agglomeration, and drying in a single unit.
- **Oscillating Granulator**: Used for sizing and achieving uniform pellet size.

Importance of Controlling Process Parameters
Uniform Pellet Size and Shape:

- **Extrusion Speed and Pressure**: Control the uniformity of extrudates, affecting pellet size and shape.
- **Spheronization Time and Speed**: Influence the roundness and surface smoothness of pellets.
- **Granulating Liquid**: The amount and type of liquid affect the consistency and cohesiveness of the wet mass.

Release Characteristics:

- **Binder Concentration**: Higher binder concentration can slow down drug release by creating a denser matrix.
- **Coating Thickness**: Thicker coatings generally result in slower drug release, providing sustained or controlled release profiles.

4.3 Pellets
4.3.3 Equipment for Manufacture
Types of Equipment Used for the Manufacture of Pellets
The manufacture of pellets requires specialized equipment to achieve the desired size, shape, and release characteristics. Key equipment includes

extruders, spheronizers, fluid bed coaters, and high-shear mixers. Understanding the working principles and specifications of each type of equipment is essential for selecting the appropriate machinery based on the formulation and desired pellet characteristics.

Extruders
Working Principles:

- **Single-Screw Extruders**: The wet mass is fed into a cylindrical barrel where a single rotating screw pushes the material through a die. The pressure and shear forces generated by the screw help to form cylindrical extrudates.
- **Twin-Screw Extruders**: Two intermeshing screws rotate within a barrel, providing more intensive mixing and shear. This type is particularly suitable for formulations requiring thorough mixing and high throughput.

Specifications:

- **Barrel Diameter**: Typically ranges from 1 mm to several centimeters, depending on the scale of production.
- **Screw Speed**: Adjustable speed settings, generally between 20-200 rpm.
- **Die Configuration**: Various die shapes and sizes to produce different extrudate diameters.

Selection Criteria:

- **Formulation Viscosity**: High-viscosity formulations may require twin-screw extruders for better processing.
- **Scale of Production**: Single-screw extruders are suitable for small to medium-scale production, while twin-screw extruders are ideal for large-scale manufacturing.

Spheronizers
Working Principles:

- Spheronizers consist of a rotating friction plate with a grooved surface. The extrudates are placed on the rotating plate, where centrifugal forces and friction break them into smaller segments and round them into spherical pellets.

Specifications:

- **Plate Diameter:** Typically ranges from 200 mm to 1000 mm.
- **Rotation Speed:** Adjustable speed settings, usually between 100-2000 rpm.
- **Groove Configuration:** Different groove patterns to optimize pellet shape and size.

Selection Criteria:

- **Desired Pellet Size and Shape:** The groove pattern and rotation speed can be adjusted to achieve the desired pellet characteristics.
- **Throughput Requirements:** Larger plates and higher speeds are suitable for high-throughput production.

Fluid Bed Coaters
Working Principles:

- Fluid bed coaters use a stream of heated air to suspend and fluidize the pellets while simultaneously spraying a coating solution. The coating is applied uniformly as the pellets are dried by the heated air.

Specifications:

- **Airflow Rate:** Adjustable to maintain proper fluidization without damaging the pellets.
- **Spray Rate:** Controlled to ensure uniform coating without overwetting.
- **Temperature Control:** Precise temperature settings to optimize drying and coating quality.

Selection Criteria:

- **Coating Requirements:** The type and thickness of the coating needed will determine the appropriate airflow and spray rate settings.
- **Batch Size:** Fluid bed coaters come in various sizes, from laboratory-scale units to large industrial systems, to match the scale of production.

High-Shear Mixers
Working Principles:

- High-shear mixers use a rapidly rotating impeller to create intense mixing and shear forces, ensuring thorough blending of the powder ingredients and the granulating liquid. This process forms a wet mass suitable for extrusion.

Specifications:

- **Impeller Speed**: Typically ranges from 100 to 3000 rpm, adjustable to control the intensity of mixing.
- **Bowl Capacity**: Varies from small laboratory models (1-10 liters) to large industrial machines (up to 1000 liters).
- **Chopper Speed**: Secondary chopper blades help break down agglomerates and improve mixing.

Selection Criteria:

- **Formulation Characteristics**: High-shear mixers are suitable for formulations requiring intensive mixing and uniform wet mass consistency.
- **Scale of Production**: The capacity of the mixer should match the batch size requirements, ensuring efficient and scalable production.

CHAPTER FIVE

Parenteral Products

5.1 Introduction and Types

5.1.1 Definition

Parenteral products are sterile preparations intended for administration by injection, infusion, or implantation into the body. These products bypass the gastrointestinal tract, delivering medications directly into systemic circulation or specific tissues. The term "parenteral" is derived from the Greek words "para" (beside) and "enteron" (intestine), indicating routes other than the digestive tract. Parenteral products are critical in medical treatments where rapid onset of action, precise dosing, and direct delivery of drugs are required.

Routes of Administration

Intravenous (IV): Intravenous administration involves injecting the drug directly into the bloodstream, providing immediate therapeutic effects. It is the preferred route for emergency medications, fluids, electrolytes, and blood transfusions. Common drugs administered intravenously include antibiotics (e.g., vancomycin), chemotherapy agents (e.g., cisplatin), and anesthetics (e.g., propofol).

Intramuscular (IM): Intramuscular injections are administered into the muscle tissue, allowing for rapid absorption of the drug into the bloodstream. This route is suitable for medications that need to be absorbed more slowly than IV injections but faster than subcutaneous injections. Examples of IM drugs include vaccines (e.g., influenza vaccine), hormonal therapies (e.g., testosterone), and antibiotics (e.g., ceftriaxone).

Subcutaneous (SC): Subcutaneous injections are administered into the fatty tissue just beneath the skin. This route provides slower, more sustained drug absorption compared to IM and IV routes. It is commonly used for medications that require gradual absorption and for patients who need to self-administer injections. Examples include insulin for diabetes, heparin for anticoagulation, and certain vaccines.

Intradermal (ID): Intradermal injections are administered into the dermis, the layer of skin just below the epidermis. This route is primarily used for diagnostic purposes, allergy testing, and local anesthesia. The absorption is slow and limited, making it ideal for small volumes of medication. Examples include tuberculin skin tests (Mantoux test) and allergy tests.

5.1.2 Advantages and Limitations

Advantages of Parenteral Products

Rapid Onset of Action: Parenteral administration allows for the immediate delivery of drugs into the bloodstream or target tissues, leading to a rapid onset of action. This is crucial in emergency situations where quick therapeutic effects are necessary, such as in the administration of epinephrine for anaphylaxis or thrombolytics for acute myocardial infarction.

Precise Dosing: Parenteral routes provide accurate and controlled dosing, ensuring that the exact amount of medication reaches the systemic circulation. This precision is particularly important for drugs with narrow therapeutic indices, such as digoxin and warfarin, where slight variations in dosage can lead to toxicity or therapeutic failure.

Suitability for Patients Unable to Take Oral Medications: Parenteral products are essential for patients who cannot take oral medications due to conditions like vomiting, unconsciousness, or gastrointestinal malabsorption. For example, patients undergoing surgery or those with severe gastrointestinal disorders may rely on parenteral nutrition or IV antibiotics.

Bypassing the First-Pass Metabolism: Parenteral administration avoids the first-pass metabolism in the liver, enhancing the bioavailability of drugs that are extensively metabolized when taken orally. Drugs like lidocaine and nitroglycerin benefit from this route as they exhibit higher bioavailability when administered parenterally.

Limitations and Challenges of Parenteral Administration

Risks of Infection: Parenteral administration carries a higher risk of infection due to the breach of the skin barrier. Strict aseptic techniques and sterile equipment are required to minimize the risk of introducing pathogens during the injection process. For example, central line-associated bloodstream infections (CLABSIs) are a significant concern in hospitals.

Need for Skilled Administration: Administering parenteral medications requires trained healthcare professionals to ensure proper technique and avoid complications. Errors in administration, such as incorrect injection site or technique, can lead to serious adverse effects, including nerve damage and tissue necrosis.

Pain and Tissue Damage: Injections can cause pain and discomfort at the injection site. Repeated injections may lead to tissue damage, fibrosis, and the formation of abscesses. For instance, frequent insulin injections can cause lipodystrophy, a condition characterized by abnormal fat distribution at the injection sites.

Higher Costs and Complexity: Parenteral products are generally more expensive and complex to manufacture and store compared to oral medications. They require stringent quality control measures, sterile packaging, and specialized storage conditions. For example, certain biologics and vaccines need to be stored at specific temperatures to maintain their efficacy.

5.2 Preformulation Factors and Essential Requirements

5.2.1 Vehicles and Additives

Vehicles in Parenteral Formulations

Aqueous Solutions: Aqueous vehicles are the most commonly used vehicles in parenteral formulations. They include water for injection (WFI), saline, and dextrose solutions. These vehicles are preferred because they are compatible with body fluids and do not cause adverse reactions.

- **Water for Injection (WFI)**: This is highly purified water free from pyrogens. It is used as a solvent for many injectable drugs due to its high purity and safety.
- **Saline Solution (0.9% NaCl)**: An isotonic solution commonly used as a vehicle for diluting drugs and as a fluid replacement therapy.
- **Dextrose Solution (5% Dextrose)**: An isotonic solution used for providing calories and as a vehicle for drugs.

Oils: Oil-based vehicles are used for drugs that are poorly soluble in water. They provide a sustained release of the drug, making them suitable for depot injections.

- **Vegetable Oils**: Commonly used oils include soybean oil, sesame oil, and olive oil. These oils are biocompatible and non-toxic.

- **Examples**: Testosterone propionate and progesterone are often formulated in oil-based vehicles for intramuscular injection.

Emulsions: Emulsions are mixtures of oil and water phases stabilized by emulsifying agents. They are used to improve the solubility of lipophilic drugs and provide controlled release.

- **Oil-in-Water (O/W) Emulsions**: The oil phase is dispersed in the aqueous phase, making it suitable for intravenous administration.
- **Water-in-Oil (W/O) Emulsions**: The aqueous phase is dispersed in the oil phase, typically used for intramuscular or subcutaneous administration.
- **Examples**: Lipid emulsions for parenteral nutrition (e.g., Intralipid) and propofol (an anesthetic agent) are formulated as emulsions.

Additives in Parenteral Formulations

Preservatives: Preservatives are added to multi-dose parenteral formulations to prevent microbial growth during storage and use.

- **Benzyl Alcohol**: Commonly used as a preservative in multi-dose vials.
- **Methylparaben and Propylparaben**: Often used in combination to provide broad-spectrum antimicrobial activity.

Stabilizers: Stabilizers help maintain the stability and potency of the active ingredient by preventing degradation.

- **Antioxidants**: Ascorbic acid and sodium metabisulfite are used to prevent oxidation of susceptible drugs.
- **Chelating Agents**: EDTA (ethylenediaminetetraacetic acid) is used to bind metal ions that can catalyze degradation reactions.

Buffering Agents: Buffering agents are used to maintain the pH of the parenteral formulation within a range that ensures stability and compatibility with body fluids.

- **Phosphate Buffers**: Commonly used to maintain a physiological pH.
- **Acetate Buffers**: Used when a slightly acidic pH is required for stability.

Examples of Commonly Used Vehicles and Additives

- **Vehicle**: Water for Injection (WFI) - Used as a solvent for a wide range of injectable drugs.
- **Additive**: Benzyl Alcohol - Used as a preservative in multi-dose vials of medications like lidocaine.
- **Additive**: Ascorbic Acid - Used as an antioxidant in formulations containing epinephrine to prevent oxidation.

5.2.2 Importance of Isotonicity

Definition and Importance of Isotonicity

Isotonicity refers to the osmotic pressure exerted by a solution relative to the osmotic pressure of body fluids. An isotonic solution has the same osmotic pressure as blood plasma, ensuring that cells maintain their normal shape and function when exposed to the solution. In parenteral formulations, isotonicity is crucial to prevent cell damage and irritation at the injection site.

Physiological Impact of Hypotonic and Hypertonic Solutions

Hypotonic Solutions: Solutions with a lower osmotic pressure than body fluids can cause water to enter cells, leading to cell swelling and lysis. This can result in tissue damage and inflammation at the injection site.

Hypertonic Solutions: Solutions with a higher osmotic pressure than body fluids can cause water to exit cells, leading to cell shrinkage and dehydration. This can cause pain, irritation, and damage to blood vessels and surrounding tissues.

Methods to Achieve Isotonicity in Parenteral Products

Adjusting Solute Concentration: The concentration of solutes, such as salts and sugars, can be adjusted to achieve isotonicity. For example, adding sodium chloride or dextrose can make a solution isotonic.

Use of Isotonic Solutions as Vehicles: Using pre-prepared isotonic solutions like 0.9% saline or 5% dextrose as vehicles ensures that the final parenteral product is isotonic.

Buffer Systems: Buffer systems can help maintain the isotonicity and pH of the solution. For instance, phosphate buffers can be used to adjust both the pH and osmolarity of the formulation.

Examples of Commonly Used Isotonic Solutions

- **0.9% Sodium Chloride (Normal Saline)**: Widely used as a vehicle for diluting drugs and for intravenous fluid replacement.
- **5% Dextrose Solution**: Used to provide calories and as a vehicle for medications.
- **Lactated Ringer's Solution**: Contains sodium chloride, potassium chloride, calcium chloride, and sodium lactate. It is used for fluid and electrolyte replenishment.

5.3 Production Procedure and Facilities

5.3.1 Aseptic Processing

Principles of Aseptic Processing in the Production of Parenteral Products

Aseptic processing is a crucial method in the production of parenteral products, designed to prevent contamination by microorganisms, particulates, and pyrogens. It involves maintaining sterility throughout the manufacturing process, ensuring that the final product is safe for patient use.

Key Steps Involved in Aseptic Processing
Sterilization of Equipment:

- **Sterilization Methods**: Equipment and components are sterilized using various methods such as steam sterilization (autoclaving), dry heat sterilization, ethylene oxide gas, and gamma irradiation. The choice of method depends on the nature of the equipment and materials.
- **Validation**: Sterilization processes are validated to ensure they effectively eliminate microbial contamination. This involves biological indicators and chemical integrators to confirm the efficacy of the sterilization process.

Preparation of Sterile Solutions:

- **Preparation Area**: Solutions are prepared in a controlled environment to minimize contamination. Laminar flow hoods or isolators are used to provide a sterile working area.
- **Filtration**: Solutions are passed through sterile filters (typically 0.22 microns) to remove any microorganisms. The filters are validated to ensure they do not adsorb the active ingredients or additives.

Aseptic Filling:

- **Filling Equipment**: Sterile filling machines, such as peristaltic pumps and volumetric fillers, are used to transfer the sterile solution into pre-sterilized containers (vials, ampoules, syringes) without introducing contaminants.
- **Sealing**: After filling, the containers are immediately sealed using sterile closures (e.g., rubber stoppers, aluminum caps) to maintain sterility.

Maintaining a Sterile Environment
Cleanroom Standards:

- **Classification**: Production areas are classified based on the level of cleanliness required, ranging from ISO Class 5 (highest cleanliness) to ISO Class 8. Aseptic processing typically occurs in ISO Class 5 environments.
- **Air Quality**: High-efficiency particulate air (HEPA) filters are used to maintain clean air by removing particles and microorganisms. Laminar airflow systems ensure a continuous flow of clean air over critical areas.

Personnel Practices:

- **Gowning Procedures**: Personnel entering the cleanroom must follow strict gowning procedures, including wearing sterile gowns, gloves, masks, and shoe covers to minimize contamination.
- **Training**: Staff involved in aseptic processing receive specialized training in aseptic techniques, contamination control, and good manufacturing practices (GMP).

Environmental Monitoring:

- **Microbial Monitoring**: Regular sampling of air, surfaces, and personnel is conducted to detect microbial contamination. This includes settle plates, contact plates, and active air sampling.
- **Particulate Monitoring**: Continuous monitoring of airborne particulates is performed using particle counters to ensure compliance with cleanroom standards.

Importance of Maintaining a Sterile Environment

Maintaining a sterile environment is vital to ensure the safety and efficacy of parenteral products. Any breach in sterility can lead to contamination, posing significant risks to patient health, including infections and other adverse reactions. Rigorous aseptic processing standards and practices are essential to prevent contamination and ensure that parenteral products meet the stringent quality requirements necessary for patient safety.

5.3.2 Quality Control Measures

Quality Control Measures Implemented During the Production of Parenteral Products

Quality control measures are integral to the production of parenteral products, ensuring that they meet the required standards for sterility, potency, and safety. These measures involve comprehensive testing and monitoring throughout the production process.

Environmental Monitoring

Microbial Monitoring:

- **Air Sampling**: Active air samplers collect airborne microorganisms in the cleanroom. Samples are cultured and analyzed to detect any microbial presence.
- **Surface Sampling**: Contact plates and swabs are used to sample surfaces, equipment, and personnel to detect contamination.
- **Personnel Monitoring**: Gown and glove samples are taken from operators to assess microbial contamination.

Particulate Monitoring:

- **Particle Counters**: Continuous particle counting is performed to ensure the cleanroom environment meets the required cleanliness standards (e.g., ISO Class 5).

In-Process Controls

Sterility Testing:

- **Membrane Filtration**: Samples from the production process are filtered through a membrane to capture microorganisms, which are then cultured to check for growth.

- **Direct Inoculation**: Samples are directly inoculated into a growth medium and incubated to detect microbial contamination.

Potency Testing:

- **Assay of Active Ingredient**: The concentration of the active pharmaceutical ingredient (API) is measured using techniques such as high-performance liquid chromatography (HPLC) to ensure it meets the specified range.

Endotoxin Testing:

- **Limulus Amebocyte Lysate (LAL) Test**: This test detects endotoxins, which are toxic substances produced by Gram-negative bacteria. Endotoxins can cause severe adverse reactions if present in parenteral products.

Final Product Testing
Sterility Testing:

- **Batch Release Testing**: Samples from each batch of the final product are tested for sterility using membrane filtration or direct inoculation methods.

Pyrogen Testing:

- **Rabbit Test**: Historically used to detect pyrogens by injecting the product into rabbits and monitoring for fever.
- **LAL Test**: More commonly used now due to its sensitivity and specificity.

Particulate Matter Testing:

- **Visual Inspection**: Each unit is visually inspected for particulate matter using magnification and proper lighting.
- **Light Obscuration Method**: Automated particle counters measure the number and size of particulates in the solution.

Container Closure Integrity Testing:

- **Dye Ingress Test**: Containers are exposed to a dye solution under vacuum, and the presence of dye inside the container indicates a breach in the seal.
- **Helium Leak Test**: Measures the escape of helium from sealed containers to detect leaks.

Importance of Quality Control Measures

Quality control measures are essential to ensure that parenteral products are safe, effective, and meet regulatory standards. Environmental monitoring helps maintain a sterile production environment, while in-process controls ensure that the product remains within specified parameters throughout manufacturing. Final product testing verifies that each batch meets the required standards for sterility, potency, and safety before release.

Examples of Specific Tests and Checks

- **Microbial Monitoring**: Regular air sampling and surface testing to detect and control microbial contamination in the cleanroom.
- **Potency Testing**: Assay of active ingredient concentration using HPLC to ensure accurate dosing.
- **Endotoxin Testing**: LAL test to detect and quantify endotoxins, ensuring the product is free from pyrogenic substances.
- **Sterility Testing**: Batch release sterility testing to confirm that the final product is free from microbial contamination.
- **Particulate Matter Testing**: Visual inspection and light obscuration methods to ensure the absence of particulate contamination.

5.4 Formulation of Injections

5.4.1 Sterile Powders

Formulation and Preparation of Sterile Powders for Injection

Sterile powders are an important dosage form for injectable drugs that are unstable in liquid form. The formulation involves several steps to ensure the product's stability, sterility, and efficacy.

Formulation:

- **Active Pharmaceutical Ingredient (API)**: The API is carefully selected and processed to ensure it remains stable and potent during storage and after reconstitution.
- **Excipients**: Stabilizers, buffers, and bulking agents may be added to enhance the stability and solubility of the API. Common excipients include mannitol, lactose, and sodium phosphate.
- **Lyophilization (Freeze-Drying)**: The solution containing the API and excipients is sterile-filtered and filled into vials. The vials are then subjected to lyophilization, where the solution is frozen, and the water is removed by sublimation under vacuum. This process results in a dry, porous powder that is stable and easy to reconstitute.

Advantages of Using Sterile Powders:

- **Stability**: Sterile powders are more stable than liquid formulations, especially for drugs that are sensitive to hydrolysis or oxidation. The absence of water in the formulation significantly reduces the risk of degradation.
- **Ease of Storage**: Sterile powders have a longer shelf life and can be stored at room temperature, reducing the need for refrigeration. This is particularly beneficial for drugs that require extended storage periods.
- **Convenience**: The reconstitution process allows healthcare providers to prepare the exact dose required immediately before administration, reducing waste and ensuring accurate dosing.

Reconstitution Process:

- **Procedure**: Before administration, the sterile powder must be reconstituted with a suitable diluent. The diluent is added to the vial, and the vial is gently swirled or shaken until the powder is completely dissolved.
- **Choice of Diluent**: The choice of diluent depends on several factors, including the solubility of the drug, the desired pH, and the compatibility with the patient's physiological conditions. Common diluents include sterile water for injection, normal saline (0.9% sodium chloride solution), and dextrose solution (5% dextrose in water).
- **Factors Influencing Choice**: The diluent must be compatible with the drug and the patient's physiology. It should not cause precipitation or

degradation of the API. The pH and osmolarity of the reconstituted solution should be suitable for injection to avoid irritation or adverse reactions.

5.4.2 Large Volume Parenterals

Formulation and Production of Large Volume Parenterals (LVPs)

Large volume parenterals (LVPs) are sterile solutions intended for administration in volumes typically greater than 100 mL. They are used for a variety of medical purposes, including hydration, electrolyte balance, and nutrition.

Formulation:

- **Vehicles**: The primary vehicle for LVPs is usually water for injection. Electrolytes, sugars, amino acids, and other nutrients are dissolved in the water to create the final formulation.
- **Components**: Common components of LVPs include sodium chloride, potassium chloride, calcium chloride, magnesium sulfate, glucose, and amino acids. These components are chosen based on their compatibility, stability, and physiological roles.
- **pH and Osmolarity**: The pH and osmolarity of LVPs are carefully controlled to ensure they are compatible with the patient's blood and tissues. Buffering agents may be added to maintain the desired pH.

Typical Uses of LVPs:

- **Intravenous Fluids**: LVPs are widely used as intravenous fluids to maintain or restore fluid balance in patients. They provide hydration and help maintain electrolyte balance in cases of dehydration, surgery, or illness.
- **Electrolyte Balance**: LVPs containing electrolytes are used to correct imbalances in sodium, potassium, calcium, and other essential ions. They are critical in the management of conditions such as hypokalemia, hyponatremia, and hypercalcemia.
- **Parenteral Nutrition**: LVPs can provide total parenteral nutrition (TPN) to patients who cannot consume food orally or enterally. These formulations include glucose, amino acids, lipids, vitamins, and trace elements to meet the nutritional needs of the patient.

Challenges in Ensuring Sterility and Stability of LVPs
Sterility:

- **Aseptic Processing**: The production of LVPs requires strict aseptic processing to prevent microbial contamination. This involves sterilization of equipment, filtration of solutions, and aseptic filling of containers.
- **Terminal Sterilization**: LVPs are often subjected to terminal sterilization methods such as autoclaving, where the final product is sterilized in its sealed container. This provides an additional layer of assurance that the product is free from contaminants.

Stability:

- **Chemical Stability**: Ensuring the chemical stability of the components in LVPs is crucial. Incompatibilities between components can lead to precipitation, degradation, or loss of efficacy. Stability studies are conducted to determine the shelf life of the product.
- **Physical Stability**: LVPs must remain clear and free from particulates throughout their shelf life. This requires careful control of the formulation and production processes to prevent issues such as crystallization or phase separation.

Quality Control Measures:

- **Sterility Testing**: Routine sterility testing is conducted to ensure that LVPs are free from microbial contamination. This includes testing of raw materials, in-process samples, and the final product.
- **Endotoxin Testing**: LVPs are tested for endotoxins using the Limulus Amebocyte Lysate (LAL) test to ensure they are free from pyrogens, which can cause fever and other adverse reactions.
- **Particulate Matter Testing**: The final product is inspected for particulate matter using methods such as light obscuration particle count and visual inspection to ensure it meets regulatory standards.
- **Stability Testing**: Long-term and accelerated stability testing are conducted to verify that the LVPs remain stable throughout their intended shelf life. This includes testing for changes in pH, osmolarity, and the concentration of active ingredients.

5.4 Formulation of Injections

5.4.3 Lyophilized Products

Process of Lyophilization (Freeze-Drying) and Its Application in Parenteral Products

Lyophilization, or freeze-drying, is a dehydration process used to preserve perishable materials, improve the stability of sensitive drugs, and extend the shelf life of parenteral products. The process involves three main stages: freezing, primary drying (sublimation), and secondary drying (desorption).

Freezing:

- The solution containing the active pharmaceutical ingredient (API) and excipients is frozen at a low temperature, typically between -40°C and -80°C. This step solidifies the water present in the solution.

Primary Drying (Sublimation):

- Under a vacuum, the frozen water (ice) is directly converted to vapor without passing through the liquid phase. This process is known as sublimation. The temperature and pressure are carefully controlled to ensure efficient removal of water while maintaining the structural integrity of the product.

Secondary Drying (Desorption):

- After the primary drying phase, some bound water remains in the product. The temperature is gradually increased to remove this residual moisture. The final product is a dry, porous cake that can be easily reconstituted.

Application in Parenteral Products:

- Lyophilization is commonly used for drugs that are unstable in aqueous solutions, such as antibiotics, vaccines, and biologics. It helps maintain the potency and efficacy of these sensitive drugs by removing water, which can cause hydrolysis and degradation.

Advantages of Lyophilized Products

Extended Shelf Life:

- Lyophilized products have a significantly longer shelf life compared to liquid formulations. The removal of water prevents hydrolytic degradation, making them more stable and suitable for long-term storage.

Stability of Sensitive Drugs:

- Sensitive drugs, such as proteins, peptides, and nucleic acids, are better preserved in a lyophilized state. The low-temperature process minimizes thermal degradation, and the dry state prevents chemical reactions that can occur in aqueous environments.

Ease of Transport and Storage:

- Lyophilized products are lighter and more compact, making them easier to transport and store. They do not require refrigeration, which is particularly beneficial for distribution in regions with limited cold chain infrastructure.

Reconstitution Process and Factors Affecting Quality
Reconstitution Process:

- Before administration, lyophilized products must be reconstituted with a suitable diluent. The diluent is added to the vial, and the vial is gently swirled or agitated to dissolve the lyophilized powder. The choice of diluent depends on the solubility and stability of the drug, as well as the intended route of administration.

Factors Affecting Quality:

- **Residual Moisture Content:** The amount of residual moisture left in the lyophilized product can affect its stability and shelf life. Lower residual moisture content generally improves stability but must be balanced with the risk of over-drying, which can damage the product.
- **Reconstitution Time:** The time required to fully dissolve the lyophilized powder is critical. It should be short and consistent to ensure ease of use

in clinical settings. Factors such as the particle size and porosity of the lyophilized cake influence reconstitution time.

- **Appearance and Integrity**: The lyophilized product should have a uniform appearance, typically a porous cake that maintains its structure. Collapse or shrinkage of the cake can indicate problems with the lyophilization process and affect the product's quality and stability.

5.5 Containers and Closures
5.5.1 Selection Criteria
Criteria for Selecting Containers and Closures for Parenteral Products
Selecting appropriate containers and closures for parenteral products is crucial to ensure the stability, safety, and efficacy of the formulation. Key criteria include compatibility, protection, and convenience.
Compatibility:

- **Material Compatibility**: The container and closure materials must be compatible with the formulation to prevent chemical reactions, adsorption, or leaching of container components into the product.
- **Examples**: Glass is inert and widely used for its excellent barrier properties, while certain plastics like polyethylene (PE) and polypropylene (PP) offer flexibility and durability.
- **Chemical Stability**: The materials should not react with the drug or excipients. For instance, certain drugs may adsorb onto glass surfaces or react with plasticizers in plastic containers.

Protection:

- **Barrier Properties**: Containers should provide an effective barrier against light, moisture, and oxygen to protect the formulation from degradation.
- **Sterility**: The container and closure system must maintain sterility throughout the product's shelf life. This involves ensuring that the closure provides an airtight seal to prevent microbial contamination.

Convenience:

- **Ease of Use**: The container and closure should be easy to handle, open, and administer. For example, single-dose vials with flip-off caps are convenient for quick access in clinical settings.

- **Storage and Transport**: The design should facilitate efficient storage and transport. Lightweight and shatterproof materials are preferred for ease of handling and to reduce breakage during distribution.

Common Materials Used for Containers and Closures
Glass:

- **Advantages**: Glass is chemically inert, provides an excellent barrier to gases and moisture, and is transparent, allowing for easy inspection of the contents.
- **Disadvantages**: Glass can be brittle and prone to breakage. Certain types of glass (e.g., Type I borosilicate) are used to minimize interactions with the formulation.

Plastic:

- **Advantages**: Plastics like polyethylene (PE) and polypropylene (PP) are lightweight, flexible, and resistant to breakage. They are suitable for large volume parenterals and certain single-dose applications.
- **Disadvantages**: Plastics can be permeable to gases and may interact with certain drug formulations. Additives in plastic materials may leach into the product.

Rubber Stoppers:

- **Advantages**: Rubber stoppers provide a secure seal and are used in combination with aluminum caps to maintain sterility. They are compatible with most drugs and can be easily punctured by needles for administration.
- **Disadvantages**: Certain rubber formulations may interact with specific drugs, leading to potential leaching of additives or adsorption of the API.

Aluminum Seals:

- **Advantages**: Aluminum seals provide a tamper-evident closure and protect the integrity of the rubber stopper. They are durable and can withstand autoclaving and other sterilization processes.

- **Disadvantages**: Aluminum seals require specialized equipment for crimping and may not be suitable for all types of closures.

5.5.2 Filling and Sealing Techniques
Techniques Used for Filling and Sealing Parenteral Products
Aseptic Filling:

- **Description**: Aseptic filling involves filling the sterile product into pre-sterilized containers under sterile conditions. The process is carried out in a cleanroom environment (ISO Class 5) to prevent contamination.
- **Equipment**: Peristaltic pumps, rotary piston pumps, and filling needles are commonly used. The process is often automated to ensure precision and minimize contamination risks.
- **Importance**: Ensures that the product remains sterile throughout the filling process, which is critical for parenteral products that cannot undergo terminal sterilization.

Terminal Sterilization:

- **Description**: Terminal sterilization involves filling and sealing the product in non-sterile conditions, followed by sterilizing the final product in its sealed container. Methods include autoclaving (steam sterilization), dry heat, and gamma irradiation.
- **Equipment**: Autoclaves, dry heat ovens, and gamma irradiators are used for terminal sterilization.
- **Importance**: Provides a high assurance of sterility by sterilizing the entire product, including the container and closure.

Blow-Fill-Seal (BFS) Technology:

- **Description**: BFS technology integrates the formation, filling, and sealing of containers in a continuous, automated process. Molten plastic is extruded to form the container, which is then filled and sealed in one operation.
- **Equipment**: BFS machines, such as those manufactured by Rommelag and Weiler Engineering, are used to perform the entire process in a single step.

- **Importance**: BFS technology minimizes human intervention, reducing the risk of contamination. It is ideal for large-scale production of single-dose units.

Maintaining Sterility During Filling and Sealing
Cleanroom Environment:

- **Description**: The filling and sealing processes are conducted in cleanrooms with controlled air quality, temperature, and humidity. HEPA filters are used to maintain a sterile environment.
- **Importance**: Prevents contamination by airborne particles and microorganisms, ensuring the sterility of the product.

Personnel Practices:

- **Description**: Personnel involved in aseptic processing follow strict gowning and hygiene protocols to minimize contamination risks. This includes wearing sterile gowns, gloves, masks, and shoe covers.
- **Importance**: Reduces the introduction of contaminants from operators, maintaining the sterility of the product.

Equipment Sterilization:

- **Description**: All equipment used in the filling and sealing processes is sterilized before use. Sterilization methods include steam autoclaving, dry heat, and chemical sterilants.
- **Importance**: Ensures that all contact surfaces are free from microorganisms, preventing contamination of the product.

Examples of Challenges and Solutions in Filling and Sealing Parenteral Products
Challenge: Maintaining Sterility:

- **Solution**: Implement strict aseptic processing protocols, including environmental monitoring, personnel training, and the use of advanced aseptic filling equipment.

Challenge: Ensuring Consistent Fill Volume:

- **Solution**: Use automated filling systems with precise control mechanisms, such as peristaltic pumps and rotary piston pumps, to ensure accurate and consistent fill volumes.

Challenge: Preventing Container Breakage:

- **Solution**: Choose appropriate container materials (e.g., plastic for large volumes) and design packaging to minimize handling stress. Implement quality control checks to identify and remove defective containers.

5.6 Quality Control Tests

Quality control tests are essential to ensure the safety, efficacy, and quality of parenteral products. These tests include sterility testing, pyrogenicity testing, particulate matter testing, and assay of active ingredients. Each test plays a crucial role in verifying that the product meets stringent regulatory standards.

Sterility Testing

Description: Sterility testing is performed to ensure that the parenteral product is free from viable microorganisms.

Methods:

- **Membrane Filtration**: The product is passed through a membrane filter that captures any microorganisms. The filter is then incubated in a suitable growth medium to detect microbial growth.
- **Direct Inoculation**: The product is directly inoculated into a growth medium and incubated to observe any microbial growth.

Significance:

- Ensures that the product is sterile and safe for administration, preventing infections and other complications in patients.
- Verifies the effectiveness of the aseptic processing and sterilization methods used during production.

Regulatory Requirements:

- The United States Pharmacopeia (USP), European Pharmacopeia (EP), and other pharmacopeias provide guidelines for sterility testing, including specific media, incubation conditions, and acceptance criteria.

Pyrogenicity Testing

Description: Pyrogenicity testing assesses the presence of pyrogens, which are fever-inducing substances, typically derived from bacterial endotoxins.

Methods:

- **Rabbit Pyrogen Test**: The product is injected into rabbits, and their body temperature is monitored. An increase in temperature indicates the presence of pyrogens.
- **Limulus Amebocyte Lysate (LAL) Test**: The product is mixed with LAL reagent, which reacts with endotoxins to produce a detectable change (e.g., gel clot, color change).

Significance:

- Ensures that the product is free from pyrogens, which can cause fever, shock, and other severe reactions in patients.
- Confirms the effectiveness of endotoxin removal and prevention measures during production.

Regulatory Requirements:

- Regulatory guidelines, such as those from the USP and EP, specify the procedures, reagents, and acceptance criteria for pyrogen testing.

Particulate Matter Testing

Description: Particulate matter testing detects and quantifies visible and sub-visible particles in parenteral products.

Methods:

- **Visual Inspection**: Each container is visually inspected for visible particles using proper lighting and magnification.
- **Light Obscuration Method**: An automated particle counter measures the number and size of sub-visible particles in the product.
- **Microscopic Particle Count Test**: The product is filtered, and the particles on the filter are counted and measured under a microscope.

Significance:

- Ensures that the product is free from harmful particulate contamination, which can cause adverse reactions such as embolism and inflammation.
- Verifies the effectiveness of filtration and other particulate removal processes during production.

Regulatory Requirements:

- Standards for particulate matter testing are outlined in pharmacopeias, such as USP <788> for injectable products, which specify acceptable limits for visible and sub-visible particles.

Assay of Active Ingredients

Description: The assay of active ingredients measures the concentration of the active pharmaceutical ingredient (API) in the parenteral product.

Methods:

- **High-Performance Liquid Chromatography (HPLC):** A common analytical technique used to separate, identify, and quantify the API.
- **UV-Vis Spectrophotometry:** Measures the absorbance of the API at specific wavelengths to determine its concentration.
- **Mass Spectrometry (MS):** Provides precise quantification and identification of the API and its impurities.

Significance:

- Ensures that the product contains the correct amount of API, providing the intended therapeutic effect.
- Verifies the consistency and accuracy of the formulation and manufacturing processes.

Regulatory Requirements:

- Pharmacopeial standards (e.g., USP, EP) provide specific methods and acceptance criteria for the assay of APIs in parenteral products, ensuring they meet the required potency and purity.

Additional Quality Control Tests
pH Testing:

- **Description**: Measures the acidity or alkalinity of the parenteral product to ensure it is within the acceptable range for administration.
- **Significance**: Ensures the product is safe and comfortable for injection, preventing irritation and tissue damage.

Osmolarity Testing:

- **Description**: Measures the osmolarity of the product to ensure it is isotonic or appropriately adjusted for its intended use.
- **Significance**: Prevents adverse effects related to osmotic imbalances, such as cell lysis or dehydration.

Container Closure Integrity Testing:

- **Description**: Tests the integrity of the container and closure system to ensure it maintains sterility throughout the product's shelf life.
- **Methods**: Include dye ingress testing, helium leak testing, and high-voltage leak detection.
- **Significance**: Ensures the product is protected from contamination and maintains its sterility and stability over time.

Regulatory Requirements and Standards
Regulatory bodies such as the FDA, EMA, and various pharmacopeias set stringent standards for the quality control of parenteral products. These standards ensure that products are safe, effective, and of high quality. Key regulatory requirements include:

- **Good Manufacturing Practices (GMP)**: Guidelines that ensure products are consistently produced and controlled according to quality standards.
- **Pharmacopeial Standards**: Specific tests and acceptance criteria outlined in pharmacopeias such as the USP, EP, and JP.
- **Batch Release Testing**: Comprehensive testing of each batch to ensure it meets all specifications before release.

CHAPTER SIX

Ophthalmic Preparations

6.1 INTRODUCTION AND FORMULATION CONSIDERATIONS

Ophthalmic preparations are specialized pharmaceutical forms designed for application to the eyes, aimed at treating various ocular conditions. These preparations primarily include **eye drops, ointments, and lotions**, each serving distinct purposes based on the nature and severity of the eye ailment. Eye drops are aqueous solutions or suspensions used for delivering drugs to the eye for conditions such as infections, inflammations, or glaucoma. Ointments, being more viscous, provide a longer residence time on the ocular surface, making them suitable for severe or chronic conditions. Lotions, though less common, are used for their soothing and lubricating properties.

Formulating ophthalmic products requires meticulous attention to several critical factors to ensure their safety, efficacy, and patient compliance. **Sterility** is paramount as the eye is highly susceptible to infections. This necessitates the use of sterile manufacturing conditions and the inclusion of preservatives in multi-dose containers to prevent microbial contamination. The **pH** of ophthalmic preparations must be carefully controlled to match the natural pH of the tears, typically around 7.4. Deviations from this pH can cause discomfort and damage to the eye tissues.

Another crucial factor is **isotonicity**. Ophthalmic solutions should be isotonic with the natural tears to avoid irritation and osmotic damage to the ocular tissues. This is usually achieved by adding isotonic agents like sodium chloride or dextrose to the formulation. **Viscosity** also plays a significant role in ophthalmic preparations. An optimal viscosity ensures that the drug remains on the eye surface long enough for absorption without causing blurring of vision or discomfort. Polymers like polyvinyl alcohol or carbomers are often added to adjust viscosity.

Patient comfort and compliance are vital considerations in the development of ophthalmic formulations. Comfort is significantly influenced by the factors mentioned above – sterility, pH, isotonicity, and viscosity. Additionally, the formulation should be non-irritating and should not cause stinging or burning upon application. The **ease of administration** is also crucial; thus, formulations should be easy to instill and should not blur vision, especially for individuals who need to drive or operate machinery.

Ensuring patient compliance involves designing formulations that require fewer administrations per day, as frequent dosing can be cumbersome and reduce adherence to the treatment regimen. Therefore, **sustained-release formulations** or those with longer duration of action are often preferred.

6.2 FORMULATION OF EYE DROPS, OINTMENTS, AND LOTIONS
6.2.1 METHODS OF PREPARATION

The preparation of ophthalmic products, including **eye drops, ointments, and lotions**, requires a rigorous approach to ensure **sterility, stability, and efficacy**. Each type of formulation has unique preparation methods, but maintaining sterility throughout the process is of utmost importance to prevent infections and ensure patient safety.

Eye Drops

The preparation of eye drops involves several critical steps. Initially, the **solution preparation** phase entails dissolving the active pharmaceutical ingredient (API) and any excipients in a suitable solvent, usually sterile water for injection. The solution must be carefully mixed to ensure uniformity. Key considerations include adjusting the pH, isotonicity, and viscosity to match the physiological conditions of the eye. Buffers, tonicity adjusters, and viscosity enhancers are added accordingly.

Once the solution is prepared, **sterilization** is typically achieved using filtration. A membrane filter with a pore size of 0.22 micrometers is commonly used to remove any microbial contaminants. In some cases, the solution may also be subjected to heat sterilization, provided the API and excipients are heat-stable.

After sterilization, the **packaging** step involves filling the sterile solution into sterile containers. This is usually done in a controlled environment, such as a laminar flow hood or a cleanroom, to prevent contamination. The containers are then sealed, labeled, and packaged for distribution. Multi-dose containers often contain preservatives to maintain sterility after opening, while single-dose containers are preservative-free to avoid potential eye irritation.

Ointments

The preparation of ophthalmic ointments involves the **incorporation of active ingredients** into an ointment base. The base is typically a mixture of petrolatum, mineral oil, or lanolin. The API is finely powdered and mixed with a portion of the base to form a smooth paste. This paste is then gradually incorporated into the remaining base using techniques such as levigation or trituration to ensure a homogeneous mixture.

Sterilization of ointments can be challenging due to their semi-solid nature. Heat sterilization is commonly used, where the ointment is heated to a temperature that kills microbial contaminants but does not degrade the API or the base. Alternatively, the individual components of the ointment may be sterilized separately before mixing.

The sterile ointment is then transferred to **filling equipment** under aseptic conditions. The ointment is filled into sterile tubes or jars, which are then sealed and labeled. The entire process, from mixing to filling, must be carried out in a clean environment to prevent contamination.

Lotions

The preparation of ophthalmic lotions involves an **emulsification process**, where the API is dispersed in either an oil-in-water (O/W) or water-in-oil (W/O) emulsion. The choice of emulsion type depends on the desired properties of the final product. The API and emulsifying agents are dissolved in the appropriate phases, and the phases are then mixed under high shear to form a stable emulsion.

Sterilization of lotions is achieved through filtration, similar to eye drops. The emulsion is passed through a 0.22-micrometer filter to remove any microbial contaminants. Heat sterilization is less common due to the potential for emulsion breakdown at high temperatures.

The sterile lotion is then **packaged** under aseptic conditions. It is filled into sterile bottles or tubes, sealed, and labeled. Maintaining sterility throughout the preparation and packaging process is crucial to ensure the safety and efficacy of the product.

Importance of Maintaining Sterility

Maintaining sterility throughout the preparation process of ophthalmic products is essential to prevent infections and ensure patient safety. The eye is highly sensitive and vulnerable to infections, which can lead to severe complications. Therefore, strict aseptic techniques, cleanroom environments, and appropriate sterilization methods are employed to eliminate microbial contamination at every stage of the preparation process.

6.2.2 LABELING AND CONTAINERS

Labeling

Labeling of ophthalmic preparations is critical for ensuring the safe and effective use of the products. The label must provide clear and comprehensive information to the user and healthcare professionals. Key elements that must be included on the label are:

- **Active Ingredients**: The label should clearly state the active ingredients present in the formulation along with their concentrations. This information is crucial for identifying the medication and understanding its potency.
- **Concentration**: The concentration of each active ingredient should be specified to ensure accurate dosing.
- **Expiration Date**: The label must indicate the expiration date of the product, beyond which the product may no longer be safe or effective.
- **Storage Instructions**: Proper storage conditions are vital to maintain the stability and efficacy of the product. The label should provide detailed storage instructions, such as "store in a cool, dry place" or "refrigerate".
- **Usage Instructions**: Instructions on how to use the product, including the dosage and frequency of administration, should be included.
- **Warnings and Precautions**: Any potential side effects, contraindications, or special precautions should be clearly mentioned to avoid misuse and ensure patient safety.
- **Manufacturer Information**: Details about the manufacturer, including name, address, and contact information, should be provided for traceability and in case of any issues.

Containers

The choice of containers for ophthalmic products is crucial to protect the formulation from contamination and degradation while ensuring patient convenience. Common types of containers used for ophthalmic products include:

Dropper Bottles

Dropper bottles are widely used for dispensing eye drops. They are typically made from plastic materials like low-density polyethylene (LDPE) or high-density polyethylene (HDPE).

- **Advantages**: These materials are lightweight, flexible, and provide a good barrier against moisture and oxygen, which helps in maintaining the stability of the formulation. Dropper bottles are also convenient for patients to use, allowing for precise dosing of the medication.
- **Disadvantages**: Plastic dropper bottles may have a tendency to absorb certain active ingredients or preservatives, potentially altering the efficacy of the product. They may also be prone to microbial contamination if not used properly.

Tubes

Tubes are commonly used for ophthalmic ointments. They are usually made from aluminum or plastic laminates.

- **Advantages**: Aluminum tubes offer excellent protection against light, air, and moisture, preserving the stability of the ointment. Plastic laminate tubes provide flexibility and are less likely to break or dent, making them convenient for patient use.
- **Disadvantages**: Aluminum tubes can be less flexible and harder to squeeze, which might be inconvenient for some patients. Plastic laminate tubes, while more flexible, may not provide as strong a barrier against environmental factors as aluminum.

Single-Dose Containers

Single-dose containers are used for both eye drops and lotions. They are typically made from plastic materials and are designed for one-time use.

- **Advantages**: Single-dose containers eliminate the need for preservatives, reducing the risk of irritation and allergic reactions. They also minimize the risk of contamination since each dose is individually packaged and used only once.
- **Disadvantages**: These containers can be more expensive to produce compared to multi-dose containers. They also generate more waste, which can be a concern from an environmental perspective.

Materials Used for Containers

The materials used for ophthalmic containers play a significant role in protecting the product and ensuring patient safety and convenience. Common materials include:

- **Low-Density Polyethylene (LDPE):** LDPE is commonly used for dropper bottles due to its flexibility and moisture barrier properties. It is also relatively inexpensive.
- **High-Density Polyethylene (HDPE):** HDPE is more rigid than LDPE and offers excellent protection against moisture and chemicals. It is often used for larger containers.
- **Aluminum:** Aluminum is used for tubes and provides excellent protection against light, air, and moisture. It is, however, less flexible and can be more difficult to handle.
- **Plastic Laminates:** These materials are used for tubes and combine the flexibility of plastic with the barrier properties of aluminum. They provide a balance between protection and ease of use.

6.3 EVALUATION OF OPHTHALMIC PREPARATIONS
6.3.1 QUALITY CONTROL TESTS

The quality control of ophthalmic preparations involves a series of rigorous tests to ensure their **safety, efficacy, and stability**. These tests are designed to verify that the products meet the required specifications and are free from contaminants. Below are the key quality control tests conducted on ophthalmic preparations:

Sterility Test

Sterility testing is paramount for ophthalmic products to ensure they are free from viable microorganisms. This test is typically performed using membrane filtration or direct inoculation methods.

- **Significance:** Ensures the product is free from microbial contamination, preventing infections when applied to the sensitive ocular area.
- **Method:** In membrane filtration, the product is passed through a sterile membrane filter that captures any microorganisms. The filter is then incubated in a culture medium to detect microbial growth. Direct inoculation involves directly adding the product to a culture medium and incubating it.

Particulate Matter Test

This test checks for the presence of visible and sub-visible particles in the ophthalmic solution.

- **Significance**: Particulate matter can cause irritation or damage to the eye tissues. Ensuring the absence of particles maintains the product's safety and comfort for the user.
- **Method**: Visual inspection under specific lighting conditions is used to detect visible particles. For sub-visible particles, instruments like light obscuration or microscopic particle counters are employed.

pH Test

The pH of the ophthalmic preparation is measured to ensure it is within the acceptable range.

- **Significance**: Maintaining an appropriate pH is crucial to avoid irritation and discomfort to the eye. The ideal pH for ophthalmic solutions is around 7.4, matching the natural pH of tears.
- **Method**: The pH is measured using a calibrated pH meter.

Osmolarity Test

Osmolarity testing ensures the solution's osmotic pressure is similar to that of natural tears.

- **Significance**: Solutions that are too hypo- or hyperosmotic can cause discomfort or damage to the eye. Isotonicity with natural tears prevents such issues.
- **Method**: Osmolarity is measured using an osmometer, which determines the osmotic pressure of the solution.

Viscosity Test

Viscosity measurement ensures the solution has the appropriate thickness to remain on the ocular surface without causing discomfort.

- **Significance**: Appropriate viscosity enhances the drug's residence time on the eye surface, improving absorption while preventing blurred vision or discomfort.
- **Method**: Viscosity is measured using viscometers or rheometers, which assess the flow properties of the solution.

Assay of Active Ingredients

The assay determines the concentration of the active pharmaceutical ingredients (APIs) in the formulation.

- **Significance**: Ensures the product contains the correct amount of API, guaranteeing its efficacy and safety.
- **Method**: High-performance liquid chromatography (HPLC), ultraviolet (UV) spectroscopy, or other suitable analytical techniques are used to quantify the APIs.

Each of these quality control tests plays a critical role in ensuring that ophthalmic preparations are safe, effective, and comfortable for the patient. By adhering to stringent testing protocols, manufacturers can produce high-quality ophthalmic products that meet regulatory standards and provide therapeutic benefits without adverse effects.

6.3.2 STABILITY TESTING

Importance of Stability Testing

Stability testing is a critical aspect of pharmaceutical development, ensuring that ophthalmic preparations remain **safe, effective, and of high quality** throughout their shelf life. The primary objective of stability testing is to determine how the quality of a drug substance or drug product varies with time under the influence of various environmental factors such as temperature, humidity, and light. This information is crucial for establishing the **shelf life**, optimal storage conditions, and proper packaging of the product.

Types of Stability Tests

Accelerated Stability Testing

Accelerated stability testing involves storing the ophthalmic preparation at elevated stress conditions to speed up the chemical degradation or physical changes.

- **Parameters Monitored**: Physical appearance, pH, assay of active ingredients, viscosity, osmolarity, and microbial contamination.
- **Purpose**: Provides an estimate of the product's shelf life in a shorter time frame, allowing for quicker market release.
- **Conditions**: Typically involves storing the product at higher temperatures (e.g., 40°C ± 2°C) and higher humidity (e.g., 75% ± 5% RH).

Long-Term Stability Testing

Long-term stability testing evaluates the product under recommended storage conditions over an extended period, usually up to the expected shelf life of the product.

- **Parameters Monitored**: Physical appearance, pH, assay of active ingredients, viscosity, osmolarity, and microbial contamination.
- **Purpose**: Confirms the shelf life and storage conditions derived from accelerated stability testing.
- **Conditions**: Typically involves storing the product at standard conditions (e.g., 25°C ± 2°C) and ambient humidity (e.g., 60% ± 5% RH).

Parameters Monitored During Stability Testing

Physical Appearance: Monitoring for changes in color, clarity, and the presence of precipitates or particles. Any significant change can indicate degradation or contamination.

pH: Ensuring the pH remains within the acceptable range is crucial for maintaining the product's comfort and efficacy. Changes in pH can affect the stability and activity of the active ingredients.

Assay of Active Ingredients: Regularly measuring the concentration of active ingredients ensures the product maintains its therapeutic efficacy. Any significant decrease in the assay can indicate degradation.

Viscosity: Monitoring viscosity ensures the product maintains its intended application properties, such as ease of administration and retention time on the ocular surface.

Osmolarity: Ensuring the osmolarity remains within the isotonic range is essential to prevent ocular irritation or discomfort.

Microbial Contamination: Ensuring sterility throughout the shelf life is critical for ophthalmic products to prevent infections. Regular microbial testing is conducted to ensure the product remains free from contamination.

Stability-Indicating Methods

High-Performance Liquid Chromatography (HPLC): HPLC is commonly used to separate and quantify the active ingredients and any degradation products. It is a robust method for evaluating the chemical stability of the product.

UV-Visible Spectroscopy: This method can be used to monitor changes in the concentration of active ingredients by measuring their absorbance at specific wavelengths.

Gas Chromatography (GC): GC can be used to detect and quantify volatile degradation products, ensuring the chemical integrity of the ophthalmic preparation.

Microbial Testing: Techniques such as membrane filtration and direct inoculation are used to monitor microbial contamination, ensuring the product remains sterile throughout its shelf life.

Visual Inspection: Regular visual inspection under controlled lighting conditions is used to detect any changes in physical appearance, such as discoloration or particulate formation.

CHAPTER SEVEN

Cosmetics

7.1 INTRODUCTION TO COSMETIC PREPARATIONS

Cosmetic preparations are products applied to the body, particularly the skin, hair, and nails, to **enhance or alter the appearance, fragrance, and texture**. The primary purpose of cosmetics is to improve aesthetic appeal and maintain personal hygiene. Regulatory definitions of cosmetics, as provided by organizations like the Food and Drug Administration (FDA) and the European Commission, emphasize that cosmetics are substances or mixtures intended to be placed in contact with various external parts of the human body, such as the skin, hair, nails, lips, and external genital organs, or with the teeth and the mucous membranes of the oral cavity, to clean, perfume, change appearance, protect, keep in good condition, or correct body odors.

Categories of Cosmetics

Skincare: Products designed to improve and maintain the condition of the skin. Examples include moisturizers, cleansers, exfoliants, and anti-aging creams. These products aim to hydrate, cleanse, rejuvenate, and protect the skin.

Haircare: Products used to maintain and enhance the appearance and health of the hair. Common products include shampoos, conditioners, hair oils, and styling products. Haircare cosmetics aim to clean, condition, nourish, and style the hair.

Oral Care: Products intended for cleaning the teeth, gums, and mouth, such as toothpaste, mouthwash, and dental floss. These products help maintain oral hygiene, prevent dental issues, and freshen breath.

Decorative Cosmetics: Also known as color cosmetics, these include products used to enhance or change the appearance of the face and body. Examples are lipsticks, foundations, eye shadows, and nail polishes. They provide color, coverage, and sometimes added benefits like hydration or sun protection.

Importance of Safety, Efficacy, and Consumer Appeal

Safety: Cosmetic products must be safe for use, free from harmful substances, and should not cause adverse reactions. Regulatory bodies have strict guidelines and testing requirements to ensure the safety of cosmetic products.

Efficacy: Cosmetics should deliver the promised benefits effectively. This requires thorough research and testing to prove that the product performs as intended, whether it's moisturizing the skin, providing long-lasting color, or protecting from UV rays.

Consumer Appeal: The success of a cosmetic product largely depends on its appeal to consumers. This includes factors like texture, fragrance, packaging, ease of application, and overall experience. Products must be attractive, pleasant to use, and meet consumer expectations.

Examples of Common Cosmetic Products and Their Benefits

- **Moisturizers:** Hydrate and soften the skin, prevent dryness and improve skin texture.
- **Shampoos:** Cleanse the hair and scalp, remove dirt and oil, and can provide additional benefits like volume or dandruff control.
- **Toothpaste:** Clean the teeth, prevent cavities, reduce plaque, and freshen breath.
- **Lipsticks:** Provide color to the lips, enhance their appearance, and can include moisturizing or long-lasting properties.

7.2 FORMULATION AND PREPARATION OF VARIOUS COSMETICS

7.2.1 LIPSTICKS

Formulation and Preparation Process of Lipsticks

Lipsticks are one of the most popular decorative cosmetics, designed to add color, texture, and protection to the lips. The formulation and preparation process of lipsticks involves a combination of key ingredients and meticulous manufacturing steps to achieve the desired properties.

Key Ingredients

- **Waxes:** Provide structure and stability to the lipstick. Common waxes used include beeswax, carnauba wax, and candelilla wax. They help in maintaining the shape and preventing the product from melting at high temperatures.

- **Oils**: Add smoothness and glide to the lipstick. Common oils include castor oil, mineral oil, and lanolin. They help in spreading the color evenly and provide a moisturizing effect.
- **Pigments**: Provide the color to the lipstick. Pigments can be organic or inorganic and are chosen based on the desired shade and intensity. Common pigments include iron oxides, titanium dioxide, and D&C dyes.
- **Emollients**: Moisturize and soften the lips. Emollients like shea butter, cocoa butter, and vitamin E are added to improve the texture and provide a hydrating effect.

Manufacturing Process

1. **Melting**: The waxes and oils are melted together in a controlled environment to create a uniform base. This step ensures that the ingredients are thoroughly mixed and any solid particles are dissolved.
2. **Mixing**: Pigments and emollients are added to the melted base and mixed thoroughly to achieve a consistent color and texture. The mixture is stirred continuously to ensure uniform distribution of pigments.
3. **Molding**: The molten lipstick mixture is poured into molds and allowed to cool and solidify. The molds are designed to give the lipstick its final shape. This step is crucial for achieving the desired appearance and texture.
4. **Cooling**: The molded lipsticks are cooled to room temperature to solidify completely. Proper cooling is essential to prevent cracking and ensure a smooth surface.

Importance of Texture, Color, and Stability

Achieving the right texture, color, and stability is essential for the success of a lipstick product. The texture should be smooth and creamy for easy application, without being too soft or too hard. The color should be vibrant and uniform, providing full coverage with a single application. Stability is crucial to ensure that the lipstick does not melt or break under normal conditions and remains effective throughout its shelf life.

Examples of Different Types of Lipsticks

- **Matte Lipsticks**: Provide a flat, non-shiny finish. They are long-lasting and often have a higher concentration of pigments for intense color.

- **Glossy Lipsticks**: Offer a shiny, lustrous finish. They often contain more oils and emollients for added hydration and a glossy appearance.
- **Long-Lasting Lipsticks**: Formulated to provide extended wear without frequent reapplication. They may contain special film-forming agents to adhere to the lips for longer periods.

7.2.2 SHAMPOOS

Formulation and Preparation of Shampoos

Shampoos are an essential part of personal care, designed to cleanse the scalp and hair, remove dirt, oil, and other impurities, and often provide additional benefits such as conditioning, dandruff control, or color protection. The formulation and preparation of shampoos involve a careful selection of ingredients and meticulous production processes to ensure they meet consumer expectations for cleansing efficiency, safety, and sensory attributes.

Main Ingredients

- **Surfactants**: These are the primary cleansing agents in shampoos. They reduce surface tension, allowing water to mix with oil and dirt for effective removal. Common surfactants include sodium lauryl sulfate (SLS), sodium laureth sulfate (SLES), and ammonium lauryl sulfate. Surfactants are categorized into anionic, cationic, nonionic, and amphoteric, each providing different properties like foaming, mildness, and conditioning.
- **Conditioning Agents**: These ingredients improve the feel and manageability of hair. They can be silicones (e.g., dimethicone), quaternary ammonium compounds (e.g., cetrimonium chloride), or natural oils (e.g., argan oil). Conditioners help to smooth the hair cuticle, reduce static, and add shine.
- **Thickeners**: Thickeners are added to improve the viscosity of the shampoo, giving it a desirable texture and making it easier to apply. Common thickeners include xanthan gum, hydroxyethyl cellulose, and sodium chloride.
- **Preservatives**: These are essential to prevent microbial growth and extend the shelf life of the product. Common preservatives include parabens, phenoxyethanol, and benzyl alcohol.

Steps Involved in Shampoo Production

1. **Mixing**: The process begins with the preparation of the aqueous phase, where water-soluble ingredients like surfactants, thickeners, and preservatives are dissolved in water. This phase is typically heated to ensure complete dissolution and to help mix oil-soluble ingredients.

2. **Homogenization**: Once the aqueous phase is prepared, conditioning agents, fragrances, and other additives are incorporated. Homogenization ensures a uniform mixture, preventing separation of ingredients and ensuring consistent product quality.

3. **pH Adjustment**: The pH of the shampoo is adjusted to be within the range of 4.5 to 5.5, which is close to the natural pH of the scalp and hair. This helps to maintain the health of the hair and scalp, preventing irritation and maintaining the hair's natural balance.

4. **Foam Production**: Foaming properties are crucial for consumer perception. Surfactants are responsible for foam production, which enhances the cleansing process and gives a sensory indication of cleanliness. Foam boosters like cocamidopropyl betaine may be added to improve lather.

5. **Cleansing Efficiency**: Ensuring the shampoo effectively removes dirt, oil, and product buildup is essential. This is achieved through the careful balance of surfactants and other cleansing agents.

6. **Packaging**: Once the formulation is complete and quality tests are passed, the shampoo is filled into bottles or containers under sterile conditions. Packaging must be done in a way that maintains the product's integrity and protects it from contamination and degradation.

Specialized Shampoos

- **Anti-Dandruff Shampoos**: Formulated with active ingredients like zinc pyrithione, ketoconazole, or selenium sulfide, these shampoos help to control dandruff by reducing the yeast on the scalp and alleviating symptoms like flaking and itching.

- **Color-Protecting Shampoos**: Designed for color-treated hair, these shampoos contain mild surfactants to prevent color stripping and ingredients like UV filters and antioxidants to protect the hair color from fading.

- **Sulfate-Free Shampoos**: Free from harsh sulfates like SLS and SLES, these shampoos use gentler surfactants such as cocamidopropyl betaine and decyl glucoside. They are suitable for sensitive scalps and color-treated hair, offering mild cleansing without stripping natural oils.

7.2.3 COLD CREAM AND VANISHING CREAM

Formulation and Preparation of Cold Creams and Vanishing Creams

Cold creams and vanishing creams are two distinct types of cosmetic creams, each designed to serve different purposes and offer unique benefits. Understanding their formulation, preparation, and key differences is essential for developing effective and consumer-friendly products.

Cold Cream

Ingredients and Intended Uses

Cold cream is an emulsion of water in oil (W/O) designed to cleanse and moisturize the skin. It is typically used as a makeup remover, moisturizer, or night cream, providing a rich, oily texture that leaves the skin feeling soft and hydrated.

- **Emollients:** These are the primary moisturizing agents in cold creams, providing a rich, occlusive layer that prevents water loss from the skin. Common emollients include mineral oil, lanolin, and beeswax.
- **Humectants:** Ingredients like glycerin and propylene glycol attract water from the environment to the skin, enhancing hydration.
- **Emulsifiers:** Emulsifiers like borax and sodium borate help to stabilize the water-in-oil emulsion, ensuring a consistent and smooth texture.
- **Preservatives:** To prevent microbial growth and extend shelf life, preservatives like parabens or phenoxyethanol are added.

Manufacturing Process

1. **Emulsification:** The oil phase (containing emollients and emulsifiers) and the water phase (containing humectants and preservatives) are heated separately. The water phase is then slowly added to the oil phase with continuous stirring to form a stable emulsion.
2. **Cooling:** After emulsification, the mixture is cooled gradually while stirring to ensure uniform consistency and prevent separation of phases.
3. **Packaging:** The cooled cream is filled into jars or tubes under sterile conditions to maintain product integrity.

Desired Texture and Skin Feel

Cold creams should have a thick, rich texture that spreads easily and leaves a protective, moisturizing layer on the skin. The cream should feel smooth and non-greasy after application.

Common Formulations and Benefits

- **Classic Cold Cream**: Contains mineral oil, beeswax, borax, and water. It is excellent for removing makeup and providing deep hydration, especially in dry or cold climates.

Vanishing Cream

Ingredients and Intended Uses

Vanishing cream is an oil-in-water (O/W) emulsion designed to provide a light, non-greasy moisturizer that "vanishes" into the skin, leaving it matte and smooth. It is often used as a day cream or base for makeup.

- **Emollients**: Provide a light moisturizing effect without leaving an oily residue. Common emollients include stearic acid and cetyl alcohol.
- **Humectants**: Ingredients like glycerin attract moisture to the skin, enhancing hydration without heaviness.
- **Emulsifiers**: Emulsifiers like potassium hydroxide and triethanolamine help to stabilize the oil-in-water emulsion, ensuring a smooth and consistent product.
- **Preservatives**: Preservatives like parabens or methylisothiazolinone prevent microbial growth and ensure product safety.

Manufacturing Process

1. **Emulsification**: The oil phase (containing emollients and emulsifiers) and the water phase (containing humectants and preservatives) are heated separately. The oil phase is then slowly added to the water phase with continuous stirring to form a stable emulsion.
2. **Cooling**: After emulsification, the mixture is cooled gradually while stirring to ensure uniform consistency and prevent separation of phases.
3. **Packaging**: The cooled cream is filled into jars or tubes under sterile conditions to maintain product integrity.

Desired Texture and Skin Feel

Vanishing creams should have a light, smooth texture that spreads easily and absorbs quickly into the skin, leaving a matte finish without any greasy residue. The cream should feel refreshing and non-sticky after application.

Common Formulations and Benefits

- **Classic Vanishing Cream**: Contains stearic acid, potassium hydroxide, glycerin, and water. It provides light hydration and a matte finish, making it suitable for use under makeup or in humid climates.

Key Differences Between Cold Cream and Vanishing Cream

- **Emulsion Type**: Cold creams are water-in-oil (W/O) emulsions, providing a rich, oily texture, while vanishing creams are oil-in-water (O/W) emulsions, offering a light, non-greasy feel.
- **Use and Benefits**: Cold creams are ideal for deep moisturizing and makeup removal, especially in dry conditions, whereas vanishing creams are perfect for light hydration and a matte finish, making them suitable for daytime use and as a makeup base.

7.2.4 TOOTHPASTES

Formulation and Preparation of Toothpastes

Toothpastes are essential oral care products designed to clean teeth, prevent dental diseases, and enhance oral hygiene. The formulation and preparation of toothpastes involve a combination of active and inactive ingredients to achieve the desired properties and efficacy. Understanding the key ingredients and the production process is crucial for developing effective toothpaste formulations.

Main Ingredients

- **Abrasives**: These are the primary cleaning agents that help remove plaque, stains, and food particles from the teeth. Common abrasives include calcium carbonate, hydrated silica, and dicalcium phosphate. The abrasiveness must be balanced to effectively clean without damaging the enamel.
- **Fluoride**: An active ingredient that helps to prevent cavities by strengthening tooth enamel and promoting remineralization. Sodium fluoride, stannous fluoride, and sodium monofluorophosphate are commonly used fluoride compounds.

- **Humectants:** These ingredients prevent the toothpaste from drying out and maintain its moisture content. Common humectants include glycerin, sorbitol, and propylene glycol.
- **Thickeners:** Thickeners provide the desired consistency and texture to the toothpaste, making it easy to apply and use. Common thickeners include xanthan gum, carrageenan, and carboxymethyl cellulose.
- **Flavoring Agents:** These agents improve the taste and acceptability of the toothpaste. Mint flavors (such as peppermint and spearmint) are commonly used, along with sweeteners like saccharin and xylitol to enhance the flavor.

Steps Involved in Toothpaste Production

1. **Mixing:** The production process begins with the mixing of water and humectants to form the base. The abrasive agents, fluoride compounds, thickeners, and other ingredients are then added to this base. The mixing must be thorough to ensure uniform distribution of all components.
2. **Homogenization:** The mixed paste is subjected to homogenization to achieve a smooth and consistent texture. This process involves high-shear mixing or milling to break down any lumps and ensure a uniform product.
3. **pH Adjustment:** The pH of the toothpaste is adjusted to ensure it is within the acceptable range, typically around neutral (pH 7), to be safe and effective for oral use.
4. **Filling:** The homogenized toothpaste is then filled into tubes or containers. This step is performed under hygienic conditions to prevent contamination. The filled containers are sealed and labeled for distribution.

Importance of Consistency, Abrasiveness, and Stability

- **Consistency:** The toothpaste must have the right consistency to be easily squeezed out of the tube and applied to the toothbrush. It should not be too runny or too thick.
- **Abrasiveness:** The abrasiveness of the toothpaste must be balanced to effectively clean the teeth without causing damage to the enamel or gums. This is measured using the Relative Dentin Abrasivity (RDA) value.

- **Stability**: The toothpaste must remain stable throughout its shelf life, maintaining its efficacy, texture, and flavor. This involves ensuring that the ingredients do not separate or degrade over time.

Examples of Different Types of Toothpastes

- **Whitening Toothpastes**: These contain additional abrasives or chemical agents like hydrogen peroxide to help remove surface stains and whiten the teeth. Examples include Crest 3D White and Colgate Optic White.
- **Sensitive Toothpastes**: Formulated with desensitizing agents like potassium nitrate or strontium chloride, these toothpastes help reduce tooth sensitivity by blocking the pathways to the nerves. Examples include Sensodyne and Colgate Sensitive Pro-Relief.
- **Anti-Cavity Toothpastes**: These are fortified with higher levels of fluoride to provide enhanced protection against cavities and tooth decay. Examples include Colgate Total and Crest Pro-Health.

7.2.5 HAIR DYES

Formulation and Preparation of Hair Dyes

Hair dyes are cosmetic products designed to alter the color of the hair, either temporarily or permanently. The formulation and preparation of hair dyes involve a careful selection of ingredients and meticulous manufacturing processes to ensure consistent color results, safety, and hair conditioning.

Types of Hair Dyes

Permanent Hair Dyes: These dyes provide long-lasting color by penetrating the hair shaft and forming color molecules inside the hair. They often require a developer to oxidize the dye and fix it within the hair.

Semi-Permanent Hair Dyes: These dyes deposit color on the surface of the hair shaft and partially penetrate it. They do not require a developer and gradually fade with washing, typically lasting for several weeks.

Temporary Hair Dyes: These dyes coat the surface of the hair and can be easily washed out with one or two shampoos. They are ideal for short-term color changes and special occasions.

Key Ingredients

- **Colorants**: These are the primary ingredients that provide the desired color. In permanent dyes, these are usually oxidative dyes that react with a developer to form larger, color-fast molecules inside the hair. In semi-permanent and temporary dyes, direct dyes are used that do not require oxidation.

- **Developers**: Typically hydrogen peroxide, developers are used in permanent hair dyes to oxidize the colorants and help them penetrate the hair shaft. They also lighten the natural pigment of the hair, allowing the new color to show more effectively.
- **Conditioning Agents**: These ingredients help to protect and nourish the hair during the coloring process. Common conditioning agents include cationic surfactants, silicones, and natural oils like argan oil.
- **pH Adjusters**: These are used to maintain the desired pH level of the dye formulation, ensuring optimal performance and stability. Ammonia or monoethanolamine (MEA) are commonly used in permanent dyes to raise the pH, opening the hair cuticle for better dye penetration.

Manufacturing Process

1. **Mixing**: The process begins with mixing the colorants, conditioning agents, and other ingredients to create a uniform base. In the case of permanent dyes, the colorants are mixed with a developer.
2. **Emulsification**: The mixture is then emulsified to ensure a smooth and homogeneous product. This involves high-shear mixing to evenly distribute all components.
3. **pH Adjustment**: The pH of the mixture is adjusted to the desired level using pH adjusters. For permanent dyes, this typically involves adding ammonia or MEA to achieve an alkaline pH.
4. **Quality Control**: Before packaging, the product undergoes rigorous quality control tests to ensure consistency in color, viscosity, pH, and stability. Microbial testing is also conducted to ensure the product is free from contamination.
5. **Packaging**: The finished product is filled into tubes, bottles, or kits under sterile conditions. Proper packaging is essential to maintain product stability and ease of use for the consumer.

Importance of Consistent Color Results, Safety, and Hair Conditioning

- **Consistent Color Results**: Achieving uniform and predictable color results is crucial for consumer satisfaction. This requires precise formulation and quality control to ensure that each batch of hair dye performs identically.
- **Safety**: Hair dyes must be safe for use, with no harmful side effects or allergic reactions. This involves using safe ingredients and conducting thorough safety testing.
- **Hair Conditioning**: The dye should not damage the hair but instead leave it feeling soft and conditioned. Conditioning agents are added to protect the hair during the coloring process and improve its texture and manageability.

Examples of Common Hair Dye Formulations and Their Applications

- **Permanent Hair Dye**: Typically contains oxidative colorants, hydrogen peroxide as the developer, conditioning agents like cationic surfactants, and ammonia as a pH adjuster. Used for long-lasting color changes and gray coverage. Examples include L'Oréal Paris Excellence Creme and Garnier Nutrisse.
- **Semi-Permanent Hair Dye**: Contains direct dyes, conditioning agents, and no developer or ammonia. Provides a less damaging option for those seeking a temporary color change. Examples include Clairol Natural Instincts and Manic Panic.
- **Temporary Hair Dye**: Contains direct dyes and conditioning agents, designed to wash out easily. Used for short-term color changes or special occasions. Examples include L'Oréal Colorista Hair Makeup and Spray On Hair Color.

7.2.6 SUNSCREENS

Formulation and Preparation of Sunscreens

Sunscreens are essential cosmetic products designed to protect the skin from the harmful effects of ultraviolet (UV) radiation. The formulation and preparation of sunscreens involve a careful selection of ingredients and precise manufacturing processes to ensure effective UV protection, stability, and consumer satisfaction.

Key Ingredients

- **UV Filters**: These are the active ingredients that provide protection against UV radiation. They can be divided into chemical (organic) and physical (inorganic) filters.

    - **Chemical Filters**: These absorb UV radiation and convert it into harmless heat. Common chemical filters include avobenzone, octocrylene, oxybenzone, and octinoxate.
    - **Physical Filters**: These reflect and scatter UV radiation. Common physical filters include zinc oxide and titanium dioxide. They are often used in formulations for sensitive skin due to their mildness and broad-spectrum protection.

- **Emollients**: These ingredients help to moisturize and soften the skin, enhancing the feel and spreadability of the sunscreen. Common emollients include glycerin, isopropyl myristate, and dimethicone.
- **Emulsifiers**: These agents help to stabilize the mixture of oil and water phases in the sunscreen, creating a uniform and consistent product. Common emulsifiers include cetyl alcohol, glyceryl stearate, and polysorbates.
- **Preservatives**: These are used to prevent microbial growth and ensure the product's shelf life. Common preservatives include parabens, phenoxyethanol, and ethylhexylglycerin.

Steps Involved in Sunscreen Production

1. **Mixing**: The production begins with the preparation of the oil and water phases separately. UV filters, emollients, and oil-soluble ingredients are mixed in the oil phase, while water-soluble ingredients, including preservatives and some emulsifiers, are mixed in the water phase.
2. **Emulsification**: The oil and water phases are then combined through emulsification. This process involves high-shear mixing to create a stable emulsion. The emulsifiers help to keep the oil and water phases uniformly mixed, preventing separation.
3. **Homogenization**: The emulsion is further homogenized to ensure a smooth and consistent texture. This step ensures that the sunscreen has a uniform distribution of UV filters and other ingredients.
4. **Cooling and pH Adjustment**: The mixture is cooled to room temperature while being stirred. The pH of the sunscreen is adjusted to

a skin-friendly level, typically between 5 and 7, using pH adjusters like citric acid or sodium hydroxide.

5. **Quality Control:** The final product undergoes rigorous quality control tests to ensure it meets the required standards for SPF, stability, and microbial safety. Tests include measuring the SPF, checking for homogeneity, and ensuring there are no microbial contaminants.

6. **Packaging:** The sunscreen is filled into tubes, bottles, or sprays under sterile conditions. Proper packaging is crucial to maintain product integrity and ensure ease of use for the consumer.

Importance of Achieving the Right SPF, Photostability, and Skin Feel

- **SPF (Sun Protection Factor):** The SPF indicates the level of protection the sunscreen provides against UVB radiation. Achieving the right SPF is crucial for ensuring effective sun protection. The SPF is tested through standardized methods to ensure accuracy and reliability.
- **Photostability:** Sunscreens must remain effective when exposed to sunlight. Photostability ensures that the UV filters do not degrade upon exposure to UV radiation, maintaining their protective effect.
- **Skin Feel:** The texture and feel of the sunscreen on the skin are important for consumer acceptance. The product should spread easily, absorb well, and leave a pleasant, non-greasy feel.

Examples of Different Types of Sunscreens

- **Broad-Spectrum Sunscreens:** These provide protection against both UVA and UVB radiation. They typically contain a combination of chemical and physical UV filters. Examples include products with avobenzone, octocrylene, zinc oxide, and titanium dioxide.
- **Water-Resistant Sunscreens:** Formulated to remain effective even when exposed to water or sweat. They often include film-forming agents that help the product adhere to the skin. Examples include sunscreens labeled as water-resistant for 40 or 80 minutes.
- **Sensitive Skin Formulations:** These sunscreens use mild and non-irritating ingredients, focusing on physical UV filters like zinc oxide and titanium dioxide. They avoid common allergens and irritants. Examples include sunscreens marketed as hypoallergenic or for sensitive skin.

CHAPTER EIGHT

Pharmaceutical Aerosols

8.1 DEFINITION AND TYPES OF AEROSOL SYSTEMS

Definition and Significance of Pharmaceutical Aerosols

Pharmaceutical aerosols are dosage forms that contain therapeutically active ingredients dissolved, suspended, or emulsified in a propellant or a mixture of solvent and propellant. They are dispensed as fine mist, spray, or foam upon activation. These systems are significant in drug delivery due to their ability to provide rapid onset of action, targeted delivery to specific sites, and ease of use. Aerosols are particularly important in treating respiratory conditions, as they allow direct delivery of medication to the lungs, leading to efficient and effective treatment.

Types of Aerosol Systems

Metered-Dose Inhalers (MDIs)

Working Mechanism

Metered-dose inhalers (MDIs) deliver a specific amount of medication in aerosol form using a propellant. When the inhaler is activated, the propellant forces the medication out through a nozzle, creating a fine mist that can be inhaled into the lungs.

Applications

MDIs are commonly used to treat respiratory conditions such as asthma and chronic obstructive pulmonary disease (COPD). They provide rapid relief from bronchospasm and inflammation.

Examples of Common Drugs

- **Albuterol**: A bronchodilator used for quick relief of asthma symptoms.
- **Beclomethasone**: A corticosteroid used for long-term control of asthma.
- **Ipratropium**: An anticholinergic agent used for managing COPD.

Dry Powder Inhalers (DPIs)

Working Mechanism

Dry powder inhalers (DPIs) deliver medication in a dry powdered form. The patient inhales deeply through the device, which disperses the powder into fine particles that can reach the lower respiratory tract. DPIs rely on the patient's inhalation effort to generate the necessary airflow for drug delivery.

Applications

DPIs are used for both acute and chronic management of respiratory diseases, providing a convenient alternative to MDIs, especially for patients who have difficulty coordinating inhalation with device activation.

Examples of Common Drugs

- **Fluticasone/Salmeterol**: A combination of a corticosteroid and a long-acting beta agonist used for asthma and COPD.
- **Budesonide/Formoterol**: Another combination therapy for long-term management of asthma and COPD.
- **Tiotropium**: A long-acting anticholinergic used for COPD maintenance.

Nebulizers

Working Mechanism

Nebulizers convert liquid medication into a fine mist using compressed air or ultrasonic waves. The mist is then inhaled through a mouthpiece or mask, making it suitable for patients who cannot use MDIs or DPIs effectively.

Applications

Nebulizers are often used for severe respiratory conditions, including acute asthma attacks and advanced COPD, where higher doses of medication or longer administration times are required.

Examples of Common Drugs

- **Albuterol**: Used in nebulized form for acute relief of bronchospasm.
- **Ipratropium**: Often combined with albuterol for enhanced bronchodilation in COPD.
- **Budesonide**: A corticosteroid used in nebulized form for chronic management of asthma.

8.2 PROPELLANTS, CONTAINERS, AND VALVES
Role of Propellants in Aerosol Systems

Propellants are crucial components in aerosol systems as they create the force needed to expel the medication from the container in the form of a fine mist, spray, or foam. They work by building pressure inside the container, which, upon activation of the valve, releases the product in the desired form. Propellants not only help in the efficient delivery of the medication but also influence the particle size, spray pattern, and overall performance of the aerosol product.

Types of Propellants
Chlorofluorocarbons (CFCs)
Advantages

- CFCs were widely used due to their excellent propellant properties, including stability, non-flammability, and effectiveness in delivering fine particles.

Disadvantages

- CFCs have been largely phased out due to their detrimental effects on the ozone layer. Their environmental impact led to the development of more eco-friendly alternatives.

Hydrofluoroalkanes (HFAs)
Advantages

- HFAs are non-ozone-depleting and have similar performance characteristics to CFCs, making them suitable replacements.
- They are chemically stable and non-toxic, providing a safe option for medical aerosols.

Disadvantages

- HFAs are more expensive than CFCs and require modifications in the formulation and design of the aerosol system to ensure compatibility and performance.

Hydrocarbons
Advantages

- Hydrocarbons like propane, butane, and isobutane are cost-effective and widely available.
- They provide good propellant properties and are commonly used in non-medical aerosols.

Disadvantages

- Hydrocarbons are flammable, which poses safety risks, especially in medical applications.
- They may also react with certain formulation components, affecting the stability and efficacy of the product.

Selection Criteria for Containers and Valves
Containers
Materials Used

- **Aluminum**: Lightweight, corrosion-resistant, and provides excellent barrier properties to protect the formulation from light and moisture. Aluminum containers are commonly used for MDIs and other medical aerosols.
- **Stainless Steel**: Offers superior strength and corrosion resistance, making it suitable for pressurized containers that require high durability. Stainless steel is often used for reusable or specialty aerosol systems.
- **Plastic**: Used for certain applications due to its flexibility and lower cost. However, plastic containers may have compatibility issues with some formulations and propellants, limiting their use in medical aerosols.

Compatibility with Formulation

- The container material must be compatible with both the propellant and the active ingredients to prevent reactions that could degrade the product or compromise its safety and efficacy.
- Proper selection ensures the stability of the formulation over its shelf life and maintains the integrity of the container under pressure.

Valves
Importance of Valve Design

- **Accurate Dosing**: The valve design is critical in ensuring precise and consistent dosing of the medication. Metered-dose valves are specifically designed to release a fixed amount of medication with each actuation.
- **Proper Delivery**: The valve must be designed to deliver the medication effectively, whether as a fine mist, spray, or foam. It should create an appropriate spray pattern and particle size for optimal absorption and therapeutic effect.
- **Material Compatibility**: Valves are often made from materials like stainless steel, aluminum, and plastic, selected based on their compatibility with the formulation and propellant. The materials must withstand the pressure and chemical nature of the contents without degradation.

Examples of Valve Components

- **Actuator**: The part of the valve that the user presses to release the medication. It is designed for ease of use and precise control.
- **Stem**: Connects the actuator to the valve body, allowing the passage of the product during actuation.
- **Gasket**: Ensures a tight seal to prevent leakage and maintain pressure inside the container.

8.3 FORMULATION AND MANUFACTURE OF AEROSOLS

Formulation Considerations for Pharmaceutical Aerosols

The formulation of pharmaceutical aerosols requires careful selection and combination of various components to ensure the safety, efficacy, and stability of the final product. Key considerations include the choice of active ingredients, solvents, propellants, and other excipients.

Active Ingredients

The selection of active ingredients depends on the therapeutic purpose of the aerosol. The active ingredient must be stable in the formulation and compatible with other components. It should also be able to be delivered in a fine mist or spray form for optimal absorption and therapeutic effect.

Solvents

Solvents are used to dissolve or disperse the active ingredients and other excipients. They must be compatible with the propellant and should not react with the active ingredients. Common solvents include ethanol, water, and other organic solvents. The choice of solvent can influence the solubility, stability, and delivery of the active ingredient.

Propellants

Propellants are critical for the delivery of the aerosol. The choice between chemical propellants (such as CFCs, HFAs, and hydrocarbons) depends on regulatory considerations, compatibility with the active ingredients, and the desired performance characteristics of the aerosol.

Excipients

Other excipients, such as surfactants, stabilizers, and preservatives, are included to enhance the stability, efficacy, and safety of the formulation. Surfactants help to disperse the active ingredients uniformly, while stabilizers and preservatives ensure the long-term stability and sterility of the product.

Steps Involved in the Manufacture of Aerosols

1. **Mixing**

The active ingredients, solvents, and excipients are mixed to create a uniform solution or suspension. This step ensures that all components are evenly distributed throughout the formulation. The mixing process must be carried out under controlled conditions to maintain the integrity and stability of the active ingredients.

1. **Filling**

The mixed formulation is filled into aerosol containers. This is typically done using automated filling machines that ensure precise and accurate filling of each container. The filling process must be conducted in a sterile environment to prevent contamination.

3. **Crimping**

After filling, the containers are sealed with a valve and actuator assembly. Crimping ensures that the valve is securely attached to the container, preventing leakage and maintaining the pressure inside the container. This step is crucial for ensuring the proper functioning of the aerosol system.

4. **Propellant Addition**

The propellant is added to the filled and crimped containers. This can be done through a process known as pressure filling or cold filling, depending on the type of propellant used. Pressure filling involves adding the propellant under high pressure, while cold filling involves cooling the formulation and propellant to low temperatures before combining them.

5. Testing

The final product undergoes rigorous testing to ensure its quality, safety, and efficacy. Tests include checking the pressure, valve functionality, spray characteristics, and particle size distribution. Microbial testing is also conducted to ensure the sterility of the product.

Importance of Maintaining Sterility and Stability

Maintaining sterility throughout the manufacturing process is critical to prevent contamination and ensure the safety of the aerosol product. This requires strict adherence to aseptic techniques and the use of sterile equipment and facilities. Ensuring the stability of the formulation is also essential for maintaining the efficacy and shelf life of the product. This involves selecting stable active ingredients and excipients, optimizing the formulation, and conducting stability testing under various conditions.

Challenges in Aerosol Formulation and How They Can Be Addressed

Compatibility Issues

Compatibility between the active ingredients, propellants, and other excipients can be challenging. Incompatibility can lead to degradation of the active ingredients or changes in the formulation. This can be addressed by conducting thorough compatibility studies during the formulation development stage and selecting compatible components.

Particle Size Control

Achieving the desired particle size distribution is critical for the effectiveness of aerosol products. Inconsistent particle sizes can affect the delivery and absorption of the active ingredient. This can be addressed by optimizing the mixing and homogenization processes and using appropriate surfactants to ensure uniform particle size distribution.

Valve Functionality

Ensuring the proper functioning of the valve is essential for accurate dosing and effective delivery of the aerosol. Malfunctioning valves can lead to under-dosing or over-dosing. This can be addressed by rigorous testing of valve components and ensuring that the crimping process is properly controlled.

Stability Issues

Maintaining the stability of the formulation over its shelf life is a common challenge. This can be addressed by selecting stable active ingredients and excipients, optimizing the formulation, and conducting stability testing under various conditions to identify and address potential stability issues.

8.4 EVALUATION AND QUALITY CONTROL

Quality control is essential in the production of pharmaceutical aerosols to ensure their safety, efficacy, and performance. Various tests are conducted to evaluate different aspects of the aerosol product. Below are key quality control tests and their significance.

Particle Size Distribution

Description

This test measures the size of the particles in the aerosol spray. Particle size affects the deposition of the drug in the respiratory tract and its therapeutic effectiveness.

Significance

- **Efficacy**: Smaller particles can reach the deeper parts of the lungs, enhancing drug absorption.
- **Safety**: Ensures particles are not too large, which could cause throat irritation or reduced effectiveness.
- **Regulatory Compliance**: Consistent particle size distribution is required to meet regulatory standards for inhalation products.

Method

Laser diffraction or cascade impactors are commonly used to measure particle size distribution. These methods provide detailed information on the size range and distribution of particles in the aerosol.

Valve Performance

Description

This test evaluates the functionality of the valve, ensuring it delivers the correct amount of medication with each actuation.

Significance

- **Accurate Dosing**: Ensures the patient receives the correct dose each time.

- **Consistency**: Verifies that each actuation delivers a consistent dose.
- **Patient Safety**: Prevents under-dosing or overdosing.

Method

Valve performance is tested by actuating the aerosol and measuring the amount of medication delivered. This includes testing for spray volume, weight, and consistency over multiple actuations.

Spray Pattern

Description

This test examines the shape, size, and distribution of the aerosol spray as it exits the container.

Significance

- **Drug Delivery**: A uniform spray pattern ensures effective drug delivery and coverage.
- **Device Performance**: Confirms the aerosol device is functioning correctly.
- **Patient Compliance**: Ensures ease of use for patients.

Method

Aerosol spray pattern is analyzed using high-speed photography or laser imaging systems to capture and evaluate the spray characteristics.

Leak Testing

Description

Leak testing checks for any leaks in the aerosol container and valve assembly.

Significance

- **Product Integrity**: Ensures the product remains sterile and effective until the expiration date.
- **Safety**: Prevents loss of propellant and medication, which could lead to incorrect dosing.
- **Regulatory Compliance**: Ensures the product meets safety standards.

Method

Leak testing is performed using pressure decay methods or immersion tests, where the container is submerged in water and observed for bubbles, indicating leaks.

Content Uniformity

Description

This test ensures that each aerosol container contains the correct amount of active ingredient and that the content is uniformly distributed.

Significance

- **Efficacy**: Ensures each dose contains the correct amount of medication.
- **Consistency**: Verifies that the product is uniform across different batches.
- **Regulatory Compliance**: Required to meet pharmacopoeial standards and regulatory guidelines.

Method

Content uniformity is tested by sampling multiple containers from a batch and analyzing the amount of active ingredient using techniques such as high-performance liquid chromatography (HPLC) or gas chromatography (GC).

Regulatory Requirements and Standards

Quality control for pharmaceutical aerosols is governed by regulatory bodies such as the U.S. Food and Drug Administration (FDA), European Medicines Agency (EMA), and other national health authorities. Key regulatory requirements include:

- **Good Manufacturing Practices (GMP)**: Ensures products are consistently produced and controlled according to quality standards.
- **International Conference on Harmonisation (ICH) Guidelines**: Provides guidelines on stability testing, validation, and quality risk management.
- **Pharmacopoeial Standards**: Specifications set by pharmacopoeias (e.g., USP, EP) for aerosol products, including tests for particle size, content uniformity, and sterility.
- **Documentation and Reporting**: Detailed records of all quality control tests, batch production, and any deviations must be maintained and available for regulatory inspection.

8.5 STABILITY STUDIES

Importance of Stability Studies for Pharmaceutical Aerosols

Stability studies are essential for pharmaceutical aerosols to ensure that the products remain safe, effective, and of high quality throughout their shelf life. These studies help to identify any potential changes in the formulation, container, or delivery system that could affect the product's performance or safety. Stability studies also provide the necessary data to establish expiration dates, storage conditions, and handling guidelines.

Types of Stability Tests

Accelerated Stability

Description

Accelerated stability testing involves storing the aerosol product under elevated conditions of temperature and humidity to speed up the rate of chemical and physical changes.

Purpose

- **Predict Shelf Life**: Provides an estimate of the product's shelf life in a shorter time frame.
- **Identify Potential Issues**: Helps to identify potential stability issues that may occur over time under normal storage conditions.

Conditions

Typically involves storing the product at temperatures such as 40°C ± 2°C with relative humidity of 75% ± 5%.

Long-Term Stability

Description

Long-term stability testing evaluates the product under recommended storage conditions over an extended period, usually up to the expected shelf life of the product.

Purpose

- **Confirm Shelf Life**: Confirms the shelf life and storage conditions derived from accelerated stability testing.
- **Monitor Real-Time Changes**: Observes any changes in the product under normal storage conditions.

Conditions

Typically involves storing the product at standard conditions such as 25°C ± 2°C with relative humidity of 60% ± 5%.

In-Use Stability

Description

In-use stability testing assesses the product's stability and performance during and after repeated use over a specified period.

Purpose

- **Ensure Consistency**: Ensures the product remains stable and effective throughout its intended period of use by the patient.
- **Evaluate Durability**: Evaluates the durability of the packaging and delivery system under normal usage conditions.

Conditions

Simulates the typical use conditions, such as repeated actuations, exposure to environmental conditions, and handling by the user.

Parameters Monitored During Stability Tests

Physical Appearance

- **Significance**: Changes in color, clarity, or phase separation can indicate degradation or contamination.
- **Method**: Visual inspection under controlled lighting conditions.

Particle Size

- **Significance**: Consistent particle size ensures effective delivery and absorption of the active ingredient.
- **Method**: Measured using laser diffraction or cascade impactors.

Pressure

- **Significance**: Ensures the propellant maintains the necessary pressure for effective delivery.
- **Method**: Pressure gauges or other pressure measurement devices.

Assay of Active Ingredients

- **Significance**: Ensures the correct amount of active ingredient is present and remains stable over time.
- **Method**: High-performance liquid chromatography (HPLC), gas chromatography (GC), or other suitable analytical techniques.

Stability-Indicating Methods
High-Performance Liquid Chromatography (HPLC)

- **Description**: Separates and quantifies the active ingredients and any degradation products.
- **Application**: Used to monitor the chemical stability and assay of active ingredients over time.

Gas Chromatography (GC)

- **Description**: Detects and quantifies volatile components and degradation products.
- **Application**: Used to evaluate the stability of propellants and other volatile ingredients.

Laser Diffraction

- **Description**: Measures the size distribution of particles in the aerosol.
- **Application**: Used to ensure consistent particle size for effective drug delivery.

Pressure Decay Testing

- **Description**: Measures changes in internal pressure over time.
- **Application**: Used to monitor the stability of the propellant and ensure proper functionality of the delivery system.

Microbial Testing

- **Description**: Ensures the product remains free from microbial contamination.
- **Application**: Conducted periodically to confirm sterility, especially for products intended for respiratory use.

Examples of Stability-Indicating Methods

- **Accelerated Stability**: HPLC and GC are used to monitor chemical stability, while laser diffraction assesses particle size distribution.

- **Long-Term Stability**: Regular visual inspection, HPLC for assay of active ingredients, and pressure measurement.
- **In-Use Stability**: Particle size analysis using laser diffraction, pressure monitoring, and microbial testing to ensure sterility.

CHAPTER NINE

Packaging Materials Science

9.1 MATERIALS USED FOR PACKAGING OF PHARMACEUTICAL PRODUCTS

Packaging materials play a crucial role in ensuring the safety, stability, and efficacy of pharmaceutical products. Different materials are used depending on the type of product and its specific packaging needs. The primary materials include glass, plastics, metals, and paperboard. Each material has unique characteristics, advantages, and disadvantages, making them suitable for various applications in pharmaceutical packaging.

Glass

Characteristics

- Inert and non-reactive, making it ideal for sensitive pharmaceuticals.
- Transparent, allowing easy visual inspection of the contents.
- Rigid and provides excellent barrier properties against gases and moisture.

Advantages

- Chemical stability ensures no interaction with the product.
- High resistance to heat and sterilization processes.
- Reusable and recyclable.

Disadvantages

- Fragile and prone to breakage, requiring careful handling.
- Heavier compared to other packaging materials, increasing transportation costs.

Applications

- **Vials**: Used for injectable medications and vaccines, providing a sterile environment.
- **Ampoules**: Single-dose containers for parenteral administration, ensuring product sterility and integrity.
- **Bottles**: Used for liquid medications, including syrups and oral solutions.

Plastics
Characteristics

- Lightweight and versatile, with varying degrees of flexibility and rigidity.
- Can be molded into various shapes and sizes.
- Good barrier properties against moisture and gases, depending on the type of plastic.

Advantages

- Durable and less prone to breakage compared to glass.
- Cost-effective and easy to produce in large quantities.
- Lightweight, reducing transportation costs.

Disadvantages

- Potential for chemical interaction with certain pharmaceutical products.
- Environmental concerns due to plastic waste and non-biodegradability.

Applications

- **Blister Packs**: Used for unit-dose packaging of tablets and capsules, providing protection from moisture and contamination.
- **Bottles**: Widely used for solid and liquid oral medications, including pills, syrups, and suspensions.
- **Syringes and Tubes**: For injectable medications and topical creams, ensuring ease of use and accurate dosing.

Metals
Characteristics

- Excellent barrier properties against light, moisture, and gases.
- Strong and durable, providing physical protection to the contents.
- Can be coated or lined to prevent interaction with the product.

Advantages

- High resistance to external factors, ensuring long-term stability.
- Can be sterilized and used for aseptic packaging.
- Recyclable, contributing to environmental sustainability.

Disadvantages

- Higher cost compared to plastics and paperboard.
- Potential for corrosion if not properly coated or lined.

Applications

- **Tubes**: Used for ointments, creams, and gels, providing a protective barrier and easy application.
- **Foil Blisters**: Combined with plastic to form blister packs, offering superior protection for sensitive tablets and capsules.
- **Cans**: For aerosol products, ensuring the integrity and stability of pressurized contents.

Paperboard
Characteristics

- Made from paper pulp, providing a lightweight and flexible packaging option.
- Can be easily printed and customized for branding and information purposes.
- Often used as secondary packaging, providing additional protection and support.

Advantages

- Cost-effective and widely available.
- Biodegradable and recyclable, making it environmentally friendly.

- Versatile and easy to handle.

Disadvantages

- Limited barrier properties, requiring additional layers or coatings for moisture and gas protection.
- Less durable compared to glass and metals, offering less physical protection.

Applications

- **Cartons**: Used as outer packaging for bottles, blister packs, and vials, providing structural support and protection during transport.
- **Labels and Inserts**: For providing product information, instructions, and branding.
- **Secondary Packaging**: For grouping multiple units of a product, facilitating handling and distribution.

9.2 FACTORS INFLUENCING CHOICE OF CONTAINERS

The choice of containers for pharmaceutical products is influenced by several critical factors to ensure the safety, efficacy, and stability of the drug. Key considerations include compatibility with the drug formulation, protection from environmental factors, mechanical strength, ease of use, and patient compliance. Below are detailed discussions of these factors and examples of their application in selecting containers for different types of pharmaceutical products.

Compatibility with the Drug Formulation

Considerations

- **Chemical Compatibility**: The container material must not react with the drug formulation, which could lead to degradation of the active ingredients or contamination.
- **Physical Compatibility**: The container should not alter the physical properties of the drug, such as viscosity, particle size, or appearance.

Examples

- **Tablets**: Plastic bottles made from high-density polyethylene (HDPE) are commonly used because they are chemically inert and do not interact with the tablet ingredients.
- **Liquids**: Glass bottles are often preferred for liquid formulations to prevent chemical interactions and provide an inert barrier.
- **Injectables**: Glass vials are used for injectables to maintain the purity and stability of the drug, avoiding any reactions with the container material.

Protection from Environmental Factors
Considerations

- **Light**: Some drugs are sensitive to light and require containers that provide protection from UV and visible light.
- **Moisture**: Moisture can degrade many pharmaceutical products, so containers must provide an effective barrier against humidity.
- **Oxygen**: Oxidation can lead to the degradation of active ingredients, so containers must prevent oxygen permeation.

Examples

- **Tablets**: Blister packs with aluminum foil provide excellent protection from light and moisture, ensuring the stability of light-sensitive and hygroscopic tablets.
- **Liquids**: Amber glass bottles protect light-sensitive liquid formulations from UV light.
- **Injectables**: Sealed glass ampoules and vials prevent exposure to oxygen and moisture, maintaining the sterility and stability of the drug.

Mechanical Strength
Considerations

- **Durability**: The container must withstand physical stresses during transportation, storage, and handling without breaking or deforming.
- **Protection**: The container should protect the drug from physical damage, such as crushing or impact.

Examples

- **Tablets**: Rigid plastic bottles offer good mechanical strength, protecting tablets from crushing and impact.
- **Liquids**: Glass bottles, while fragile, provide a strong barrier and are often protected with additional packaging to prevent breakage.
- **Injectables**: Glass vials are strong and resistant to high pressure, ensuring the integrity of the injectable product.

Ease of Use
Considerations

- **Accessibility**: The container should allow easy access to the drug, especially for patients with limited dexterity.
- **Dosage Accuracy**: The design should facilitate accurate dosing to ensure the patient receives the correct amount of medication.

Examples

- **Tablets**: Flip-top or screw-cap plastic bottles are easy to open and provide quick access to the medication.
- **Liquids**: Dropper bottles or measuring spoons provided with liquid medications ensure accurate dosing.
- **Injectables**: Prefilled syringes enhance ease of use and ensure accurate dosing, especially for patients who self-administer their medication.

Patient Compliance
Considerations

- **Convenience**: The container design should promote ease of use, storage, and portability to encourage regular use of the medication.
- **Safety Features**: Child-resistant closures and tamper-evident seals enhance safety and compliance.

Examples

- **Tablets**: Unit-dose blister packs provide convenience and help patients track their medication usage, improving compliance.
- **Liquids**: Measuring caps or syringes with liquid medications promote accurate dosing and convenience, enhancing compliance.

- **Injectables**: Auto-injectors or pen injectors make it easier for patients to administer their medication, increasing adherence to the prescribed regimen.

9.3 LEGAL AND OFFICIAL REQUIREMENTS

Pharmaceutical packaging must adhere to stringent legal and official requirements to ensure the safety, efficacy, and integrity of the products. Regulatory agencies such as the FDA (Food and Drug Administration), EMA (European Medicines Agency), and WHO (World Health Organization) play pivotal roles in setting standards and guidelines for packaging materials. These standards ensure that pharmaceutical products are consistently produced, stored, and distributed in a manner that preserves their quality and safety.

Role of Regulatory Agencies

FDA (Food and Drug Administration)

The FDA regulates pharmaceutical packaging in the United States, ensuring that it meets safety and quality standards. The FDA's guidelines cover various aspects, including material compatibility, labeling requirements, and packaging design. Key documents include the Code of Federal Regulations (CFR), particularly Title 21, which provides detailed requirements for pharmaceutical packaging and labeling.

EMA (European Medicines Agency)

The EMA oversees the regulation of pharmaceutical packaging within the European Union. It ensures that packaging materials and processes comply with EU regulations, such as the EU Good Manufacturing Practice (GMP) guidelines. The EMA also issues specific guidelines on packaging materials, labeling, and safety features, ensuring harmonized standards across member states.

WHO (World Health Organization)

The WHO provides international guidelines and standards for pharmaceutical packaging, particularly for developing countries. The WHO's guidelines focus on ensuring that packaging protects the product, provides necessary information, and promotes safe use. These guidelines are part of the WHO's broader efforts to improve global health standards and ensure the availability of safe medicines worldwide.

Specific Requirements for Pharmaceutical Packaging
Labeling
Requirements

- **Content**: Labels must include the drug name, dosage form, strength, storage conditions, expiration date, batch number, and manufacturer information.
- **Legibility**: Labels must be clear, legible, and durable, ensuring that the information remains intact throughout the product's shelf life.
- **Regulatory Compliance**: Labels must comply with specific regulatory guidelines, such as the FDA's labeling requirements in 21 CFR Part 201 and the EMA's labeling guidelines.

Examples

- Prescription medications must include detailed usage instructions, warnings, and contraindications.
- Over-the-counter (OTC) products must have clear instructions for use, active ingredients, and dosage recommendations.

Tamper-Evidence Requirements

- **Tamper-Evident Features**: Packaging must include features that provide visible evidence if the package has been tampered with, such as seals, bands, or wrappers.
- **Regulatory Standards**: These features must comply with regulatory standards to ensure their effectiveness in preventing tampering and ensuring product integrity.

Examples

- Blister packs with tamper-evident seals that show if the package has been opened.
- Bottles with tamper-evident bands or seals under the cap.

Child-Resistance Requirements

- **Child-Resistant Packaging**: Certain medications, especially those that are harmful if ingested by children, must be packaged in child-resistant containers.

- **Testing and Certification**: Packaging must undergo testing to ensure it is difficult for children to open but accessible to adults. This is often guided by standards such as the Consumer Product Safety Commission (CPSC) guidelines in the U.S.

Examples

- Prescription medications with child-resistant caps that require a specific combination of actions to open.
- Household medications like acetaminophen or ibuprofen packaged in child-resistant blister packs.

Traceability Requirements

- **Batch and Lot Numbers**: Packaging must include batch or lot numbers to enable traceability of the product throughout the supply chain.
- **Serialization**: Unique identifiers must be assigned to each package, allowing for tracking and verification of authenticity.

Examples

- Serialization codes on packaging that allow tracking from manufacturing to the end user, ensuring authenticity and traceability.
- Barcodes or QR codes that provide detailed information about the product's origin and distribution.

Regulations and Guidelines
U.S. FDA

- **21 CFR Part 211**: Covers current Good Manufacturing Practice (cGMP) for finished pharmaceuticals, including requirements for packaging and labeling control.
- **21 CFR Part 201**: Provides specific labeling requirements for prescription and OTC drugs.

European Medicines Agency (EMA)

- **EU GMP Guidelines**: Detailed requirements for the manufacture and packaging of pharmaceuticals.
- **Directive 2001/83/EC**: On the Community code relating to medicinal products for human use, including packaging and labeling requirements.

World Health Organization (WHO)

- **WHO Technical Report Series**: Provides guidelines on Good Manufacturing Practices for pharmaceuticals, including packaging requirements.
- **Guidelines on Packaging for Pharmaceutical Products**: Offers comprehensive guidance on the selection and evaluation of packaging materials and systems.

9.4 STABILITY ASPECTS OF PACKAGING MATERIALS

Stability Aspects of Packaging Materials in Pharmaceutical Products

The stability of pharmaceutical products is significantly influenced by the materials used in their packaging. Packaging materials must protect the drug product from environmental factors and prevent any interactions that could compromise the product's quality, safety, and efficacy. Understanding the stability aspects of packaging materials is crucial for ensuring the long-term stability and shelf life of pharmaceuticals.

Impact of Packaging Materials on Drug Stability and Shelf Life

Packaging materials play a vital role in maintaining the stability of drug products by providing a barrier against external factors such as light, moisture, oxygen, and microbial contamination. However, the choice of packaging material can also affect the stability of the drug product through interactions between the material and the formulation. These interactions can lead to various stability issues that may reduce the product's effectiveness or safety.

Importance of Conducting Stability Studies

Stability studies are essential to evaluate the interaction between the packaging material and the drug formulation. These studies help to identify potential stability issues and ensure that the packaging material provides adequate protection throughout the product's shelf life. Stability studies typically involve storing the packaged product under various environmental conditions and monitoring changes in physical, chemical, and microbiological properties over time.

Examples of Common Stability Issues Related to Packaging Materials

Leaching

Description

Leaching occurs when chemicals from the packaging material migrate into the drug formulation. This can happen with certain plasticizers, stabilizers, or other additives used in the packaging material.

Impact

- **Chemical Contamination**: Leached substances can contaminate the drug product, potentially leading to adverse reactions or reduced efficacy.
- **Regulatory Compliance**: The presence of leached chemicals can violate regulatory standards for pharmaceutical purity and safety.

Examples

- Plastic containers may leach phthalates or bisphenol A (BPA) into liquid formulations, affecting the drug's stability and safety.
- Rubber stoppers in vials may release sulfur compounds into injectable solutions.

Adsorption

Description

Adsorption refers to the process by which drug molecules adhere to the surface of the packaging material. This can lead to a reduction in the available concentration of the active ingredient.

Impact

- **Reduced Efficacy**: Adsorption can decrease the effective dose of the drug, compromising its therapeutic efficacy.
- **Stability Testing**: Adsorption issues must be identified and addressed during stability testing to ensure consistent drug delivery.

Examples

- Proteins and peptides may adsorb to the surface of glass vials or rubber stoppers, leading to a loss of active ingredient.

- Certain drugs may adsorb to plastic surfaces, reducing their concentration in solution.

Permeability
Description
Permeability refers to the ability of the packaging material to allow the passage of gases, moisture, or other substances. High permeability can lead to degradation of the drug product.
Impact

- **Moisture Ingress**: Permeable packaging can allow moisture to enter, leading to hydrolysis or degradation of moisture-sensitive drugs.
- **Oxygen Ingress**: Oxygen permeability can result in oxidation of the drug, reducing its potency and stability.

Examples

- Plastic blister packs may allow moisture to penetrate, affecting the stability of tablets and capsules.
- Polyethylene containers may allow oxygen to permeate, leading to oxidation of sensitive drug formulations.

Conducting Stability Studies
Stability studies involve exposing the packaged drug product to various environmental conditions and monitoring changes over time. These conditions typically include:

- **Accelerated Stability Testing**: High temperature and humidity conditions (e.g., 40°C ± 2°C / 75% ± 5% RH) to predict long-term stability.
- **Long-Term Stability Testing**: Real-time conditions (e.g., 25°C ± 2°C / 60% ± 5% RH) to confirm the product's shelf life.
- **Stress Testing**: Extreme conditions (e.g., freeze-thaw cycles, light exposure) to identify potential stability issues.

Parameters Monitored

- **Physical Appearance**: Changes in color, clarity, or phase separation.

- **Chemical Stability**: Assay of active ingredients, identification of degradation products.
- **Moisture Content**: Monitoring moisture levels in the drug product and packaging.
- **Microbial Stability**: Ensuring the product remains free from microbial contamination.

9.5 QUALITY CONTROL TESTS FOR PACKAGING MATERIALS

Quality control tests for packaging materials are essential to ensure their suitability for pharmaceutical use. These tests evaluate the physical properties, chemical compatibility, barrier properties, and potential for microbial contamination. Each test plays a crucial role in ensuring the packaging material can protect the pharmaceutical product effectively and maintain its quality and safety.

Physical Properties

Tensile Strength

Description

Tensile strength measures the resistance of a material to breaking under tension. It determines how much force the material can withstand before breaking.

Significance

- **Durability**: Ensures that the packaging can withstand handling, transportation, and storage without breaking.
- **Protection**: Provides confidence that the material will protect the contents from physical damage.

Method

A sample of the packaging material is stretched until it breaks using a tensile testing machine. The force required to break the material is measured.

Thickness

Description

Thickness measurement ensures that the packaging material has a consistent and appropriate thickness throughout.

Significance

- **Consistency**: Ensures uniformity in protection and performance across all packaging units.
- **Barrier Properties**: Thickness can influence the material's barrier properties, such as moisture and gas permeability.

Method
Thickness is measured using micrometers or other specialized thickness gauges.

Chemical Compatibility
Description
Chemical compatibility tests assess whether the packaging material reacts with the pharmaceutical product or any of its components.

Significance

- **Stability**: Prevents chemical reactions that could degrade the drug product or compromise its safety.
- **Integrity**: Ensures that the packaging material does not leach harmful substances into the product.

Method
Samples of the packaging material are exposed to the drug formulation under controlled conditions, and any changes in the chemical composition of the product or packaging material are analyzed using techniques like HPLC or GC.

Barrier Properties
Moisture Vapor Transmission Rate (MVTR)
Description
MVTR measures the amount of moisture that can pass through the packaging material over a specific period.

Significance

- **Moisture Protection**: Ensures that the packaging protects moisture-sensitive drugs from humidity, preventing degradation.
- **Shelf Life**: Helps in predicting the product's shelf life by understanding how well the packaging can maintain low moisture levels.

Method

MVTR is measured by placing a sample of the packaging material between two chambers, one with a known humidity level and one with a desiccant. The amount of moisture that passes through the material is measured over time.

Oxygen Transmission Rate (OTR)

Description

OTR measures the amount of oxygen that can pass through the packaging material over a specific period.

Significance

- **Oxygen Protection**: Ensures that the packaging protects oxygen-sensitive drugs from oxidation, which can degrade the product.
- **Product Stability**: Helps in predicting the product's stability by understanding how well the packaging can maintain low oxygen levels.

Method

OTR is measured by placing a sample of the packaging material between two chambers, one with pure oxygen and one with an oxygen-free environment. The amount of oxygen that passes through the material is measured over time.

Microbial Contamination

Description

Microbial contamination tests ensure that the packaging material is free from harmful microorganisms that could contaminate the pharmaceutical product.

Significance

- **Sterility**: Ensures that the packaging does not introduce microbial contamination, especially for sterile products like injectables.
- **Safety**: Protects patients from infections and ensures the product remains safe for use.

Method

Packaging materials are tested for microbial contamination using methods such as direct inoculation or membrane filtration, followed by incubation and microbial count analysis.

Regulatory Standards and Guidelines

FDA (Food and Drug Administration)

The FDA provides guidelines for the quality control of packaging materials in the pharmaceutical industry through the Code of Federal Regulations (CFR). Key sections include:

- **21 CFR Part 211**: Current Good Manufacturing Practice (cGMP) for Finished Pharmaceuticals, which includes requirements for packaging materials.
- **21 CFR Part 820**: Quality System Regulation for medical devices, applicable to certain types of pharmaceutical packaging.

EMA (European Medicines Agency)

The EMA oversees packaging material standards in the EU through various guidelines:

- **EU GMP Guidelines**: Detailed requirements for the manufacture and quality control of packaging materials.
- **ICH Q1A(R2)**: Stability Testing of New Drug Substances and Products, which includes guidelines for packaging material testing.

WHO (World Health Organization)

The WHO provides international guidelines for the quality control of packaging materials:

- **WHO Technical Report Series**: Guidelines on Good Manufacturing Practices for pharmaceuticals, including packaging material standards.
- **Guidelines on Packaging for Pharmaceutical Products**: Comprehensive guidance on the selection and evaluation of packaging materials.

CHAPTER TEN

Quality Assurance and Regulatory Requirements

10.1 OVERVIEW OF QUALITY ASSURANCE IN PHARMACEUTICAL MANUFACTURING

Definition and Significance of Quality Assurance (QA)

Quality Assurance (QA) in pharmaceutical manufacturing is a comprehensive system designed to ensure that pharmaceutical products are consistently produced and controlled to meet the quality standards appropriate for their intended use. QA encompasses all aspects of the manufacturing process, from raw material selection to final product release, ensuring the safety, efficacy, and quality of pharmaceutical products.

Significance of QA

- **Safety**: Ensures that pharmaceutical products are free from contaminants and impurities that could harm patients.
- **Efficacy**: Guarantees that products perform as intended, providing the therapeutic benefits claimed.
- **Quality**: Maintains high standards of quality throughout the production process, from raw materials to finished products.
- **Regulatory Compliance**: Ensures adherence to regulatory requirements and standards, facilitating market approval and maintaining public trust.

Key Components of a QA System

Quality Control (QC)

Definition

Quality Control is a subset of QA focused on testing and inspecting materials and products to ensure they meet specified standards.

Role in QA

- **Testing**: Conducts analytical and microbiological tests on raw materials, in-process materials, and finished products to verify their quality.
- **Inspection**: Regularly inspects production processes and equipment to ensure they operate within defined parameters.
- **Documentation**: Maintains records of all tests and inspections, providing a traceable history of product quality.

Quality Risk Management (QRM)

Definition

QRM is a systematic process for assessing, controlling, communicating, and reviewing risks to the quality of the pharmaceutical product across its lifecycle.

Role in QA

- **Risk Assessment**: Identifies potential risks to product quality and evaluates their impact and likelihood.
- **Risk Control**: Implements measures to mitigate identified risks, ensuring they remain within acceptable levels.
- **Risk Review**: Continuously monitors and reviews risk control measures to ensure their effectiveness.

Documentation Practices

Definition

Documentation practices involve the creation, management, and maintenance of records related to the manufacturing process.

Role in QA

- **Traceability**: Provides a comprehensive and traceable record of all manufacturing activities, enabling quick identification and resolution of issues.
- **Compliance**: Ensures compliance with regulatory requirements for documentation, including Good Manufacturing Practices (GMP).
- **Continuous Improvement**: Facilitates ongoing review and improvement of processes based on documented evidence and historical data.

Continuous Improvement

Definition

Continuous improvement is an ongoing effort to enhance products, services, or processes to increase efficiency, effectiveness, and quality.

Role in QA

- **Process Optimization**: Regularly reviews and optimizes manufacturing processes to improve quality and efficiency.
- **Feedback Mechanisms**: Utilizes feedback from QC testing, audits, and customer complaints to identify areas for improvement.
- **Training and Development**: Ensures that staff are continuously trained on the latest QA practices and regulatory requirements.

Role of QA in Meeting Regulatory Requirements and Maintaining Compliance

Regulatory Requirements

QA systems are designed to comply with regulatory requirements set by agencies such as the FDA, EMA, and WHO. These regulations include:

- **Good Manufacturing Practices (GMP)**: Detailed guidelines for the production, testing, and quality assurance of pharmaceutical products.
- **Pharmacopoeial Standards**: Standards set by pharmacopoeias (e.g., USP, EP) for the quality, purity, and strength of pharmaceutical products.

Maintaining Compliance

- **Audits and Inspections**: Regular internal and external audits ensure ongoing compliance with regulatory standards.
- **Standard Operating Procedures (SOPs)**: Clearly defined and documented procedures ensure consistent application of QA practices.
- **Regulatory Submissions**: Comprehensive documentation and evidence of QA practices are submitted to regulatory bodies for product approval and ongoing compliance monitoring.

10.2 GOOD MANUFACTURING PRACTICES (GMP) AND GOOD LABORATORY PRACTICES (GLP)

Good Manufacturing Practices (GMP) and Good Laboratory Practices (GLP) are critical regulatory frameworks in pharmaceutical manufacturing and testing, ensuring the quality, safety, and integrity of pharmaceutical products and laboratory data.

Good Manufacturing Practices (GMP)
Principles of GMP

- **Quality Management**: Establishes a comprehensive quality management system covering all aspects of production, from raw materials to final product.
- **Standard Operating Procedures (SOPs)**: Clearly defined and documented procedures for every aspect of the manufacturing process to ensure consistency and control.
- **Documentation**: Comprehensive recording of all activities and processes to provide traceability and accountability.
- **Personnel**: Adequately trained and qualified personnel to perform and supervise manufacturing processes.
- **Facilities and Equipment**: Proper design, maintenance, and cleaning of facilities and equipment to prevent contamination and ensure product quality.
- **Validation**: Thorough validation of manufacturing processes to ensure they consistently produce products meeting their intended specifications.
- **Quality Control**: Rigorous testing of raw materials, in-process materials, and finished products to verify their quality and compliance with specifications.

Application of GMP

GMP guidelines apply to the entire manufacturing process, ensuring that pharmaceutical products are consistently produced and controlled according to quality standards appropriate for their intended use.

Good Laboratory Practices (GLP)
Principles of GLP

- **Study Planning**: Detailed and approved study plans outlining objectives, methodologies, and protocols.
- **Personnel**: Qualified and trained personnel to conduct and supervise laboratory studies.
- **Facilities**: Proper design and maintenance of laboratory facilities to ensure a controlled environment for testing.

- **Equipment**: Calibration, maintenance, and validation of laboratory equipment to ensure accurate and reliable data.
- **Standard Operating Procedures (SOPs)**: Documented procedures for all laboratory activities to ensure consistency and reproducibility.
- **Documentation**: Comprehensive and accurate recording of all study-related activities and data to ensure traceability.
- **Quality Assurance**: Independent quality assurance unit to monitor compliance with GLP and verify the integrity of study data.

Application of GLP

GLP guidelines apply to non-clinical laboratory studies that evaluate the safety and efficacy of pharmaceutical products, ensuring the reliability and integrity of laboratory data.

Regulatory Agencies and Guidelines
FDA (Food and Drug Administration)

- **GMP**: Governed by the Code of Federal Regulations (CFR), particularly 21 CFR Parts 210 and 211, which outline requirements for the manufacturing, processing, packing, or holding of drugs.
- **GLP**: Governed by 21 CFR Part 58, which outlines the standards for non-clinical laboratory studies.

EMA (European Medicines Agency)

- **GMP**: Detailed in the EU GMP guidelines, which are part of the EudraLex Volume 4, covering the manufacture of medicinal products in the EU.
- **GLP**: Governed by the OECD Principles of GLP, adopted by the EMA for non-clinical studies.

WHO (World Health Organization)

- **GMP**: Outlined in the WHO GMP guidelines, providing a global standard for the production and quality control of pharmaceutical products.
- **GLP**: Detailed in the WHO Handbook on GLP, which aligns with the OECD Principles of GLP and provides guidance for laboratory studies.

Examples of GMP and GLP in Ensuring Product Safety, Consistency, and Compliance

GMP in Manufacturing

- **Consistency**: By following validated processes and SOPs, manufacturers ensure that every batch of product meets the same quality standards.
- **Safety**: Rigorous quality control testing and proper handling of raw materials prevent contamination and ensure the safety of the final product.
- **Compliance**: Adherence to GMP guidelines ensures that products comply with regulatory requirements, facilitating market approval and maintaining public trust.

GLP in Laboratory Testing

- **Integrity**: Detailed documentation and traceability of study data ensure the integrity and reliability of laboratory results.
- **Reliability**: Calibrated and validated equipment, along with qualified personnel, ensure that laboratory studies produce accurate and reproducible data.
- **Compliance**: Adherence to GLP guidelines ensures that non-clinical study data meet regulatory standards, supporting the safety and efficacy claims of pharmaceutical products.

10.3 REGULATORY REQUIREMENTS FOR PHARMACEUTICAL PRODUCTS

10.3.1 CENTRAL DRUG STANDARD CONTROL ORGANIZATION (CDSCO)

Role and Responsibilities of CDSCO

The Central Drug Standard Control Organization (CDSCO) is the primary national regulatory authority in India responsible for regulating pharmaceutical products and ensuring their safety, efficacy, and quality. CDSCO operates under the Ministry of Health and Family Welfare and plays a crucial role in public health by overseeing the regulation of drugs, cosmetics, and medical devices.

Key Responsibilities

- **Approval of New Drugs**: CDSCO evaluates and approves new drug applications based on clinical trial data and other relevant information to ensure safety and efficacy before the drugs can be marketed.

- **Clinical Trials**: CDSCO grants permission to conduct clinical trials in India, ensuring that they are conducted ethically and scientifically.
- **Manufacturing Licenses**: CDSCO issues licenses for the manufacture of pharmaceuticals, ensuring compliance with Good Manufacturing Practices (GMP).
- **Marketing Authorizations**: CDSCO provides marketing authorizations for pharmaceutical products, allowing them to be sold and distributed in India.
- **Pharmacovigilance**: Monitors the safety of marketed drugs and takes necessary actions in case of adverse drug reactions or other safety concerns.
- **Regulation of Medical Devices and Cosmetics**: Ensures the safety and quality of medical devices and cosmetics through rigorous regulatory oversight.
- **Quality Control**: Ensures the quality of drugs through testing and inspection of manufacturing facilities.

Regulation of Pharmaceutical Products
Approval Process for New Drugs

1. **New Drug Application (NDA)**: Pharmaceutical companies must submit a New Drug Application to CDSCO, including detailed information on preclinical and clinical data, manufacturing processes, quality control, and proposed labeling.
2. **Evaluation and Review**: CDSCO reviews the NDA, focusing on the safety, efficacy, and quality of the drug. This involves rigorous assessment by experts and technical committees.
3. **Clinical Trial Approval**: Before approval, clinical trial data must be reviewed. If necessary, CDSCO may require additional studies or trials.
4. **Approval and Authorization**: If the data supports the safety and efficacy of the drug, CDSCO grants marketing authorization, allowing the drug to be marketed in India.

Clinical Trials

1. **Application for Clinical Trials**: Sponsors must submit a clinical trial application, including the trial protocol, investigator details, and ethical approvals.

2. **Ethical Review**: Clinical trials must be reviewed and approved by an Ethics Committee.
3. **Regulatory Approval**: CDSCO evaluates the application to ensure that the trial will be conducted ethically and scientifically.
4. **Monitoring and Inspection**: CDSCO monitors ongoing clinical trials to ensure compliance with approved protocols and regulatory requirements.

Manufacturing Licenses

1. **Application for License**: Manufacturers must apply for a license, providing details about the manufacturing facility, equipment, and quality control systems.
2. **Inspection and Compliance**: CDSCO inspects the manufacturing facility to ensure compliance with GMP standards.
3. **Issuance of License**: If the facility meets the required standards, CDSCO issues a manufacturing license.

Marketing Authorizations

1. **Application for Marketing Authorization**: Companies must submit applications for marketing authorization, including detailed information on the drug's safety, efficacy, and quality.
2. **Evaluation and Approval**: CDSCO evaluates the application and, if satisfied, grants marketing authorization, allowing the product to be marketed.

Organizational Structure of CDSCO
Central Level

- **Drugs Controller General of India (DCGI)**: The head of CDSCO, responsible for overseeing all regulatory activities.
- **Deputy Drugs Controllers**: Assist the DCGI in various regulatory functions.
- **Assistant Drugs Controllers**: Support the DCGI and Deputy Drugs Controllers in specific regulatory areas.
- **Technical Committees**: Expert committees that evaluate new drug applications, clinical trial proposals, and other regulatory submissions.

Zonal and Sub-Zonal Offices

- **Zonal Offices**: CDSCO has several zonal offices across India that carry out regulatory activities at the regional level.
- **Sub-Zonal Offices**: Sub-zonal offices further support zonal offices in their regulatory functions.

Interaction with Other Regulatory Bodies
National Level

- **State Drug Control Authorities**: CDSCO collaborates with state drug control authorities to ensure uniform enforcement of drug regulations across India.
- **Indian Pharmacopoeia Commission (IPC)**: Works with IPC to set standards for drugs and pharmaceuticals in India.

International Level

- **World Health Organization (WHO)**: CDSCO collaborates with WHO on international regulatory standards and guidelines.
- **US Food and Drug Administration (FDA)** and **European Medicines Agency (EMA)**: Engages with international regulatory bodies to harmonize regulations and ensure the quality and safety of pharmaceuticals globally.

10.3.2 STATE LICENSING AUTHORITIES
Role of State Licensing Authorities in Regulating Pharmaceutical Products

State licensing authorities in India play a crucial role in regulating pharmaceutical products within their respective jurisdictions. They work in tandem with the Central Drug Standard Control Organization (CDSCO) to ensure the safety, efficacy, and quality of pharmaceutical products. While CDSCO oversees national regulatory activities, state licensing authorities focus on the local implementation and enforcement of these regulations.

Responsibilities of State Licensing Authorities
Issuing Manufacturing Licenses

1. **Application Review**: State licensing authorities review applications for manufacturing licenses submitted by pharmaceutical companies. This includes verifying the details of the manufacturing facility, the qualifications of personnel, and the adequacy of quality control measures.
2. **Inspections**: Before issuing a license, state authorities conduct thorough inspections of the manufacturing facility to ensure compliance with Good Manufacturing Practices (GMP) and other regulatory standards.
3. **Licensing**: If the facility meets all requirements, the state licensing authority issues the manufacturing license, allowing the company to produce pharmaceutical products within the state.

Conducting Inspections

1. **Routine Inspections**: State licensing authorities conduct regular inspections of pharmaceutical manufacturing and distribution facilities to ensure ongoing compliance with GMP and other regulatory standards.
2. **Investigative Inspections**: In response to complaints or reports of non-compliance, state authorities may conduct targeted inspections to investigate potential violations and ensure corrective actions are taken.
3. **Sampling and Testing**: Inspectors may take samples of pharmaceutical products for testing to verify their quality, potency, and purity.

Enforcing Compliance with Regulatory Standards

1. **Monitoring and Surveillance**: State licensing authorities continuously monitor the pharmaceutical market to identify and address issues related to product quality, safety, and efficacy.
2. **Enforcement Actions**: In cases of non-compliance, state authorities have the power to take enforcement actions such as issuing warning letters, imposing fines, suspending or revoking licenses, and initiating legal proceedings.
3. **Recalls**: State authorities can mandate the recall of pharmaceutical products that are found to be unsafe, ineffective, or of poor quality.

Comparison of Roles: State Licensing Authorities vs. CDSCO
Scope of Authority

- **State Licensing Authorities**: Primarily responsible for regulating pharmaceutical manufacturing, distribution, and sale within their respective states. They focus on local implementation and enforcement of national regulatory standards.
- **CDSCO**: Oversees national regulatory activities, including the approval of new drugs, clinical trials, and the establishment of national policies and guidelines. CDSCO also coordinates with state authorities to ensure uniform implementation of regulations across the country.

Regulatory Focus

- **State Licensing Authorities**: Emphasize local enforcement, conducting inspections, issuing licenses, and taking enforcement actions within the state. They ensure that manufacturers and distributors within the state comply with national and state-specific regulations.
- **CDSCO**: Focuses on national-level activities, such as the approval of new drug applications, clinical trial oversight, and the development of regulatory standards. CDSCO also plays a key role in coordinating with international regulatory bodies and ensuring compliance with global standards.

Responsibilities in Ensuring Safety, Efficacy, and Quality

- **State Licensing Authorities**:

  - **Manufacturing Licenses**: Issue and renew licenses for pharmaceutical manufacturing facilities within the state.
  - **Inspections**: Conduct routine and investigative inspections to ensure compliance with GMP and other standards.
  - **Local Enforcement**: Take enforcement actions against non-compliant facilities and products.

- **CDSCO**:

  - **New Drug Approvals**: Evaluate and approve new drug applications based on clinical trial data and other relevant information.
  - **Clinical Trials**: Grant permissions and oversee clinical trials conducted in India.

- ◦ **National Policies**: Develop and implement national regulatory policies and guidelines.
- ◦ **Coordination**: Work with state authorities and international bodies to ensure consistent regulatory practices.

10.4 STABILITY TESTING AND DOCUMENTATION

Stability Testing and Documentation Requirements for Pharmaceutical Products

Stability Testing

Stability testing is a critical component of pharmaceutical development and regulatory approval. It involves assessing how the quality of a drug substance or drug product varies over time under the influence of environmental factors such as temperature, humidity, and light. The purpose of stability testing is to determine the shelf life, appropriate storage conditions, and degradation pathways of the drug, ensuring that it remains safe, effective, and of high quality throughout its intended shelf life.

Importance of Stability Studies

- **Shelf Life**: Stability studies help establish the expiration date of the product, indicating the period during which the drug remains effective and safe for use.
- **Storage Conditions**: These studies determine the optimal storage conditions to maintain the drug's stability, such as specific temperature and humidity ranges.
- **Degradation Pathways**: Understanding how a drug degrades over time helps identify potential impurities and degradation products, which can inform formulation adjustments and packaging decisions.

Regulatory Guidelines for Conducting Stability Testing

ICH Guidelines

The International Council for Harmonisation of Technical Requirements for Pharmaceuticals for Human Use (ICH) provides comprehensive guidelines for stability testing. These guidelines are widely accepted by regulatory authorities worldwide, including the FDA, EMA, and WHO.

ICH Q1A(R2): Stability Testing of New Drug Substances and Products

This guideline outlines the general requirements for stability testing, including:

- **Types of Stability Studies:**

  - **Accelerated Stability Studies**: Conducted at elevated stress conditions (e.g., 40°C ± 2°C / 75% ± 5% RH) to quickly predict the product's stability and shelf life.
  - **Long-Term Stability Studies**: Conducted at recommended storage conditions (e.g., 25°C ± 2°C / 60% ± 5% RH) to confirm the product's stability over its intended shelf life.
  - **Intermediate Stability Studies**: Conducted at intermediate conditions (e.g., 30°C ± 2°C / 65% ± 5% RH) if the product fails accelerated testing or if it's intended for specific climatic zones.

- **Parameters Monitored:**

  - **Physical Appearance**: Evaluating changes in color, texture, or phase separation.
  - **Assay**: Measuring the active ingredient's concentration to ensure it remains within specified limits.
  - **Degradation Products**: Identifying and quantifying degradation products to ensure they remain within acceptable limits.
  - **Moisture Content**: Measuring moisture levels to ensure the product remains stable and free from hydrolysis.
  - **pH**: Monitoring pH changes, especially for liquid formulations.
  - **Dissolution Rate**: Ensuring tablets and capsules dissolve as expected to release the active ingredient.

Documentation Requirements
Stability Testing Protocol

- A detailed stability testing protocol must be prepared, outlining the study design, including storage conditions, time points, and tests to be conducted.
- The protocol should specify the criteria for evaluating the stability data and the acceptance criteria for each test parameter.

Stability Data

- Comprehensive records of all stability tests and results must be maintained.
- Data should include the conditions under which the studies were conducted, the time points tested, and the results for each parameter monitored.
- Any deviations from the protocol or unexpected results should be documented and investigated.

Stability Report

- A stability report summarizes the stability study findings, including data analysis, interpretation, and conclusions.
- The report should discuss the product's shelf life, recommended storage conditions, and any identified degradation pathways.
- Stability reports are essential components of regulatory submissions, supporting product registration and label claims.

Role of Stability Data in Regulatory Submissions
Product Registration

- Stability data is critical for obtaining regulatory approval for new drug substances and products. It demonstrates that the product will remain stable and effective throughout its intended shelf life.
- Regulatory authorities require stability data as part of the dossier submitted for product registration.

Label Claims

- Stability studies support the claims made on the product label regarding shelf life, storage conditions, and any specific handling requirements.
- Accurate label claims are essential for ensuring proper use and storage of the product by consumers and healthcare providers.

Regulatory Submissions

- Stability data is included in regulatory submissions such as New Drug Applications (NDAs), Abbreviated New Drug Applications (ANDAs), and Marketing Authorization Applications (MAAs).

- Ongoing stability studies are required for post-approval changes to the formulation, manufacturing process, or packaging.

CHAPTER ELEVEN

Glossary

A

- **Active Pharmaceutical Ingredient (API):** The substance in a pharmaceutical drug that has therapeutic effects.
- **Aseptic Processing:** A manufacturing process in which drug products are sterilized separately from packaging and then combined in a sterile environment.
- **Amorphous:** A solid that lacks a well-defined crystalline structure.

B

- **BCS (Biopharmaceutics Classification System):** A system to classify drugs based on their solubility and permeability which helps predict drug absorption.
- **Bioavailability:** The rate and extent to which the active ingredient is absorbed and becomes available at the site of action.
- **Biostatistics:** The application of statistics to a wide range of topics in biology.

C

- **Capsules:** A solid dosage form in which the drug is enclosed within a soluble container or shell.

  - **Hard Gelatin Capsules:** Capsules made from gelatin and water, used to enclose powdered or granular drugs.
  - **Soft Gelatin Capsules:** Capsules made from a more flexible, plasticized gelatin, used to contain oils and active ingredients in liquid

form.

- **Coating**: A layer applied to the surface of a dosage form, such as a tablet, for protection or to control release.

    ◦ **Film Coating**: A thin, polymer-based coating that protects the tablet and controls its release.
    ◦ **Sugar Coating**: A coating of sugar that improves taste and appearance.

- **Cold Cream**: An emulsion of water in oil used as a moisturizer or makeup remover.
- **Containers and Closures**: Packaging materials used to contain and protect drug products.
- **Compression**: The process of compacting a powder into a solid dose form such as a tablet.
- **Crystal Form**: The solid state form of a substance characterized by a specific geometric arrangement of molecules or atoms.

D

- **Disintegration**: The process by which a tablet breaks down into smaller particles.
- **Dosage Form**: The physical form in which a drug is produced and dispensed, such as a tablet, capsule, or injection.

E

- **Elixirs**: Clear, sweetened hydroalcoholic solutions intended for oral use.
- **Emulsions**: A dosage form consisting of two immiscible liquids, one of which is dispersed as small droplets throughout the other.

F

- **Flow Properties**: Characteristics of a powder that determine its ability to flow, which affects manufacturing processes like tablet compression.
- **Formulation**: The process of designing and producing a pharmaceutical product that ensures the correct dosage, stability, and release of the

active ingredient.

G

- **Gelatin**: A protein derived from collagen, used in making capsules and as a gelling agent.
- **Good Laboratory Practice (GLP)**: A set of principles intended to ensure the quality and integrity of non-clinical laboratory studies.
- **Good Manufacturing Practice (GMP)**: Regulations that require manufacturers to ensure their products are consistently produced and controlled according to quality standards.

H

- **Hydrolysis**: A chemical reaction involving the breakdown of a compound due to reaction with water.

I

- **In-process Quality Control (IPQC)**: Tests conducted during manufacturing to ensure the product meets specified quality standards.
- **Isotonicity**: A property of a solution having the same osmotic pressure as some other solution, especially one in a cell or a body fluid.

L

- **Lyophilization**: A freeze-drying process used to preserve perishable materials or make them more convenient for transport.

M

- **Manufacturing Defects**: Flaws that occur during the production process, affecting the quality and safety of the pharmaceutical product.
- **Moisture Content**: The amount of water present in a substance, which can affect stability and shelf life.

O

- **Oral Dosage Forms**: Medications designed to be taken by mouth, including tablets, capsules, and liquid preparations.
- **Out of Specification (OOS)**: Results that fall outside the established acceptance criteria set by the manufacturer.

P

- **Parenteral**: A route of drug administration that bypasses the digestive tract, typically through injections.
- **Particle Size**: The size of the individual particles in a powder or solid dosage form, affecting dissolution and absorption.
- **Pelletization**: The process of forming small, free-flowing, spherical or semi-spherical particles.
- **Pharmacopoeia**: An official publication containing a list of medicinal drugs with their effects, directions for use, and standards for their composition and strength.
- **Polymorphism**: The occurrence of different crystal forms of a compound, which can affect the drug's stability and bioavailability.
- **Preformulation**: Studies conducted to characterize the physical and chemical properties of a drug substance to design stable and effective dosage forms.

Q

- **Quality Assurance (QA)**: A systematic process to ensure that products meet specified quality standards and regulatory requirements.
- **Quality Control (QC)**: The operational techniques and activities used to fulfill requirements for quality.

R

- **Racemisation**: The process by which an optically active compound is converted into an optically inactive mixture of equal amounts of enantiomers.
- **Raw Materials**: The basic materials used in the production of pharmaceuticals, including APIs, excipients, and other ingredients.

S

- **Solubility Profile**: The solubility characteristics of a drug substance in various solvents, affecting its formulation and bioavailability.
- **Stability Testing**: Tests conducted to determine the shelf life and storage conditions of a pharmaceutical product.
- **Suspensions**: A dosage form in which solid particles are dispersed in a liquid medium.
- **Suppositories**: Solid dosage forms designed to be inserted into body orifices where they dissolve or melt and exert local or systemic effects.

T

- **Tablets**: Solid dosage forms containing active ingredients and excipients, compressed into a small, solid, flat, or biconvex shape.
- **Technology Transfer**: The process of transferring knowledge and technologies from research and development to full-scale manufacturing.
- **Topical**: Referring to medication applied to a particular spot on the skin or mucous membranes.

U

- **USP (United States Pharmacopeia)**: A compendium of drug information, including standards for drug quality, strength, and purity.

V

- **Validation**: The process of establishing documented evidence that a process or system performs effectively and reproducibly.

W

- **Wet Granulation**: A method of granulation in which a liquid binder is added to a powder mixture to form granules.

CHAPTER TWELVE

List of Abbreviations

API: Active Pharmaceutical Ingredient

BCS: Biopharmaceutics Classification System

BE: Bioequivalence

COPP: Certificate of Pharmaceutical Product

CDSCO: Central Drug Standard Control Organization

CMC: Chemistry, Manufacturing, and Controls

DQ: Design Qualification

FDA: Food and Drug Administration

FDC: Fixed-Dose Combination

FBC: Fluidized Bed Coater

GMP: Good Manufacturing Practice

GLP: Good Laboratory Practice

HPLC: High-Performance Liquid Chromatography

IB: Investigator's Brochure

IND: Investigational New Drug

IQ: Installation Qualification

IR: Infrared

ISO: International Organization for Standardization

IV: Intravenous

LVP: Large Volume Parenteral

MoU: Memorandum of Understanding

NABL: National Accreditation Board for Testing and Calibration Laboratories

NDA: New Drug Application

OOS: Out of Specification

OQ: Operational Qualification

PAT: Process Analytical Technology

PQ: Performance Qualification

QA: Quality Assurance
QC: Quality Control
QbD: Quality by Design
QRM: Quality Risk Management
R&D: Research and Development
RDTL: Regional Drug Testing Laboratories
SOP: Standard Operating Procedure
SUPAC: Scale-Up and Post-Approval Changes
TGA: Therapeutic Goods Administration
TIFAC: Technology Information, Forecasting and Assessment Council
TQM: Total Quality Management
TT: Technology Transfer
USP: United States Pharmacopeia
WHO: World Health Organization

CHAPTER THIRTEEN

References

Aulton, M.E. (2018). Pharmaceutics: The Design and Manufacture of Medicines. 5th Edition. Churchill Livingstone. ISBN: 978-0702070051.

Ansel, H.C., Allen, L.V., & Popovich, N.G. (2011). Ansel's Pharmaceutical Dosage Forms and Drug Delivery Systems. 10th Edition. Lippincott Williams & Wilkins. ISBN: 978-0781765709.

Lachman, L., Lieberman, H.A., & Kanig, J.L. (1987). The Theory and Practice of Industrial Pharmacy. 3rd Edition. Lea & Febiger. ISBN: 978-0812107213.

Shargel, L., & Yu, A.B.C. (2015). Applied Biopharmaceutics & Pharmacokinetics. 7th Edition. McGraw-Hill Medical. ISBN: 978-0071830935.

Remington, J.P. (2020). Remington: The Science and Practice of Pharmacy. 23rd Edition. Pharmaceutical Press. ISBN: 978-0857113672.

Allen, L.V., & Ansel, H.C. (2013). Ansel's Pharmaceutical Dosage Forms and Drug Delivery Systems. 9th Edition. Lippincott Williams & Wilkins. ISBN: 978-1451188769.

Swarbrick, J. (2007). Encyclopedia of Pharmaceutical Technology. 3rd Edition. Informa Healthcare. ISBN: 978-0849393996.

Aulton, M.E., & Taylor, K.M.G. (2018). Aulton's Pharmaceutics: The Design and Manufacture of Medicines. 5th Edition. Elsevier Health Sciences. ISBN: 978-0702070051.

Indian Pharmacopoeia Commission. (2020). Indian Pharmacopoeia 2020. Government of India, Ministry of Health and Family Welfare. ISBN: 978-8193846510.

United States Pharmacopeial Convention. (2020). United States Pharmacopeia 43-National Formulary 38. ISBN: 978-1936424538.

European Directorate for the Quality of Medicines & HealthCare. (2020). European Pharmacopoeia 10th Edition. ISBN: 978-9287183903.

International Council for Harmonisation of Technical Requirements for Pharmaceuticals for Human Use (ICH). (2005). ICH Harmonised Tripartite Guideline Q8(R2): Pharmaceutical Development.

World Health Organization (WHO). (2006). WHO Expert Committee on Specifications for Pharmaceutical Preparations: WHO Technical Report Series.

Food and Drug Administration (FDA). (2018). Guidance for Industry: Q8(R2) Pharmaceutical Development.

Allen, L.V. (2013). Ansel's Pharmaceutical Dosage Forms and Drug Delivery Systems. 10th Edition. Wolters Kluwer Health. ISBN: 978-1469841864.

Sheskey, P.J., Cook, W.G., & Cable, C.G. (2017). Handbook of Pharmaceutical Excipients. 8th Edition. Pharmaceutical Press. ISBN: 978-0857112712.

Rathbone, M.J., Hadgraft, J., & Roberts, M.S. (2002). Modified-Release Drug Delivery Technology. CRC Press. ISBN: 978-0824707522.

Niazi, S.K. (2009). Handbook of Pharmaceutical Manufacturing Formulations: Semisolid Products. CRC Press. ISBN: 978-0849317480.

Sastry, S.V., Nyshadham, J.R., & Fix, J.A. (2000). Recent technological advances in oral drug delivery – a review. Pharmaceutical Science & Technology Today, 3(4), 138-145. doi: 10.1016/S1461-5347(00)00203-9.

Hickey, A.J. (2003). Pharmaceutical Inhalation Aerosol Technology. 2nd Edition. Marcel Dekker. ISBN: 978-0824708697.

Patel, G.M., Patel, G.C., Patel, R.B., Patel, J.K., & Patel, M. (2006). Nanorobot: A versatile tool in nanomedicine. Journal of Drug Targeting, 14(2), 63-67. doi: 10.1080/10611860600612862.